S0-CJM-023

YASUKUNI FUNDAMENTALISM

NANZAN LIBRARY OF ASIAN RELIGION AND CULTURE

EDITORIAL ADVISORY BOARD

Tim Graf
James W. Heisig
Kim Seung-Chul
Matthew D. McMullen
Saitō Takashi
Paul L. Swanson
Nanzan Institute for Religion and Culture

Hayashi Makoto
Aichi Gakuin University

Thomas P. Kasulis
Ohio State University

Okuyama Michiaki
Tokyo Eiwa University

James W. Heisig and John C. Maraldo, eds., *Rude Awakenings: Zen, the Kyoto School, and the Question of Nationalism* (1995)

Jamie Hubbard and Paul L. Swanson, eds., *Pruning the Bodhi Tree: The Storm over Critical Buddhism* (1997)

Mark R. Mullins, *Christianity Made in Japan: A Study of Indigenous Movements* (1998)

Jamie Hubbard, *Absolute Delusion, Perfect Buddhahood: The Rise and Fall of a Chinese Heresy* (2001)

James W. Heisig, *Philosophers of Nothingness: An Essay on the Kyoto School* (2001)

Victor Sōgen Hori, *Zen Sand: The Book of Capping Phrases for Kōan Practice* (2003)

Robert J. J. Wargo, *The Logic of Nothingness: A Study of Nishida Kitarō* (2005)

Paul L. Swanson and Clark Chilson, eds., *Nanzan Guide to Japanese Religions* (2006)

Ruth Fuller Sasaki, trans. and commentator, and Thomas Yūhō Kirchner, ed., *The Record of Linji* (2009)

James W. Heisig, Thomas P. Kasulis, and John C. Maraldo, eds., *Japanese Philosophy: A Sourcebook* (2011)

Benjamin Dorman, *Celebrity Gods: New Religions, Media, and Authority in Occupied Japan* (2012)

James W. Heisig, *Nothingness and Desire: An East-West Philosophical Antiphony* (2013)

Clark Chilson, *Secrecy's Power: Covert Shin Buddhists in Japan and Contradictions of Concealment* (2014)

Paul L. Swanson, *Clear Serenity, Quiet Insight: T'ien-t'ai Chih-i's "Mo-ho chih-kuan"* (2018)

Thomas P. Kasulis, *Engaging Japanese Philosophy: A Short History* (2018)

Yasukuni Fundamentalism

JAPANESE RELIGIONS AND THE POLITICS OF RESTORATION

Mark R. Mullins

University of Hawai'i Press
HONOLULU

© 2021 University of Hawai'i Press
All rights reserved

Printed in the United States of America

26 25 24 23 22 21   6 5 4 3 2 1

Library of Congress Cataloging-in-Publication Data

Names: Mullins, Mark, author.
Title: Yasukuni fundamentalism : Japanese religions and the politics of
   restoration / Mark R. Mullins.
Other titles: Nanzan library of Asian religion and culture.
Description: Honolulu : University of Hawai'i Press, 2021. | Series: Nanzan
   Library of Asian religion and culture | Includes bibliographical
   references and index.
Identifiers: LCCN 2020048222 (print) | LCCN 2020048223 (ebook) | ISBN
   9780824889012 (cloth) | ISBN 9780824890162 (pdf)
Subjects: LCSH: Yasukuni Jinja (Tokyo, Japan) | Shinto and politics—Japan.
   | Religious fundamentalism—Japan. | Nationalism—Religious
   aspects—Shinto.
Classification: LCC BL2223.S8 M85 2021 (print) | LCC BL2223.S8 (ebook) |
   DDC 322/.10952—dc23
LC record available at https://lccn.loc.gov/2020048222
LC ebook record available at https://lccn.loc.gov/2020048223

The design and typesetting for this book were prepared by
the Nanzan Institute for Religion and Culture.

Cover design by Claudio Bado.

University of Hawai'i Press books are printed on acid-free
paper and meet the guidelines for permanence and
durability of the Council on Library Resources.

Contents

Acknowledgments

Over a decade in the making, this book is based on a research project that was conceived back in 2008 while I was spending a portion of my sabbatical year away from Sophia University in residence at Duke University. I'm grateful to Richard Jaffe and the Asian-Pacific Studies Institute & Department of Religion for hosting me during that time. I submitted a book proposal that year to Pat Crosby, then editor at the University of Hawai'i Press, and was delighted to have a contract in hand for a volume on "Neonationalism and Religion in Contemporary Japanese Society." Although I had hoped to complete the research and writing within two to three years, the gestation period to produce this volume turned out to be far longer. This has been due in part to the continued flourishing of Shinto-related nationalism, which I felt needed to be documented. The delay was also due to some professional changes. After returning to Sophia University from sabbatical leave, I served a term as editor of *Monumenta Nipponica*, and then moved to New Zealand in 2013 for a professorship in Japanese studies at the University of Auckland.

This study represents a new area of research for me, which emerged and evolved in connection with two seemingly unrelated projects. First, it was the Aum Shinrikyō sarin incident on the Tokyo subway on 20 March 1995 that initially shifted my attention from the comparative sociology of religious minorities—Buddhists in Canada, Christians in Japan, and New Religions—to the study of religion-state issues and the relationship between religion, nationalism, and politics in contemporary Japan. Matsudo Yukio's chapter, "Back to Invented Tradition: A Nativist Response to National Crisis," in *Religion and Social Crisis in Japan* (Kisala and Mullins, 2001), alerted me to the rise of neonationalism as one important response to the destabilizing subway attack that followed the Hanshin-Awaji (Kobe) earthquake of 17 January, which began this year of disaster.

His observations prompted me to follow more closely this "nativist response," and I began to document the growing evidence for a religio-political restorationist movement in post-disaster Japan. This movement continued to develop in the wake of the 2011 "triple disaster"—earthquake, tsunami, and nuclear accident at the Fukushima Daiichi plant—which necessarily extended this project.

This serendipitously merged with a second project. Shortly after moving to Sophia University in 2002, I became aware of a popular story circulating widely, which claimed that Yasukuni Shrine was saved from destruction in the early months of the Occupation by the actions of Fr. Bruno Bitter, an important member of the Jesuit community at Sophia University, who intervened with General Douglas MacArthur. This story found its way to the homepage of Yasukuni Shrine in an article entitled "The Priest Who Defended Yasukuni Shrine" (*Yasukuni jinja o mamotta shinpu*), which recounts the Catholic priest's role and expresses deep appreciation and respect for Fr. Bitter. Many contemporary Yasukuni supporters—politicians, academics, and even the manga artist, Kobayashi Yoshinori—have found this story about a foreign priest to be useful ammunition in their responses to international criticism directed at politicians who supported the shrine by their "official" visits.

This story puzzled me and I began a period of extensive archive research in search of documentary evidence that would validate this claim, including records of the Supreme Commander of Allied Powers's (SCAP) Religions Division, Yasukuni Shrine archives, and a number of Shinto accounts of the Occupation and the early postwar period. As I read these sources it became clear to me that the Shinto experience of marginalization due to SCAP's policies is what motivated key leaders to launch a "restoration movement" once the foreign Occupation came to an end. It was in the process of tracing the genealogy of this movement that I literally backed my way into the world of Shinto scholarship. As a late-comer and interloper of sorts, I've depended upon the work of established scholars in the field of Shinto studies, which I will acknowledge extensively in what follows.

While I was already aware of the critical engagement of some Christians and New Religions with the neonationalistic trends documented in this study, I'm grateful to Ugo Dessi for introducing me to Sugahara

Ryūken and Hishiki Masaharu, two Jōdo Shinshū priests, who have been key leaders in the Buddhist legal battle with Yasukuni Shrine over postwar enshrinements. They were kind to meet with me on several occasions and generously shared legal documents, court records, and publications related to their ongoing struggle with both Yasukuni Shrine and the Japanese government.

As someone who only began serious archival research rather late in an academic career, I'm especially indebted to Ben Dorman for his helpful advice about accessing the National Archive materials related to the Occupation period and for kindly sharing his index of the religion-related files. This was an incredible time-saver as I searched for relevant materials. It turns out that other critical documents for making sense of religion during the Occupation period are scattered far and wide in a number of collections. I'd like to acknowledge the institutions and archivists who made this study possible by arranging for my visits to their collections and for kindly responding to many requests for copies of their materials: Bruce Tabb and Linda Long, Special Collections, University of Oregon Libraries; Michael P. Walsh, M.M., Maryknoll Mission Archives, New York; James Zobel, MacArthur Memorial Library & Archives, Norfolk, Virginia; and Carrie March, Special Collections, Honnold/Mudd Library, Claremont University Consortium; Tomoko Bialock and Toshiko Scot, Richard C. Rudolph East Asian Library, UCLA. I've also relied on archive materials and Shinto journals provided by Yasukuni Shrine and Kokugakuin University Library. I owe a special thanks to John Breen for his introduction to Noda Yasuhira, a Yasukuni Shrine priest and archivist at the Yūshūkan Bunko, who kindly spent many hours responding to my queries and generously provided copies of materials I requested during my visits in 2014. In addition to those mentioned above, I'd also like to thank Rich Gardner for introducing me to the family of Lt. William K. Bunce, the chief of SCAP's Religions Division during much of the Occupation. Peter Bunce generously shared some Occupation period photos from his father's personal collection, a number of which have been included in this volume.

Over the past decade, I've had many opportunities to present some of my initial research findings at international conferences, workshops, and symposia hosted by the National University of Singapore, University of Southern California, Sophia University, the City University of Hong Kong, Cornell University, Leipzig University, the University of Auckland, the University of Vienna, De Paul University, Duke University, and Otago University. Early chapter drafts were also presented at the annual meetings of a number of academic associations, including the Association for Asian Studies (2011; 2014; 2016), the Society for the Scientific Study of Religion (2016), the European Association for Japanese Studies (2011; 2017), the Australian Association for the Study of Religions (2017), the New Zealand Association for the Study of Religions (2018), and the East Asian Society for the Scientific Study of Religion (2019). I gratefully acknowledge the many expressions of collegial support and helpful feedback received along the way from many scholars, co-panelists, editors, and anonymous peer reviewers of earlier articles and book chapters, which were adapted, expanded, and updated for various sections of this larger monograph (for details of which, see the concluding Permissions). In particular, I would like to express my appreciation to Shimazono Susumu, Helen Hardacre, Ian Reader, Erica Baffelli, Nakano Kōichi, John Breen, John Nelson, Paul Swanson, Mark Teeuwen, Elisabetta Porcu, Nakano Tsuyoshi, Jeff Kingston, Sven Saaler, Okuyama Michiaki, Tsukada Hotaka, Kate Nakai, Bettina Gramlich-Oka, Esther Sanders, Chiara Formichi, David Slater, Larry Repeta, Levi McLaughlin, Emily Anderson, and Jolyon Thomas.

I would be remiss if I didn't also mention the contribution of research assistants who assisted me in tracking down materials at various stages of this project. Many thanks to Shibata Ria, Ebina Hiroshi, Iida Yōko, and Ōe Yuta, who were MA students at Sophia University during my time there, to Sugimori Yumika, an MA student at Sōka University, and to Dr. Nakamura Jun, a research associate at the University of Auckland.

Funding for research leading to this publication has been received from a number of institutions. I gratefully acknowledge the annual research funds from Sophia University (2008–2012), support from the Japan Society for the Promotion of Science Grant in Aid for the Nanzan Institute for Religion and Culture Project on the "Internationalization of Research on Religion" (2011–2013), a Faculty of Arts Research Development Fund grant from the University of Auckland (2013–2015), a Terasaki Japanese Studies Center Gordon W. Prange Collection Research and Travel Grant, UCLA

(2014), and a Japan Society for the Promotion of Science Grant in Aid for the team research project on "A Religious Studies Approach to Research on the Allied Powers' Treatment and Disposition of Postwar Asia: A Reexamination through Archives Outside Japan," which was under the direction of Professor Tsuyoshi Nakano, Soka University (2014–2016).

Over the past five years, I also received additional support for this project from the Humanities Centre for Advanced Studies at Leipzig University. I would like to thank Professors Christoph Kleine and Monika Wohlrab-Sahr for inviting me to join their "Multiple Secularities" Project as a Senior Research Fellow in 2015. This affiliation provided many opportunities for conversations with scholars working on similar issues in other contexts. In addition to attending several conferences in Leipzig, I was fortunate to be in residence for three months in late 2019, which is when I finally completed this manuscript. The chapter on Promoting Constitutional Revision actually began as a paper prepared for their 2018 Workshop on "Secularities in Japan." I'm very grateful to Christoph and Monika, as well as the other Centre staff and visiting scholars, for creating such a stimulating and supportive environment for my work.

As I wrapped up this project in 2019, I began conversations with UH editor Stephanie Chun and colleagues at Nanzan University about the possibility of including this monograph in the Nanzan Library of Asian Religion and Culture Series. I'm grateful to the Nanzan Advisory Board for agreeing to include it and to the editorial team at the Nanzan Institute, Matt McMullen, Tim Graf, Jim Heisig, and Paul Swanson, for shepherding this manuscript through the production process. I'm honored to have a second volume in the Nanzan series and would like to thank Stephanie for facilitating this arrangement with UH Press.

Since moving to New Zealand in 2013, I've returned to Japan each year for follow-up research. I'm especially grateful to good friends Yukiko and Joe Dunkle for their warm hospitality during my many sojourns back in Tokyo. And last, but certainly not least, I wish to thank Cindy, my partner of over four decades and professional in-house editor. She has not only listened to me go on about this project for far too long, but has read and offered her editorial advice on numerous chapter drafts that eventually became this book. Thanks to her editorial eye and critical feedback, the manuscript has been markedly improved. One could not ask for a better companion with whom to celebrate life's milestones.

This book is dedicated to the memory of David Reid (1927–2017), a sociologist of religion and long-time editor of the *Japanese Journal of Religious Studies*, who was a mentor to me when I returned to Japan as a young academic in the mid-1980s. He took a personal interest in my work, helped me find my bearings in the field, and kindly introduced me to his rich network of Japanese scholars. His reputation as a first-rate editor and translator was well-earned and many of us working in the field of Japanese religion and society today are indebted to him for his long career and generous investment in the work of others. May he rest in peace.

A note about macrons and Japanese names: Japanese names throughout the text are rendered in Japanese order with the surname first and the personal name second. Also, macrons are not used for Japanese place names and terms that appear in English-language dictionaries.

Introduction

Recent decades have seen a rise in religious nationalism around the world. A prominent example that immediately comes to mind is the "Make America Great Again" movement led by President Donald J. Trump, which has garnered wide support from evangelical Christians across the United States. Another is the resurgence of nationalism in India under Prime Minister Narendra Modi's leadership, which has strengthened the position of the ruling Bharatiya Janata Party and its long-held view of the country as a Hindu nation. These social expressions of nationalism emerged in very different contexts, but they nevertheless share in common an effort to shape government policies so that patriotism is promoted and linked closely to one religion. In these cases, one religion is elevated over others and is accorded special treatment. It is not surprising that religious minorities often experience a sense of marginalization as a result, fearing that their individual rights will be eroded. Although less widely known, I will argue in some detail in what follows that Japan is no exception to this recent pattern.

Manifestations of nationalism have become ubiquitous in Japanese life, and even the casual observer will notice its appearance in popular culture, organized religions, public institutions, and contemporary politics. On a visit to most bookstores, for example, one will find Kobayashi Yoshinori's popular manga series, which often focuses on nationalistic themes; and on a nearby shelf sits Prime Minister Abe Shinzō's own personal manifesto and best-seller, *Utsukushii kuni e* (2006), which outlines his vision for restoring Japanese pride and love for the motherland. Cyber-nationalism is another aspect of this growing phenomenon. Rightwing internet (*netto uyoku*) activities have also been flourishing in recent years, with such groups as Zaitoku-kai earning a reputation for hate-filled campaigns against ethnic Korean residents in Japan. The Sakura channel, likewise, provides programming on a range of topics aimed at revitalizing traditional Japanese culture and correcting the liberal press for its misguided views regarding wartime history and the "comfort women" (*ianfu*) issue, which have allegedly damaged Japan's reputation.

The promotion of patriotic rituals in public schools is another sign of the times. Over the past two decades the national government has issued new educational policies for the required use by staff and students of the national flag (Hinomaru) and anthem (Kimigayo) for all official entrance and graduation ceremonies. Related educational reforms have included initiatives for developing curriculum and textbooks that will cultivate in students a sense of national pride and patriotism. One important expression of these concerns was the organization of the Society for the Creation of New History Textbooks (Atarashii Rekishi Kyōkasho o Tsukuru Kai) in 1996. It has been actively preparing materials for public education that are widely regarded as examples of historical revisionism, conveniently excluding or denying the "so-called 'dark' chapters" of Japanese history" (Saaler 2005, 21). Apparently, national pride can only be recovered if Japan's wartime past—colonization, wartime atrocities, Nanjing massacre, and exploitation of Asian women—is removed from public view.

Some private schools have also become carriers of the revitalized nationalistic orientation. Moritomo Gakuen kindergarten in Osaka, for example, has been the focus of considerable media attention and controversy since 2017 because of its ultra-nationalistic program for young children. Daily singing of the national anthem and memorization of the Imperial Rescript on Education (*Kyōiku chokugo*, 1890), which provided the emperor-centric ideology that guided Japan until 1945, are core elements of the curriculum. The fact that Prime Minister Abe's wife, Akie, was serving as an honorary principal of the kindergarten and offered praise for its educational philosophy generated special public interest and concern about the school.

Tourism is booming these days and international guests checking into one of the APA chain of budget hotels will also encounter another expression of nationalism—complimentary bilingual books that purport to provide "the real history of Japan" and a "proposal for the revival of Japan pride." On a recent stay, I found copies of *Theoretical Modern History IV and V*, which have replaced the more familiar Gideon Bibles and Buddhist

Sutras often found in the bedside tables of other establishments. The CEO of this hotel chain, Motoya Toshio, issues these controversial books under his pen name, Seiji Fuji. His denial that Japanese troops were involved in the Nanjing massacre in 1937 is just one of the claims that has provoked protests from China and demands for the removal of the books from APA hotels. In spite of threats of boycotts by Chinese tourists from China, the hotel chain's policy is that the books will remain.

Yasukuni Shrine, the religious site that enshrines Japan's war dead, is a widely recognized symbol of contemporary nationalism and regularly attracts attention due to high profile visits by public officials and politicians. Prime Minister Abe's visit in December 2013, for example, provoked both international and domestic criticisms, as well as lawsuits for alleged violation of religion-state separation. The Prime Minister has avoided personal visits since the controversy erupted, but his wife has continued to go in his stead and has proudly publicized at least three visits to the shrine and the adjoining war museum, Yūshūkan, to her 148,824 followers on Facebook.

These few examples reveal the multi-faceted nature of nationalism across the whole range of Japanese life and institutions and reflect a significant rightward shift (*ukeika*) that has occurred in Japanese society over the past two decades.[1] In this book I am particularly interested in the role of religion in resurgent nationalism and how these various expressions are interrelated and shape public discourse and institutions. As it turns out, the "rightward shift" is closely related to some organized religions and their political efforts to reshape various dimensions of Japanese society. One aim of this study is to untangle the nature of this relationship between religion and politics, and to consider in more detail those religious nationalisms with particular relevance for the public sphere.

One difficulty in approaching this topic that must be recognized at the outset is that there is no consensus in either scholarly or popular discourse on the meaning and use of the concept of "religion" (*shūkyō*) in Japan. Even though the term was imported from the West in the late nineteenth century and has sometimes been viewed as an artificial construct that is inapplicable to the Japanese situation, it has been adopted and adapted by scholars and used widely over the past century—even by the government for official and legal purposes.[2] A careful analysis of the Japanese experience reveals that this terminology was not simply forced upon this context, but actively reinterpreted by Japanese actors as they sought to understand and define their relationship with the larger world over the past century. This means that we must navigate our way through the different ways religion is defined and understood by government officials, representatives of organized religions, and by practitioners in everyday life.

As we parse the meaning of "religion" it is also necessary to consider how it relates to other vocabulary used to make sense of human beliefs and behavior. For example, we will find that "customary practices" (*shūzokuteki kōi*) and "social rituals" (*shakaiteki girei*) are terms regularly employed to cover a range of behaviors in everyday life and events in the annual calendar. Even though these activities occur at sacred sites in the home or at shrines and temples, they are often understood to be distinct from the category of "religion." In popular consciousness, "religion" is often understood in a highly restricted way to refer only to activities by individuals who have a clear sense of membership and belonging to an organized religion—usually identified as a New Religion or Christian church. That is why Japanese usually claim to be "without religion" (*mushūkyō*), because they do not identify themselves as belonging exclusively to one particular religious group. The majority of Japanese, nevertheless, continue to participate in household and institutional rituals, festivals, and annual events, and many hold a range of beliefs related to buddhas, ancestors, protective spirits, gods, and *tatari* (fear of retribution from the spirit world). In short, it would be a mistake to interpret the "*mushūkyō*" category to mean "nonreligious" or "secular." In contemporary Japan, then, there are clearly conflicting emic interpretations of what is involved in communal events, social rituals, and public institutions. Some prefer to use the language of civic duty and customary practices with regard to their participation in a range of ritual events, while others identify these practices as "religious" and their promotion by some political leaders as actions that clearly violate the constitutional separation of religion and state.

As far as the Japanese government is concerned, religion is essentially a group phenomenon that is organized around common beliefs and practices. In order to be recognized officially by the government, a group must show that it has a doctrine that it seeks to propagate, conducts rituals and services, and provides for the educational development of its members. Groups that are recognized by the government are registered as religious juridical persons (*shūkyō hōjin*), which belong to a larger category of juridical persons (*kōeki hōjin*), that are seen as contributing to the public good (*kōeki*).[3] While paying attention to the diverse ways in which religion is understood in contemporary Japan, this study will focus on how organized religions are related to the postwar rise of neonationalism and the critical debate that has emerged surrounding the religio-political agenda to reshape public life and institutions according to a shared vision advanced by the National Association of Shrines (Jinja Honchō; NAS), the Japan Conference (Nippon Kaigi), and the rightwing of the Liberal Democratic Party (LDP).

RELIGIOUS NATIONALISMS

Nationalistic movements may be seen as one common reaction to the processes of modernization, globalization, and the weakening of traditional identities based on tribe and clan, but there are other factors that have shaped these developments in each particular context. One "classic" in the vast and growing literature in this field is Benedict Anderson's *Imagined Communities* (1983), which analyzed the cultural and religious roots of nationalism and the factors that shaped its emergence and transformation in different eras. In *The New Cold War? Religious Nationalism Confronts the Secular State*, which is a more focused treatment of this phenomenon in modern societies, Mark Juergensmeyer (1993, 2–6) observed that religious nationalism developed in many contexts—post-colonial India and the Middle East, for example—due to a fundamental dissatisfaction with secular forms of nationalism, which were based "on Western models of a nationhood" and criticized for lacking moral or spiritual values. This observation certainly holds true for some iterations of religious nationalism in postwar Japan.

Shimazono Susumu has identified three main forms of religious nationalism that have emerged in the postwar period, becoming particularly visible since the 1980s and 1990s.[4] One important stream of religious nationalism is related to the New New Religions (*shin shin shūkyō*) formed in the postwar period, which became prominent from the late 1970s (the fourth period of New Religions in Shimazono's historical framework). Examples here include such groups as Mahikari (founded in 1959), World Mate (founded in 1993), and Kōfuku no Kagaku (1986). Shimazono (2001, 116) suggests that the appearance of a "nationalistic" orientation in these New Religions is related in part to Japan's success and international status achieved as a global economic power. These "spiritual nationalisms" regard Japan as the source and foundation of the highest form of religion. Mahikari, for example, emphasizes that Japan is the origin of the human race and claims that the Japanese language is the source of all the languages of the world (Shimazono 2001, 101). Japan's destiny is to save the world from destruction. The period of Japan's economic and material prosperity is understood to be the prelude to the expansion of Japan's spiritual civilization (*reishu no bunmei*), which Mahikari will bring to the world. Along similar lines, Ōkawa Ryūhō claims that even though the age of "ethnic" gods or ethnic religion (*minzoku shūkyō*) is over, Kōfuku no Kagaku is destined to bring harmony and unity to the world.[5] More audacious claims are made by Fukami Tōshū, the founder of World Mate, who explains that it is building the spiritual foundation for Japan to rule the world in the twenty-first century (Shimazono 2001, 128).

Shimazono identifies a second stream of religious nationalism clustered around the *Nihonjinron* (Japan theory) literature and the "new spirituality movements." In the 1980s and 1990s, he explains, there were many *Nihonjinron* publications that extolled the virtues of Japan's spiritual traditions, particularly ancient Shinto and animism, and advocated their relevance for contemporary life. He notes that this vein of literature declined markedly after the 1995 Aum Shinrikyō subway gas attack. Winston Davis (1992, 268–269) has given considerable attention to *Nihonjinron* and sees parallels with prewar civil religion. "I would like to suggest," he writes, "that the blitz of books dealing with the essence of Japanese culture and society is, in reality, a groping for a new national self-identity in the face of increasing contact, competition and friction with western countries." He goes on to explain that "many of the functions of the civil religion of pre-1945 Japan— the generation of national purpose, symbolic self-defense, value-consensus, etc.—are now being assumed by the symbols, values, and imagery produced by the literature of Japan theory."[6] In Shimazono's assessment, these first two expressions of spiritual nationalism are of minimal political significance and are unlikely to have an impact on the "public sphere" for the foreseeable future.

The third form of religious nationalism considered by Shimazono (2001, 93–94)—which is my primary concern here—is closely connected to the NAS and their efforts to mobilize political leaders to restore the "public" role of Shinto. This association, which was organized in the early days of the Allied Occupation (1945–1952), has some 80,000 affiliated shrines throughout the country and has been the base institution for Shinto nationalism. While the NAS had initially been organized in early 1946 to enable Shinto shrines to survive as religious organizations during the Occupation, Shimazono (2007, 706) argues that in the postwar period it has been "primarily active as a political force in Japan. Its political aim is to revive State Shinto by promoting nationalism and reverence for the emperor." This expression of Shinto nationalism is rooted in the critical response of leaders to the secular order imposed by the Occupation authorities based on a strict interpretation of religion-state separation.

Just as Juergensmeyer identified dissatisfaction with "secular" versions of nationalism as a precipitant of religious nationalisms, Almond, Sivan, and Appleby (1995, 441) have identified secularization as "the defining and distinctive structural cause of fundamentalist movements." It is not surprising, then, that many observers have identified the postwar religious nationalism we are concerned with here as a Japanese expression of "religious fundamentalism." Over the past half century, in fact, religious nationalism and fundamentalism have evolved and coalesced to constitute one religio-political movement, which aims to repair the damage caused by the foreign occupation and restore key aspects of an idealized social order from the earlier phase of imperial Japan. There is an extensive literature on both secularization and fundamentalism that needs our attention here in order to frame this particular study of postwar religious nationalism and its significance for the public sphere.

MODERNIZATION, SECULARIZATION, AND JAPANESE RELIGIONS

The inherited wisdom from the West on the relationship between modernization and religion has been largely framed in negative terms with theories of secularization. Following Max Weber, it has been generally assumed that the necessary concomitant of modernization is the disenchantment of the world through rationalization and, ultimately, secularization. In the master narrative popularized by Weber's successors, the spread of industrial capitalism, modern science, and urbanization necessarily leads to religious decline at multiple levels—a decline in individual religiosity (micro-level), a decline in religious institutions (meso-level), and a decline in the power of religion to shape the larger society and culture (macro-level). According to Peter Berger's (1967) now classic treatment, the power of the "sacred canopy" provided by medieval Catholicism began to disintegrate in Western Europe due to the impact of the Protestant Reformation, the spread of industrial capitalism and modern science, and through the formation of the modern nation-state. In short, the modernization process in the West involved a shrinking of the "sacred canopy" and the replacement of a religious monopoly by a market situation in which various subworlds were forced to compete. It is usually understood that this increasingly pluralistic situation leads to privatization and removal of religion from the public sphere.

In *A General Theory of Secularization*, David Martin (1978, 15) provided a more cautious and nuanced analysis of the secularization process that identified variations depending upon a number of factors, including whether a country is monopolistic, pluralistic, Catholic or Protestant, for example, and whether key events in the history of a country included revolution—either united against an external force or conflict between various groups in the same society—which he refers to as a particular "frame" that shapes subsequent developments. Based on a consideration of these variables interacting in distinctive ways, Martin (1978, 59) identified different patterns of secularization, which he referred to as the American, English, Scandinavian, Mixed, Latin, Statist (right), Statist (Left), and Nationalist. Given that "multiple secularities" emerged in Western societies, we should not be surprised to find that the process of secularization in Japan has a distinctive pattern of its own.

The master narrative mentioned above has been a compelling one, but this interpretation of the impact of modernization and its model of progressive secularization based on European history does not fit the case of Japan. This is not to say that Japanese are particularly religious or that Japan is "unique," but simply to point out that modernization has "ambivalent effects" on religion (Munakata 1976, 99). It may lead to secularization—the decline of some religious beliefs, practices, or institutions—but at the same time it may reinvigorate others and even create an environment in which new forms of religion can flourish. In a word, a unilinear conception of modernization and religious decline cannot adequately account for the situation in some non-Western regions of the world.

N. J. Demerath's (2007, 16–21) typology of secularization provides a helpful framework for thinking about this process in the Japanese context.[7] His fourfold typology is based on whether the secularization process is primarily an internal (domestic) or external (foreign) one, and whether the process is non-directed or directed. The first type, "emergent secularization," is a non-directed process that is the unintended result of the processes that are a part of modernization, including industrialization, advances in modern science and education, and urbanization. This might be regarded as the "classic model" of secularization, which is more relevant for understanding recent patterns of religious decline in contemporary Japan. The second type, "diffuse secularization," refers to the process that sometimes occurs as an unintended consequence of cultural contact following the arrival of carriers of alternative systems of belief and practice, which sometimes undermine or "displace old practices, rituals, and beliefs." The third type is "coercive secularization," which is an internal top-down and purposely directed process by some actors with recognized authority within a given society. In the Japanese context, this type occurred as a result of the Meiji government's issuance in 1868 of the edict for the separation of Buddhism and Shinto (*shinbutsu bunri rei*). This edict was directed against Buddhist institutions and led to the destruction of many temples, forcing many monks to abandon monastic life and return to the secular world. The fourth type, "imperialist secularization," is also directed and coercive, but in this case orchestrated by an external or foreign authority, that is, as a process "imported or imposed from the outside." This type is particularly important for understanding the nature of secularization as it occurred during the Allied Occupation of Japan (1945–1952), which involved the top-down removal of Shinto influence from public life and institutions by "foreign" authorities. In this book, I am primarily concerned with the impact of "imperialist secularization," and will argue that a new expression of nationalism—"neonationalism"—appeared as a critical response by some Shinto leaders to their experience of marginalization during the Occupation.

Demerath's (2007, 10) theoretical perspective also includes the counter process of sacralization, which he defines as "the process whereby the secular becomes sacred, or other new forms of the sacred emerge, whether in matters of personal faith, institutional practice or political power." These two processes, he explains, "often oscillate and play off each other as partners in a dialectic" (Demerath 2007, 11). The process of secularization over the course of Japan's modern century has been accompanied by this counter process, as may be seen in the formation of a new national form of Shinto, widely referred to as State Shinto for the period from 1900 to 1945, as well as in the development of numerous new religious movements across several distinct periods.

STATE SHINTO REVISITED

Although the primary concern of this book is to understand the relationship between organized religions and nationalism in the postwar period, this needs to be considered in relation to its historical precedent and what has been widely referred to as "State Shinto." Although this terminology became more widely used following the end of the war and as a result of the "Shinto Directive" issued by the Occupation authorities, it is a term rooted in decades of Japanese scholarship and official government documents.

The term "State Shinto" has been a controversial one and the focus of considerable debate. Although scholars often mark the beginning of State Shinto from 1900, when the Bureau of Shrines (Jinja Kyoku) was established in the Home Ministry, the state actually began reshaping shrine

Shinto much earlier in the Meiji period. After the government issued the 1868 edict separating the "kami" from the eclectic kami-Buddhist shrine-temple complexes that characterized the Tokugawa religious world, it made Shrine Shinto the base institution for the expression of the restoration ideal of the "unity of rites and government" (*saisei itchi*). According to Inoue (2002, 401, 411), the state administration of shrines can be traced back to the declaration of the Council of State on 14 May 1871, which defined shrines as "public" institutions, abolished the hereditary priesthood, and began its policy to replace the local shrine traditions and ritual activities with those designated by the state.

The category of "State Shinto" had already become a part of political discourse by the early 1880s. Sakamoto (2000, 273) offers a statement by Oda Kan'ichi (1856–1909), which was addressed to a Diet committee convened to deliberate government allowances to shrine priests, to illustrate the use of this term in actual practice almost two decades before the Bureau of Shrines was even established:

> In 1882, the distinction between "religious Shinto" (*shūkyō no Shintō*) and "state Shinto" (*kokka Shintō*) was already clear enough to behold.... The Shinto that we advocate is state Shinto [as a pyramid structure] with the Ise shrines at its peak and village shrines forming its base.... Finally, in the year 1900, the government understood. It split the earlier *Shajikyoku* into a *Jinja-kyoku* and a *Shūkyōkyoku*. The former now takes responsibility for what we mean by State Shinto; the latter is charged with Christianity, Buddhism and the various sects of Shinto—what we might call religious Shinto.

In addition to the appearance and use of the term in the administrative affairs of the government, it also became a category that was subsequently adopted and developed by Japanese scholars. Katō Genchi, a leading scholar of religion at the Imperial University of Tokyo, for example, elaborated and used the term extensively in his book, *A Study of Shinto: The Religion of the Japanese Nation* (1926). In this volume, he gives considerable attention to "State Shinto" (also referred to as "Kokutai Shinto") and how it was "inculcated through the schools" and celebrated through state rituals. Although he also uses the term "secular" to refer to this form of Shinto, he maintains that it was, in fact, religious. It was Katō's work that greatly shaped the views of Daniel Clarence Holtom, and it was his book, *Modern*

Japan and Shinto Nationalism (1943), which in turn influenced the understanding of Shinto in the Religions Division of the Supreme Commander of Allied Powers (SCAP) in the early days of the Occupation. Given this genealogy of usage by Japanese in the decades before the end of the war, it was clearly a common term before it was adopted and applied extensively by SCAP's Religions Division in the early days of the Occupation.

The new national form of Shinto was created by the Meiji government in part as an effort to control the impending chaos related to the disintegration of the Tokugawa feudal order and the growing external threat of Western imperialism. European and American visions of empire and territorial expansion were accompanied by new Christian missionary initiatives throughout Asia. Over the course of several decades, the restoration government pursued a policy of uniting the people under the canopy of a state-sponsored and emperor-centric expression of Shinto, which was designed to unify and integrate a heterogeneous population and mobilize the people for nation-building, modernization, and military expansion.

The family-state ideology articulated by the Meiji Constitution and the Imperial Rescript on Education was justified with reference to the divine origin of the emperor and the people of Japan. These documents not only reinforced the traditional Confucian virtues of loyalty and filial piety, but also were used to forge a strong national identity. This meant that Buddhism lost the state patronage it had enjoyed during the Tokugawa period and a new form of Shinto was created to provide the foundation for a new political order. Here we see both the secularization of established Buddhism—apparent in the loss of power and prestige of priests as well as the destruction of Buddhist properties—as well as the sacralization process involved in the development of State Shinto. It should be noted that this first phase of secularization did not occur due to the abstract processes associated with modernization, but due to the policies implemented by political and religious elites.[8]

This new form of Shinto was eventually understood and defined by the government as a natural and "nonreligious" Way that bound all Japanese together and transcended other organized religions. In spite of the government's claims, Sarah Thal (2002, 110) has reminded us that "the rhetoric of Shinto as 'not a religion' was never entirely convincing. Because even state-supported shrines relied for most of their income on the donations of worshipers and the purchase of amulets, questions repeatedly arose concerning the religiosity of even the most public, nationally ranked shrines." In spite of the government's position, there were Japanese priests and scholars who continued to recognize the religious character of Shinto shrines during these years (Hiyane 1966, 143).

The new national religion created by the restoration bureaucrats differed considerably from the previous forms of Shinto belief and practice. It was largely an "invention of tradition" projected back on Japanese history, rather than a true restoration (Hobsbawm 1983, 1–14; Hardacre 1989, 4). In order to shift the allegiance of the majority of the population from particularistic local parish (*ujiko*) communities to the emperor and the national community, a major effort of resocialization was required on the part of the government (Davis 1977). Eventually this transformation was achieved through the effective use of the public school system, military conscription, and control of mass media. The role of public education was particularly important in the forging of a new national identity connected to the Imperial Household and symbolized by the new national shrines.[9] The role of Shinto in this system of national integration ended abruptly with Japan's defeat in World War II and surrender on 15 August 1945.

IMPERIALIST SECULARIZATION AND PLURALIZATION

Contemporary scholarship on "State Shinto" is often divided into two camps.[10] There are those—usually Shinto scholars—who operate with a "narrow" definition and understand the term to refer only to the administrative control of the shrines by the government through the Bureau of Shrines from 1900. Others adopt a "broad" definition and understand the term to also include the wider influence and diffusion of an emperor-centric version of Shinto during this period through public schools, the media, as well as the ritual traditions of the Imperial Household (Shimazono 2007, 701). The process of imperialist secularization implemented during the Allied Occupation clearly addressed both the "narrow" and "broad" aspects identified as State Shinto. The direct government control and administration of the shrines was terminated, along with the financial support of some shrines, and policies were enacted to eliminate the wider influence of Shinto in public life and institutions by instituting changes in the national calendar and the public school system. At the same time, the Occupation authorities abolished the wartime laws regulating religion, which had restricted its free practice. The new policies initiated a free-market religious economy in which most established and New Religions were allowed to exist without interference from agents of the state. Shinto institutions, however, faced censorship and some special restrictions until the end of the Occupation period.

Under these new conditions, new religious movements surged in the early decades of the postwar period, which contributed to the ongoing pluralization and growth of the institutional dimension of religion in Japan. This occurred, I should add, when Japan was focused on rebuilding a devastated country and going through a second major period of modernization. Here, again, we see the "ambivalent effects" of modernization and very different patterns of secularization depending on the level or dimension of analysis. During the Occupation and early decades of postwar Japan, for example, we see secularization at the societal level—with the removal of Shinto from the public sphere—but at the same time dynamic movements of sacralization may be seen in the emergence of literally hundreds of new religious movements. I do not want to over-emphasize the social significance of New Religions here—since probably less than 10 percent of the Japanese belong to one of these movements today—but it is remarkable, as Max Eger (1980, 18) noted years ago:

> [Japan] gave evidence of an unparalleled growth in its "religious population" at precisely the same time as its most recent "modernization." Even though the growth of the new religious movements has since tapered off, this coincidence of "modernization" and "religious growth" constitutes a remarkable confutation of the Western idea that modernization goes hand in hand with secularization.

It should be remembered that Eger's assessment appeared almost four decades ago when there were still many signs of growth and vitality in new religious movements, which is very different from the situation today.

While national statistics indicate that organized religion still has a significant presence today, it is well documented that many of these institutions are in serious trouble. Most organized forms of religion have been struggling with basic demographic realities that have accompanied postwar modernization and urbanization. This phase is an example of what Demerath refers to as "emergent secularization," that is, patterns of decline unrelated to specific anti-religious policies issued by political authorities. In the early postwar period, for example, older established Shinto and Buddhist institutions—disproportionately concentrated in rural areas or small towns)—struggled with the impact of urbanization, while a number of new religious movements emerged and initially benefited from the population shift.

Today all organized forms of religion are beginning to feel the impact of the low birthrate and aging population. While some religious groups (notably New Religions and Christian churches) have grown over the past century as a result of active membership recruitment, most religious organizations depend on natural growth, which is based on births to members and effective religious socialization. A fertility rate below 2.1 points to population decline and Japan's birthrate, which has been declining for decades, appears to have stabilized at 1.42 since 2016. This decline is especially evident in rural areas or small towns, which have the added challenge of the movement of youth to urban centers for education and employment. Some of the latest results of demographic studies of religion were helpfully summarized by journalist Ukai Hidemori in his book *Jiin shōmetsu* (2015), which projects a very gloomy future for established Buddhist temples and Shinto shrines concentrated in areas most affected by these trends. It is estimated that by 2040, some 896 small towns and municipalities will dissolve due to population decline. Given the concentration of many traditional institutions in these areas, Ishii Kenji, a sociologist of religion consulted for this study, projects that 35 percent of all registered religious organizations will also disappear (Ukai 2015, 163, 240–241).

It is not just traditional institutions in rural areas that are experiencing serious decline. The pattern of aging and decline is also apparent in most of the New Religions and many Christian churches, which are similarly suffering from a shortage of clergy and "priest-less" parishes. While there will undoubtedly be "winners" and "losers" in the shrinking religious market, it seems likely that most religious groups for the foreseeable future will be struggling to maintain their institutions and activities as the number of active clergy and members continues to decline. Reviewing postwar surveys of individual belief and behavior and institutional data, Ian Reader (2012) has made a strong case for the secularization thesis, which he captured with the subtitle, "The 'Rush Hour Away from the Gods' and the Decline of Religion in Contemporary Japan." His analysis focused on evidence from the micro- and meso-levels, however, and did not address the possible ways that religious groups are politically reengaging the larger society in the midst of very real decline, which is our key concern in this study.

DEPRIVATIZATION AND RELIGION IN THE PUBLIC SPHERE

The world has changed dramatically since Jürgen Habermas initiated scholarly debate about the nature of the public sphere over half a century ago. At the time, religion was regarded as largely irrelevant for understanding the nature of the bourgeois public sphere in modern Europe since it had already been reduced to personal piety or to the private sphere of familial relations in the wake of the Reformation.[11] Habermas was hardly alone in assuming that "privatization" was the inevitable fate of religion in modern societies. This was a central element of many secularization theories advanced in the West and accepted widely by many scholars for most of the twentieth century.

Some years ago Peter Berger (1967, 107–108) defined secularization as "the process by which sectors of society and culture are removed from the domination of religious institutions and symbols." In other words, it refers not just to institutional decline and a weakening of individual belief and practice, but also involves the privatization of religion or the removal of religion as a significant force or influence in the public sphere. Is this the inevitable and irreversible fate of religion in modern societies?

In *Public Religions in the Modern World*, José Casanova (1994, 5) challenged this taken-for-granted assumption and highlighted the fact that religions around the world were breaking out of the restricted role they had been assigned in the private sphere and were again making claims about public life and institutions, and giving birth to socially engaged religious movements. Casanova identifies this rediscovery of a public role as the process of "deprivatization." On the basis of case studies of movements in multiple national contexts, he argued that privatization is not inevitable but a process that depends in part on how religious groups interpret their religious tradition and context.

> Some religions will be induced by tradition, principle, and historical circumstances to remain basically private religions of individual salvation. Certain cultural traditions, religious doctrinal principles, and historical circumstances, by contrast will induce other religions to enter, at least occasionally, the public sphere. (Casanova 1994, 221)

Several decades ago Richard K. Fenn (1978, xii) elaborated a perspective on secularization that anticipated in some ways the argument advanced by Casanova, arguing that "individuals and groups are responsible for secularization: not impersonal or abstract forces like technology or education, but living and active human agents." Secularization occurs, he explained, as individuals and groups redefine and negotiate the boundary between the sacred and the profane. It is this changing "definition of the situation" that shapes the path toward either secularization or desecularization.

According to Fenn's framework, the process of desecularization is, in fact, theoretically possible if religious groups "assign wide scope to the sacred and require high levels of integration between personal and corporate values" (Fenn 1978, 139). Religious groups that define the sacred in broader terms represent a potential force for desecularization if they are able to effectively mobilize their members to engage the public sphere.[12] It is possible for groups—which for decades may have been largely concerned with personal piety and content with a religious life in community or congregation "separate from the world"—to discover a larger vision and adopt the view that it is their duty to engage society and influence the broader sphere of public life. This can be seen, for example, in the transformation of some fundamentalist and evangelical Protestants in the late 1970s from "separatists"—preoccupied with individual salvation and personal piety—into the "Moral Majority"—a social movement that actively sought to shape electoral politics, public schools, and legislation in America.

In more recent work, Habermas (2006, 1) has acknowledged that "religious traditions and communities of faith have gained a new, hitherto unexpected political importance," and must be included in our consideration of the public sphere. Nevertheless, his approach, as Michelle Dillon (2012, 250–251) explains, is still dominated by the "highly cognitive and rational approach to social life" that is embedded in his theory of communicative action. For that reason, he "ultimately gives short shrift to all those nonrational but highly significant sources of action and meaning in everyday life, all those things that spring from emotion and tradition." If the public sphere is an area of social life where individuals can gather and freely share their views and concerns and formulate some agenda for political action, then it is hardly limited to the types of gatherings with which Habermas was preoccupied in the European context, i.e., discursive arenas such as salons and coffee houses where "nonreligious" citizens engaged in debate and discussed matters of common concern.

It is significant that this problem highlighted by Dillon—who is primarily concerned with the deficiencies of Habermas's approach to religion in Western societies—also appears in Eiko Ikegami's (2000; 2005) revision of public sphere analysis for the Japanese cultural context. Ikegami (2000, 990, 1023) is similarly critical of Habermas's preoccupation with the "liberal public sphere" and his neglect of the "nondiscursive, nonrational, or other counterpublics." She makes the case for a "plurality of publics" and provides a broader framework that takes seriously a range of social groups—women, racial minorities, and religious groups, for example—which have been largely excluded from consideration in Eurocentric studies of the public sphere.

The significance of Japanese religions for the public sphere has recently received focused attention in relation to the response of various groups to the 2011 "triple disaster" of earthquake, tsunami, and nuclear accident in Fukushima. A number of scholars have drawn attention to the many new initiatives undertaken by Buddhist institutions and New Religions in disaster relief, spiritual counseling, social involvement with environmental and nuclear issues, and in critical engagement with the government's energy policy.[13] Given the emergency situation of northeastern Japan, these are important new developments and, to borrow Ikegami's terminology, represent emerging "counterpublics" that could eventually influence the political process and help determine the shape of public life and institutions.

Long before the disaster events stimulated the new initiatives referred to above, there was already evidence that at least some religious organizations had larger interests that extended beyond their own communities. It is well known that Sōka Gakkai, for example, the largest Buddhist New Religion in postwar Japan, was not content with cultivating the faith of its followers in the private sphere, but in 1964 formed its own political party, the Kōmeitō, with a vision of shaping public life according to its principles and ideals. Sōka Gakkai's political engagement has been the focus of considerable criticism and public debate, as well as scholarly research.[14] Another New Religion, Kōfuku no Kagaku, similarly organized its own political party, the Happiness Realization Party (Kōfuku Jitsugen Tō) in 2009, and expressed a similar concern to shape public life through electoral politics (Tsukada 2012; 2015).

Less widely known—particularly outside of Japan—are the close connections and symbiotic relationship between the Shinto establishment (i.e., leadership within the NAS) and the LDP, which is one of the defining characteristics of postwar nationalism and deserves more serious attention. Anyone following news reports on politics in Japan over the past two decades will be familiar with the broad political agenda of the LDP, which has included efforts to restore patriotic moral education in public schools, promote official visits to Yasukuni Shrine, and revise the Constitution. The close relationship between organized religions and these political initiatives remains an understudied phenomenon. It is this Shinto version of nationalism—a movement that emerged in response to a perceived inadequacy of the secular order imposed during the Occupation from 1945 to 1952—that resembles most closely the Islamic and Hindu expressions of nationalism, which were Juergensmeyer's (1993) primary concern. Our case study of this Shinto-related movement in postwar Japan will provide support from the Asian context for Casanova's (1994, 10) thesis that "the deprivatization of religion is indeed a global phenomenon."

SHINTO FUNDAMENTALISM AND RELIGION IN THE PUBLIC SPHERE

The privatization of Shinto occurred not as a result of modernization per se, but due to its forced removal from the public sphere as a result of the directives issued by SCAP and implemented by the Japanese government. Under these circumstances, it is not surprising that the process of "deprivatization" in the postwar period is closely connected to the Shinto-related neonationalistic response to the imposition of a "foreign" social order on Japan. As soon as the Occupation ended, religious and political leaders quickly mobilized forces to restore Shinto to public life and institutions.

As we will document in this study, this religio-political movement has been organized by the "elites" within the head office of the NAS, but it has failed to garner the support of most shrines or priests across the country. Nevertheless, even this relatively small association of NAS affiliated shrines has managed to mobilize a number of LDP politicians in support of its political agenda. While the NAS has been one key ideological source for this postwar movement, it has evolved into a transdenominational movement in recent decades, which now includes a larger network of religious groups and political actors, including members of the Japan Conference, who share the same restorationist vision and are working to reshape public life and institutions.

This movement has been referred to in multiple ways—as an effort to restore State Shinto (*kokka Shintō no fukkō*), as a new expression of civil religion, and as a Japanese version of religious fundamentalism. Over the past decade, for example, Shimazono Susumu has been publishing widely on State Shinto and its lingering presence in postwar Japan. His book, *Kokka Shintō to Nihonjin* (2010), and the more popular Iwanami booklet, *Kokka Shintō to senzen sengo no Nihonjin* (2014), are representative of his scholarship on this topic and also reveal his broader role as a public intellectual. One key emphasis in his work is that the Shinto traditions related to the emperor and the Imperial Household—which were key aspects of "State Shinto" in the prewar period—were given a pass by the Occupation authorities and escaped the process of imperialist secularization. This dimension of State Shinto, he argues, effectively survived into the postwar period.[15] In addition to the Shinto of the Imperial Household, other aspects of the prewar social order that were closely intertwined with Shinto institutions are also being promoted as a part of the restoration movement. These include efforts to restore the emperor-centric Imperial Rescript on Education as the foundation for moral education in public schools, a new emphasis on patriotic education, legislative attempts in the National Diet to reinstate government support of Yasukuni Shrine as a public institution, as well as promotion of official visits to the shrine by politicians.

While there are many similarities between State Shinto in the prewar period and some aspects of this restorationist movement, the actual agenda advanced by the NAS avoids any mention of returning to the prewar or wartime administrative structure, which placed Shinto shrines under the Bureau of Shrines and all other religious bodies under the Bureau of Religion (Shūkyō Kyoku). Strictly speaking, a restoration of "State Shinto" would involve a return to the direct administration of shrines by the government and an abandonment of the current registration of shrines as independent juridical persons or religious corporations. I have been unable to document any proposals by Shinto elites to return shrines to direct government management by bureaucrats, which many still regard as something that warped or damaged what some consider to be "authentic" Shinto tradition. Since this movement does not advocate a return to direct shrine administration by the Bureau of Shrines, and it has evolved into a transdenominational movement that includes supporters from Buddhist institutions and a number of New Religions, I have avoided the term "State Shinto" to identify this postwar development.

The term "civil religion" has also been adopted by some observers—both insiders and outsiders—to refer to both prewar and postwar forms of Shinto. Noguchi (1984), a scholar at Kōgakkan University, a Shinto institution, argues that State Shinto should have been regarded as a legitimate Japanese expression of "civil religion," and regrets that Robert Bellah's (1967) classic treatment of American civil religion was published some two decades too late to shape the views and policies of the Occupation. Noguchi claims that State Shinto was essentially a functional equivalent of American "civil religion" (kōmin shūkyō), which similarly unified the nation around sacred myths, a national calendar, and key sacred sites. While it was allowed to continue and flourish in the United States, the Occupation authorities dismantled the Japanese version and unfairly imposed a strict separation of religion and state and eliminated Japan's civil religion. K. Peter Takayama (1988), the late sociologist of religion, similarly used the term, referring to the postwar efforts to restore aspects of State Shinto as the "revitalization of Japanese civil religion." Although both insiders and outsiders may have embraced this term, the agenda and activities promoted by the NAS and affiliated groups remain divisive and contested. In my view, it is best to reserve the term civil religion for something that still retains the power to unify the nation. The political agenda of the neonationalist coalition is, in fact, extremely divisive and has provoked widespread criticism from a range of religious leaders and public intellectuals, and constitutes a counter-movement of sorts, which we examine in some detail in Part Two of this volume.

The contested nature of the neonationalistic political agenda has led a number of observers to regard this movement as a Japanese version of religious fundamentalism. Scholarship on fundamentalist movements around the world has flourished over the past two decades. The well-known Fundamentalism Project produced numerous tomes, and other scholars followed-up with monographs and edited collections. The first volume that emerged from The Fundamentalism Project, *Fundamentalisms Observed*, edited by Martin E. Marty and R. Scott Appleby (1991), highlighted the plural forms that fundamentalism takes in relation to a variety of religious traditions and in multiple contexts. Although the Project did not establish a consensus definition, Marty and Appleby maintain that the term fundamentalism points to a distinctive phenomena that cannot be captured by "traditionalism," "conservatism," and "orthodoxy," and proposed it as a useful construct for comparative research on a particular type of religious movement that has developed globally in response to modernization and secularization. The Project identified a number of features—referred to as "family resemblances"—that these movements often shared, but acknowledged a considerable diversity among movements, which reflected the particular religious tradition that inspired them and how they evolved in different national contexts.

For many years, fundamentalism was a term largely restricted to monotheistic "religions of the book"—Judaism, Christianity, and Islam—which tended to develop more systematic doctrinal systems of belief or creeds. This was the basis for S. N. Eisenstadt's (1999, 155, 163) observation that there was a "weakness or non-development of fundamentalist movements in Japan," which has been interpreted by some sociologists to mean that fundamentalism is actually absent from Japan (Davie 2013, 194). A sociologist with extensive research experience on Japanese religions, Winston Davis (1991), contributed a major chapter to one of the Project volumes, which provided a detailed discussion of a wide range of religious and political forms of fundamentalism that have appeared in both prewar and postwar Japan. This empirical reality challenges the taken-for-granted view that fundamentalism does not grow in Asian religious contexts.

In another contribution to the Fundamentalism Project, Ernest Gellner (1995, 280) explains that he had shared the widely held view about monotheistic doctrinal religions being "more fundamentalism prone" than the Asian religions, since the later tended to embrace multiple gods and emphasized "praxis" over "doctrine." The appearance of Hindu fundamentalism, which had once been regarded as "inconceivable," however, forced Gellner (1995, 280–281) to "make some adjustment to the theory." He put forward the following proposition:

> When a religion which has its center of gravity outside of doctrine, being rather a system of praxis, nevertheless goes fundamentalist, it can only do so by, as it were, platonizing itself a bit, by coming in some measure to resemble the more doctrinal and theological religions. This is an ad hoc hypothesis, but it may well be correct.

I will argue that Gellner's hypothesis about "platonizing" in Asian religions—a process of abstracting core and essential beliefs from a very heterogeneous heritage—is relevant not only for understanding the emergence of Hindu fundamentalism, but also for the formation of Shinto fundamentalism in the years following the Occupation.

There are several features from the cluster of characteristics identified with "fundamentalist-like" movements that are relevant for understanding the Shinto-related case in postwar Japan. First, the movement represents a response to the experience of dislocation or marginalization brought about by modernization and its attendant process of secularization. As Almond, Appleby, and Sivan (2003, 93) point out: "Fundamentalism is reactive. Fundamentalist movements form in reaction to, and in defense against, the processes of secularization and modernization which have penetrated the larger religious community." In the Japanese case, as noted earlier, the reaction is to a particular type of secularization—imperialist secularization—which was the top-down removal of Shinto from the public sphere by a foreign power. This has meant that the movement is tied inexorably to nationalist aspirations.

Second, retrieving some "essential" or "fundamental" beliefs and values from the past—what Winston Davis (1991) refers to as "symbolic regression"—is central to all fundamentalist movements, including the Shinto case under consideration. Given that Shinto communities lack the concern about inerrant scriptures and doctrinal orthodoxy so typical of fundamentalist movements rooted in Abrahamic traditions, scholars such as Sakamoto Koremaru (1994b, 179) indicate that it is difficult to determine what might constitute the "fundamentals" (*genri*) of the Shinto tradition.[16] Even without this scriptural orientation, however, there is clear evidence that the leadership in the NAS head office has managed to retrieve certain elements from the recent past and codified them into an "essentialist" vision, which constitutes both the core beliefs as well as behavioral expectations (orthopraxis) for the movement.

Third, as Marty and Appleby (1991, ix) point out, "fundamentalists begin as traditionalists who perceive some challenge or threat to their core identity, both social and personal." But they are more than traditionalists. They mobilize to engage the source of the perceived threat and "fight for" a restoration of an idealized version of the past. In other words, its public and political goals make it a different phenomenon from merely conservative religious groups that are content to practice the faith "privately" in a separate subculture. As Steve Bruce (2008, 96) has observed, what is distinctive about fundamentalist movements is that they are concerned with "society-wide obedience" and aim to gain "political power to impose the revitalized tradition." The demand for "society-wide obedience" necessarily involves coercion, which may be due to intense peer pressure or the result of legislation passed to legitimize the required conformity (Davis 1991, 785). In his study of Hindu fundamentalism in India, Peter van der Veer (1994) has identified this particular feature of fundamentalism as the "politics of inclusion," a term that captures well the aim of Yasukuni fundamentalism, which is to bring all members of society into conformity with their emperor-centric understanding of Japanese identity. The restorationists would like to bring back the "society-wide obedience" that characterized the "idealized" wartime period. As Scheid (2012, 96) reminds us: "Public ceremonies honoring the Tennō [emperor] became compulsory in schools and at universities. New national holy days in the form of shrine festivals were introduced. Shrines were defined as sites of Tennō worship that should be attended by all loyal Japanese subjects." There are aspects of this prewar pattern of coercion already reappearing in contemporary Japan as a result of the educational reforms and legislation pushed forward by the restorationists. Unlike the transnational and global aspirations of some Christian or Islamic fundamentalist movements, however, the "scope" of the political aims of the Japanese movement remains restricted to the nation.

The use of the term "fundamentalism" to capture the nature of this movement began to appear during Abe Shinzō's first term as prime minister (2006–2007). It is important to remember that Abe was not only the head of the LDP at the time, but also an active member of both the League Promoting Ties between Politics and Shinto (Shintō Seiji Renmei), and the Japan Conference. Fuwa Tetsuzō, the Director of the Japanese Communist Party Central Committee's Social Science Research Institute, used the term "Yasukuni *ha*" (sect or faction) to identify the core beliefs and agenda of the LDP's rightwing faction led by Abe. According to Fuwa (2007, 23–26), the Yasukuni faction began to consolidate itself as an organized national movement from the mid-1990s through the coordination and cooperation of political groups affiliated with the NAS and the Japan Conference. The name "Yasukuni" is attached to this movement because it shares the war memory embraced by the shrine and its museum, Yūshūkan, which claims that Japan's past invasion of its neighbors in Asia constituted a legitimate war of self-defense and a liberation of Asia from Western colonialism. It is this particular version of history, Fuwa explains, that the movement seeks to promote—actually "impose" (*oshitsuke*)—in public schools through the introduction of revisionist textbooks.

The *Akahata*, the national newspaper of the Japanese Communist Party, regularly uses this designation in its reporting about Abe's faction and his appointment of League Promoting Ties between Politics and Shinto and Japan Conference affiliated diet members to his Cabinet. All members not only share the particular war memory represented by Yūshūkan, but also promote "official visits" to Yasukuni Shrine and advocate revision of the Constitution. The strength of the Yasukuni faction and support for this agenda has only intensified since Abe began his second term as prime minister in 2012.[17] Fuwa (2007, 44–45) sees close parallels between this faction and Christian fundamentalism in America. Like Christian fundamentalists, the Yasukuni sect aims for "society-wide obedience" and aims to impose its particular values and views on the larger society through legislation, education reform, and eventually by revising the Constitution so that it conforms to their ideals.

Other observers have actually used the label "Yasukuni fundamentalism" to refer to this faction and movement. Inagaki Hisakazu (2006, 30), a Christian scholar and specialist in public philosophy, provided a more detailed treatment of Yasukuni Shrine as the center of postwar religious fundamentalism (*shūkyō teki genri shugi*) and argues that Yasukuni fundamentalism needs to be viewed alongside "Christian fundamentalism in the US, Islamic fundamentalism in various Arab countries, and Hindu fundamentalism in India." Yasukuni fundamentalism is understood here to be an umbrella term for a movement that seeks to revive and restore the social order and values expressed in the emperor-centered State Shinto of wartime Japan. In Inagaki's view, it does not represent authentic "Japanese tradition," but rather a deviation from "Japan's good tradition" (*Nihon no yoki dentō*). Although Ise Shrine is widely acknowledged as the main shrine for the NAS, it is Yasukuni Shrine that actually functions as the symbolic headquarters (*sōhonzan*) for the neonationalist movement today (Inagaki 2006, 119). Bae Boo-Gil (2007; 2008), a Korean scholar, draws on Inagaki's work and similarly uses the term "Yasukuni fundamentalism" (*Yasukuni genri shugi*) in his treatment of the postwar enshrinement of class-A war criminals.

Perhaps it is not surprising that these "outsiders" have identified the movement as the Japanese equivalent of fundamentalisms in other national contexts, but until recently it has been impossible to find the case of an "insider" using the term with reference to their own Shinto tradition. Several years ago, however, Miwa Takahiro (2016a, 2016b, 2017), the resident priest of Hiyoshi Shrine in Nagoya, began publishing his critical views of this particular version of Shinto in online reports and personal blog posts. To my knowledge, he is the first Shinto insider who has identified this restorationist movement promoted by the NAS and the Japan Conference as an authoritarian form of fundamentalism, which distorts the actual pluralism of Japanese tradition with its particularly narrow version of what constitutes authentic Japanese identity. Such public criticisms of this fundamentalist version of Shinto by priests will likely remain rare given the authority structure of the NAS, but that hardly means that its agenda fairly represents the views and concerns of priests and shrines across the country. In fact, our study will show that this particular version of Shinto and its nationalistic political agenda has been unable to garner the support of the vast majority of shrines and priests affiliated with the NAS, who remain largely focused on local communities and issues surrounding survival. Readers may decide at the end of this study whether this Shinto-related restoration movement qualifies for inclusion under the comparative rubric "fundamentalism," but I have found too many similarities to overlook and agree with Winston Davis (1991, 784) that it is a useful concept for "bringing the Japanese phenomenon into a comparative perspective."

OVERVIEW

This book is an exercise in historical sociology of religion that critically engages the contemporary debates surrounding secularization in light of postwar developments in Japanese religions. The book is divided into two main parts. Part One is concerned with the social sources of postwar nationalism and examines how and why a religio-political movement was organized to restore the public role of Shinto. The first chapter provides a detailed treatment of "imperialist secularization," which resulted from the policies implemented during the Allied Occupation of Japan. The second chapter examines how Shinto leaders and institutions responded to the foreign occupation. The first phase of their response is characterized by the process of "privatization," which resulted from policies aimed at eliminating Shinto's public influence. Their critical assessment of the impact of the "Shinto Directive" (15 December 1945) and other SCAP policies during the Occupation period provided the foundation for the second phase of "deprivatization," and the launching of a movement to restore the place of Shinto in public life and institutions.

In the two decades since 1995, there has been a surge in support for the political agenda promoted by the NAS and an increase in the number of associations, political leaders, and religious groups mobilized for the cause. In the third chapter, I examine the impact of the disaster years on the expansion of support for the neonationalist movement. First was the "double disaster" of 1995, which began with the 17 January Hanshin-Awaji earthquake and was followed by the 20 March sarin gas attack on the Tokyo subway system by members of Aum Shinrikyō. Second was the 11 March 2011 "triple disaster," which included the earthquake, tsunami, and nuclear meltdown at the Fukushima Daiichi plant. I make the case that the "social crises" generated by these events created an environment that made it possible for neonationalists to push forward their languishing agenda. Evidence reveals a steady growth in support for this movement in post-disaster Japan, particularly the increasing number of LDP politicians identifying themselves with the agenda of the NAS. The movement was strengthened by the appearance of a new organization, the Japan Conference, which was formed in 1997 through an amalgamation of conservative religious and political groups, such as Nippon o Mamoru Kai and Seichō no Ie Seiji Rengō, which had been active for several decades (Tsukada 2015, 57–80). It shared the core values and political agenda of the NAS and became a close collaborator, attracting supporters to the movement from a variety of Buddhist institutions, some New Religions, and even an indigenous Christian movement. The Cabinet of the National Diet has been dominated by politicians who belong to this religio-political coalition since Prime Minister Abe returned to power in 2012, which is evident in the support mobilized for Yasukuni Shrine, legislation passed to restore patriotic moral education in public schools, and current efforts to revise the Constitution.

Part Two shifts attention to the contested nature of this political agenda. "The nationalism appearing in Japan today may be similar to that of the 1930s," as Davis (1991, 805) has observed, "but it is forced to defend itself in a new pluralistic climate. At several crucial points it has been checked by concerned citizens (secular and religious) in ways made possible by the postwar constitutional order." The effort to reshape the public sphere according to the ideals retrieved from the invented tradition of the wartime period has been met with considerable resistance from public intellectuals and religious minorities. These alternative and critical perspectives on controversial issues, however, often fall through the cracks and disappear from the narrative. Some years ago Philip Seaton (2005, 288–289) drew attention to how media coverage often distorted the complex realities of contemporary Japan, particularly when reporting on controversial issues such as revisionist history textbooks. His review of the media reveals an "under-representation" of some groups, which refers to the "marginaliza-tion of Japanese progressives, who condemn Japan's aggression," but are rarely given equal time (to which we could add the voices of various religious minorities); there is also "the over-representation of a group (undue attention to nationalistic voices glorifying war exploits)"; and there is often "misrepresentation (the equation of the Japanese government with Japanese opinion, such as through the use of the journalistic shorthand 'Japan' to mean 'the Japanese government')."

Part Two of our study aims to bring these underrepresented perspectives back into consideration. Groups that in other contexts might appear at odds—Communists, Christians, and Buddhists—constitute a "counter-public" that has been critically engaging the agenda of the neonationalists. The fourth chapter examines key issues related to Yasukuni Shrine, par-ticularly "official visits" (*kōshiki sanpai*) and postwar enshrinements. The fifth chapter examines the debate surrounding flag and anthem and the critical response to the new policies requiring their use in public schools to promote patriotic education. Finally, the sixth chapter focuses on the pro-posal to revise the Constitution. These chapters bring into sharp relief the potential downside of embracing the political agenda of the neonationalist coalition, particularly the erosion of individual rights and freedoms.

My understanding of the issues treated in this study is based in part on many years spent as a participant observer of Japanese religious life and institutions. Over the past two decades, in particular, this has included numerous visits to Yasukuni Shrine, often accompanied by university students, and many hours spent in the adjoining museum, Yūshūkan, viewing the exhibitions and watching videos aimed at promoting a special appreciation for the enshrined "Shōwa martyrs" and nurturing a similar spirit of sacrifice for the emperor and nation. These experiences have been supplemented by numerous encounters with anti-Yasukuni activists, including priests and laity from both Buddhist and Christian organizations. These connections led to several opportunities to attend court hearings in Tokyo and Osaka, which were about lawsuits launched against the shrine and the Japanese government for facilitating postwar enshrinements. Debriefing sessions followed the hearings, which exposed me to the views and emotions of the plaintiffs, their lawyers, and supporters in response to the decision of the courts. I've also attended ecumenical gatherings and lectures organized to address concerns over proposals to revise the Constitution, as well as meetings held in support of teachers in the municipal schools of Tokyo and Osaka, who have faced disciplinary action due to their opposition to the new requirement to stand and lead students in singing the national anthem. A number of personal contacts made at these gatherings provided me with relevant court records and publications that explained their situations and views.

While all of these personal encounters and observations have enriched my understanding of the different actors involved in both the coalition and its opposition, this book does not pretend to be an ethnographic study. Given my concern with the public sphere and where political and religious actors stand in relation to a range of issues, I have used documentary evidence to support my interpretations and arguments. I have drawn upon multiple archives related to the Occupation period, diaries and letters, government records and reports, and official statements and publications from a wide range of religious organizations. Generalizations about organized religions in Japan are fraught with difficulties and it should be recognized that within most groups—whether Shinto, Buddhist, Christian, or New Religions—members hold a wide range of views about the issues considered in this study, and many disagree with the "official positions" issued by their respective leaders. Wherever possible, I provide some information that indicates the divisions that exist within representative groups. Given the scope of this study—the seventy-year period since the Occupation—I have also relied extensively on the work of other scholars in the field and, hopefully, given them credit where it is due along the way.

PART ONE

Postwar Religious Nationalism

1

Imperialist Secularization

The Restructuring of Religion
and Society in Occupied Japan

Japan's defeat and surrender on 15 August 1945 brought to an end the particular system that had been created by the government to manage religion in Japan and within the larger Japanese empire. This was a system that evolved from the early Meiji period in response to the threat of Western imperialism and the encroaching Christian missionary enterprise. Although religious freedom had been guaranteed by the Meiji Constitution, the government regarded those rituals conducted at Shinto shrines, as well as the emperor-centric rites conducted at public schools and municipal offices, as "nonreligious," and participation in such ritual activity became a normative requirement for all Japanese regardless of their personal religious commitments.

Just as the perceived threat from the West generated a "crisis" that helped launch the creation of a new form of State Shinto, it was the defeat and Occupation of Japan by the Allied Powers in August 1945 that also led to its rapid deconstruction. The principles and policies forthcoming from the Religions Division brought about a fundamental restructuring of Japanese religion and society. The colorful religion poster below, which was produced by the General Headquarters (GHQ) in 1946, provides a graphic picture of what the Division sought to achieve.[1] The profound changes brought about by the Occupation authorities provide a good example of what N. J. Demerath (2007, 72–76) has designated as "imperialist secularization," which is the coercive and top-down removal of religion from

Religion in Japan Poster, GHQ, Tokyo, December 1946. Used with the permission of Special Collections and University Archives, University of Oregon Libraries.

public institutions by a foreign power. As we have seen, this is a very different process from the one outlined in most versions of secularization, that is, the gradual decline of religion with the advance of modernization. As far as imperialist secularization is concerned, we should note that it may or may not bring about the secularization of consciousness on the part of practitioners of a given religion. In this particular case, many religious and political leaders continued to believe that Shinto should play a central role in public life and institutions and would act upon this conviction once the foreign Occupation ended.

In this chapter I briefly introduce some of the official documents and directives produced by the US State Department and the Supreme Commander of Allied Powers's (SCAP) Religions Division that laid out the principles of religious freedom and the separation of religion and state, which were to guide the treatment of religion during the Allied Occupation of Japan (1945–1952). The focus here is on the key changes affecting organized religion, particularly Shinto-related institutions, as a result of the Occupation-led reforms. As Ray A. Moore (1979, 723) has reminded us, defeated Japan "was not an empty blackboard on which Americans wrote a series of reforms"; rather, this was clearly "Japanese history, with Japanese participants and objectives, and ideals influencing events." This is certainly true as far as the treatment of religion was concerned. SCAP's Religions Division was clearly the most powerful player in determining policy, but Japanese actors—government bureaucrats, religion scholars, and priests—significantly shaped how the foreign staff came to understand Shinto as a "religion" and negotiated for the survival of Shinto institutions.

The Religions Division sought to apply a rather strict interpretation of religion-state separation to the Japanese context and encountered considerable difficulty in working with the Ministry of Education's Religions Bureau (Shūmuka) in the implementation and enforcement of their policies on the ground. The Division's stated policy to fairly apply religion-state separation to all religions was also undermined by various actors in the Occupation forces, including General MacArthur himself. This chapter will reveal the large gap that emerged between the Occupation's declared "ideals" and "actual practices" through a comparative analysis of the unequal treatment of Shinto and Christianity during this period. I will argue that the roots of religious nationalism in postwar Japan can be traced back to this Shinto experience of marginalization.

PRE-OCCUPATION PLANNING AND INITIAL DIRECTIVES

The US State Department had prepared documents to guide the Occupation, which mandated that the principles of religious freedom and the separation of religion and state would be central to the postwar social order. How these principles would be applied in Japan and impact specific institutions had to be worked out by the Religions Division staff of the Civil Information and Education (CIE) section of the SCAP. The Religions Division staff did this in consultation with Japanese government officials, scholars, and representatives of various religious bodies.

In the very early days of the Occupation, on 9 September 1945, the Office of the Commanding General of the United States Army issued an "Operational Directive" (Number 8) for the "Protection of Religious Shrines," which was to guide the behavior of the Occupation Forces on the ground (this should not be confused with the "Shinto Directive" issued several months later).[2] "In the Occupation of the Tokyo area it is desired that no religious shrines, places, or places of like nature are to be damaged or profaned by our troops. When troops occupy an area containing places of this nature the responsible commander will take the necessary steps to prevent any profanation or desecration of such places and their contents." The Directive also identified representative sites that would "require guards as US troops occupy areas in which they are located," such as the Imperial palaces, well known shrines such as Yasukuni, Tōgō, and Meiji, as well as Shinto shrines in general. This order indicates some concern that troops might damage these sacred places and provoke a hostile reaction from the local population. The Directive goes on to state, "steps will be taken to prevent the desecration of graves and the mutilation of monuments. Troops will be kept out of private homes and public baths."

Although there were those who advocated for the destruction of Shinto shrines as a part of the Occupation policy, a more cautious approach to dealing with Japanese religions had been prepared in advance. In fact, there were already rather clear and pragmatic guidelines that had been developed by a post-defeat planning group for Japan, which had been organized by the US State Department on 20 October 1943. Known as the Inter-Divisional Area Committee on the Far East, this group had met more than two hundred times by July 1945 (Takemae 2003, 204–205; Borton 1967). One important document that emerged from the planning group was a "Memorandum: Freedom of Worship" dated 15 March 1944, which became a part of the larger document entitled "Summary of United States Initial Policy related to Japan" that was finalized by the State Department on 19 April 1945.[3] The "Memorandum" apparently reached the desk of General MacArthur at GHQ sometime in October 1945.[4] This document states that "the United Nations are committed to the principle of freedom of religious worship," but recognizes that implementation of this principle in postwar Japan will be fraught with difficulties. It directly addresses the "problem" of "whether or not the occupying forces should permit freedom of worship in Japan, in view of the difficulty of differentiating Shintoism, as a religion, from extreme Nationalism." It goes on to identify certain shrines as symbolic centers of militant nationalism, including Yasukuni, Meiji, Nogi, and Tōgō, which it explains:

> could be closed without any violation of the principle of freedom of religious worship, as the Japanese Government has repeatedly asserted that National Shinto is not a religion but rather a manifestation of patriotism. It may well be, however, that tolerance of such shrines coincident with military defeat and the demobilization of the Army would do more to weaken the hold of the National Shinto cult upon the people than would the forcible closing of such shrines, which might tend to strengthen the cult.

The Memorandum (1944, 1207–1208) concluded with the following "Recommendations":

1. Freedom of religious worship should be proclaimed promptly on occupation.

2. Shrines of the ancient Shinto religion should be permitted to remain open except where it is found that such shrines are being utilized for subversive activities.

3. The Grand Shrines at Ise, dedicated to the Sun Goddess, should be permitted to remain open, unless experience indicates that it would be advisable to close them.

4. At the strictly nationalist shrines, ceremonies or gatherings which involve demonstrations or large crowds at such shrines should be forbidden. The staffs of the national shrines, other than physical caretakers, should be dismissed and not receive pay from the national treasury. *These shrines should be permitted to remain open for individual worship*, except in instances where such action appears to be contrary to public order and security. (*CAA would be well advised to obtain the guidance of Protestant and Roman Catholic missionaries in determining which are the nationalistic shrines.*)[5]

5. Care should be taken that the troops of occupation do no damage to any of the shrines.

6. No action should be necessary in regard to Buddhist temples.

7. Christian churches should be liberated by restoration of complete freedom of organization and worship.[6]

It is undeniable that many Americans thought that Shinto was at the center of Japanese militarism and some advocated "razing" Yasukuni and other so-called "national shrines." Some members of the Occupation shared this view. This, however, had not been decided in advance as a matter of policy, although popular accounts claim that the Occupation authorities had every intention of destroying Yasukuni Shrine. The Memorandum examined above indicates that those involved in planning for post-defeat Japan recommended a more cautious and pragmatic approach. This document reveals that the State Department was fully aware of the complicated nature of the situation and advised those on the ground to give due consideration to both the "intended" and "unintended" consequences of whichever policy was adopted. The authors reasoned that if one followed the logic and definition of Shinto promoted by the Japanese government, it would be possible to close shrines without violating the principle of religious freedom, since they were designated as "nonreligious" sites. Although this course of action could be legitimized given the Japanese government's interpretation of the shrines, the document clearly cautions the policymakers to think about the potential negative repercussions if such a decision were made.

Woodard (1972, 160) records that there was one staff member in the Religions Division who "claimed that the military shrines were not bona fide religious institutions and recommended that the government be directed to dissolve them and to confiscate their properties." As late as 1948 a Japanese-American from Hawaii, Francis Motofuji, also assigned to the Religions Division, still strongly opposed the continuation of Yasukuni Shrine (Nakamura 2007, 125). In this context it should be remembered, too, that in the fall of 1945 there were Japanese as well who thought that the abolition of Yasukuni Shrine should be "seriously taken into consideration."[7]

In addition to the "Memorandum: Freedom of Worship" (15 March 1944) introduced above, within the first ten weeks of the Occupation the US State Department issued several other important policy statements, which outlined the work of those responsible for addressing the religious situation in postwar Japan. The first was "US Initial Post-Surrender Policy for Japan," dated 21 September 1945.[8] Part 3 of the document included the following instructions: "Freedom of religious worship shall be proclaimed promptly on Occupation. At the same time it should be made plain to the Japanese that ultranationalistic and militaristic organizations and movements will not be permitted to hide behind the cloak of religion." This was reinforced by a memorandum issued on 4 October 1945 that instructed the Imperial Japanese government to make arrangements for the "Removal of Restrictions on Political, Civil, and Religious Liberties."⁹ Finally, the "Basic Initial Post-Surrender Directive to Supreme Commander for the Allied Powers for the Occupation and Control of Japan," sent by the Joint Chiefs of Staff on 3 November 1945, reiterated the guidelines and policies of the earlier documents and elaborated the problem of militaristic institutions in relation to Shinto as follows: "The dissemination of Japanese militaristic and ultra-nationalistic ideology and propaganda in any form will be prohibited and completely suppressed. You will require the Japanese Government to cease financial and other support of National Shinto establishments."¹⁰ These documents provided the "general principles" that were to guide the Religions Division, but the staff were required to work out the practical application of these principles. This was no easy task, since it was difficult to know how to apply the principle of religious freedom to Yasukuni and other "state-protecting" shrines (*gokoku jinja*), which SCAP referred to collectively as the "military shrines." Although Shinto ritual and protocol were used in these shrines, they were fundamentally different from many older shrines that predated the post-Meiji building of new state shrines, which were designed to provide ideological support of the military in Japan's expanding empire and ritual care of the war dead.

SCAP'S RELIGIONS DIVISION AND THE SHINTO DIRECTIVE

To address the question of how Shinto shrines survived the Occupation, it is first necessary to examine key documents and accounts related to the work of SCAP's CIE. Their aim was to bring about a fundamental re-structuring of Japanese religion and society. This was accomplished in large part due to the work of the staff assigned to the Religions Division, which was part of the CIE Section established on 22 September 1945. Within several months, the CIE was organized into separate divisions dedicated to education and religion. The CIE was essentially the Occupation administration's counterpart to the Japanese government's Ministry of Education, and it was responsible for developing SCAP's policies related to religion, the media, and education. This was a "medium-size" unit that by 1948 was staffed by "563 employees, of whom fourteen were military officers, twenty-four enlisted personnel, 202 civilian officials and 323 general staff, predominantly Japanese" (Takemae 2003, 180).

Colonel Ken R. Dyke, head of the CIE from September 1945 to May 1946, appointed Dr. William Kenneth Bunce, a Navy lieutenant, as chief of the Religions Division. This later became the Religion and Cultural Resources Division, where Bunce served until the end of the Occupation (April 1952). Bunce was trained as a historian and had earned a Ph.D. from Ohio State University. He also had some Japan experience before the war and his military assignment. From 1936 to 1939 he and his wife—the daughter of Protestant missionaries—lived in Matsuyama where he taught in the Number Twelve Higher School.[11] Given his experience in higher education in the United States, Bunce apparently thought that an assignment to the education section would have been more suitable, and he felt unqualified to deal with the religion portfolio. Nevertheless, with the assistance of various staff and Japanese scholars, before the end of the year Bunce managed to draft the "Shinto Directive Staff Study" on the problem of State Shinto (3 December 1945) and the "Shinto Directive" (15 December 1945).[12] These documents framed the work of the Religions Division and defined how Shinto, including controversial shrines like Yasukuni, would be treated throughout the Occupation period.

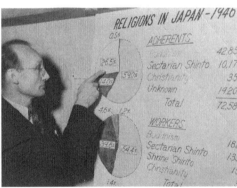

William K. Bunce at Matsuyama Number Twelve Higher School (Kōtō Gakkō) in the late 1930s, and as a staff member of the Religions Division, 17 March 1948. Photos provided from the personal files of William K. Bunce by his son Peter Bunce.

Through consultations with Japanese scholars and religious leaders, Lt. Bunce and his staff were eventually persuaded that the "religious" nature of Shinto shrines, including state-protecting shrines like Yasukuni Shrine, was more important than their connection with militarism and ultranationalism. Given that the establishment of religious freedom was one of the central tasks of the division, it was the recognition of Shinto as a religion that made it possible for even the "military shrines" to survive the Occupation.

THE ROLE OF KISHIMOTO HIDEO AND JAPANESE SCHOLARS

The documents Bunce prepared give us some idea of the various resources he drew upon for his work. An examination of citations within the 3 December "Shinto Directive Staff Study" reveals his reliance on the work of such foreign scholars as Daniel Clarence Holtom, George Sansom, and Basil Hall Chamberlain. In addition to these published resources, Bunce evidently found personal conversations and consultations with Japanese scholars during his early months on the job to be indispensable. He mentions several visits with D. T. Suzuki, who expressed strong opposition to State Shinto and "felt that Buddhism has been oppressed to some extent by government policy" (Takemae 1987, 199).

Bunce also had regular contact with several professors from Tokyo Imperial University. One key figure was Professor Miyaji Naokazu (1886–1949), who occupied the Chair for Shinto Studies. Prior to his faculty appointment in 1938, Miyaji had served in the Ministry of Home Affairs as head of the Shinto Bureau's Research Department (Jinja Kyoku Kōshōka). Although the university abolished the Chair for Shinto Studies in early 1946 in response to Bunce's recommendation, Miyaji was allowed to remain as a member of the faculty until his retirement shortly thereafter. He subsequently served as an advisor to the National Association of Shrines (Jinja Honchō; NAS), the main umbrella shrine organization of the postwar period, which was established in 1946. A second senior scholar consulted on a number of occasions was Anesaki Masaharu (1873–1949), the well-known professor of comparative religion and pioneer of religious studies in Japan. It was Kishimoto Hideo (1903–1964), however, the younger assistant professor in the same department and Anesaki's son-in-law and former student, who by all accounts was the most important scholar involved during these critical months.[13]

Shortly after CIE was organized, Colonel Dyke made a request for a Japanese consultant to facilitate communication between the various offices and institutions related to education and religion. On 11 October, Kishimoto was called to meet with Maeda Tamon (1884–1962), the minister of education, and was asked if he would be willing to serve in such a capacity. Kishimoto had spent several years at Harvard (1930–1934) and could handle English, so he was regarded as a particularly good choice for the tasks at hand. The following day he met with Dyke and agreed to serve in this role if he were allowed to continue in his academic post.[14] Thus began Kishimoto's close relationship with CIE and the Religions Division staff, which for the first three months was particularly intense. Fortunately, he left a detailed record of this period in a diary of seventy-two pages, which covers 11 October to 31 December, as well as a later substantial narrative account entitled "Shrine Shinto in the Midst of the Storm" (Kishimoto 1945; 1963).[15] These materials provide important supplementary information that helpfully contextualize the work of the Religions Division during the critical first months when the Staff Study and the Shinto Directive were being prepared.

Kishimoto Hideo, a University of Tokyo religion scholar, served as a consultant to the CIE Religions Division for several months from October 1945 and played a significant role in shaping the views of those involved in the work of the Division. He not only gave lectures to Bunce and his staff during this period, but also guided them on field trips to various shrines, temples, and New Religions, such as Tenrikyō, and exposed them to a wide variety of festivals and ritual activities. These experiences and exposure to various ritual events in a range of communities and institutions—even the controversial Yasukuni Shrine—seems to have assuaged some of the staffs' concerns regarding Shinto. It soon became clear to Bunce and his colleagues that there were various forms of Shinto and that it was not something that could be defined simply in terms of "ultranationalism and militarism" (Takagi 1993, 429).

The influence of Kishimoto and other Japanese scholars on Bunce's conclusion that Shinto must be regarded as a "religion" is apparent in the concluding section of the "Shinto Directive Staff Study" (3 December

Religions Division staff field trip with Japanese scholars to Tsurugaoka Hachi-mangū, a major Shinto shrine in Kamakura, 1946. Center rear: Warp, Bunce, Stobs, Miyajii, and Kishimoto. Photo provided from the personal files of William K. Bunce by his son Peter Bunce.

Religions Division staff field trip to Tenrikyō, a New Religion classified as sect Shinto. Front row includes Inglehart, Bunce, Warp, and Kishimoto. Tokyo, June 1946. Photo provided from the personal files of William K. Bunce by his son Peter Bunce.

Religions Division staff field trip to Mt. Nikkō and Rinnōji, a Buddhist temple, which is a part of a larger complex of religious sites, including Tōshōgū, a shrine dedicated to Tokugawa Ieyasu. On the back row second from the left is Miyaji, Kishimoto, and Bunce in the center rear. 1946. Photo provided from the personal files of William K. Bunce by his son Peter Bunce.

1945): "State Shinto is composed of both secular and religious elements, the latter predominating to such a great extent that *there is no doubt that State Shinto is a religion. Indeed, the Professor of Comparative Religion at Tokyo Imperial University estimates that State Shinto is about 80 percent religious and 20 percent secular*" (Woodard 1972, 329). This viewpoint reflects the general consensus of those Japanese scholars who surrounded the Religions Division at the time. The fact that Bunce and his staff had been exposed to the "religious" nature of Shinto—even at a "military shrine" like Yasukuni—made it difficult to issue a directive for the abolishment of any shrine without violating the principle of religious freedom, which the Initial Post-Surrender Policy had ordered them to proclaim and establish for the Japanese people.

The Shinto Directive issued on 15 December 1945 was a comprehensive document that addressed much more than the future of shrines. It dealt with many dimensions of State Shinto and required a major restructuring of Japanese religion and society. The Directive's overall aim was to establish the free practice of religion, and it was assumed that this required a clear separation of religion and state. In addition to ending government financial support for and administration of shrines, the directive instructed the Japanese government to remove Shinto elements from all public institutions. This included the removal of god-shelves (*kamidana*) from schools and public offices, the elimination of Shinto elements from textbooks and curriculum, and the termination of forced shrine visits (*sanpai*) on the part of students, teachers, and government officials.[16]

The Directive also meant that a number of "ultranationalistic" teachers would be removed from the school system. The removal of problematic teachers was under the direction of the Ministry of Education, which set-up committees in each prefecture to screen questionnaires completed by all teachers in their public schools and determine whether wartime activities warranted expulsion. According to Duke's (1973, 55) study, "the results of the rightwing purge were impressive, not because of the number of teachers removed by the committees—only about 1 percent of all teachers—but because of the total number of teachers who voluntarily resigned from the teaching profession because of the purge threat. By May 1947, when the purge was completed, 120,000 teachers, or 22 percent of the entire teaching corps, had been removed, most of them choosing the path of voluntary early retirement rather than subjecting themselves to the purge." How many of these "purged" or "voluntarily retired" teachers were also Shinto priests and to what extent their numbers declined is difficult to determine.[17] The purge extended to Tokyo Imperial University, as noted above with reference to Professor Miyaji, which abolished the Chair of Shinto Studies in response to the Directive.

The emperor's declaration of his "humanity" on 1 January 1946 was another result of the Shinto Directive. The public statement by the emperor that he was not "divine" (an *arahitogami*) clearly relativized his status and authority, and undermined one central belief of the wartime ideological system. The emperor-centric Shinto tradition was also secularized through the abolishment of the Imperial Rescript on Education (*Kyōiku chokugo*) and the Diet's passing of a new bill for education in 1947. At the time, both the emperor and the Imperial Rescript were regarded as "sacred" (*shinsei*) and understood to be the standard and source of both individual and social morality (Fukuda 1993, 538–539). The Occupation authorities thought that the continued propagation of such views in public schools was in fundamental tension with the larger goal of democratization and encouraged the Japanese government to prepare a new education policy and guidelines. The new law eliminated references to filial piety and loyalty to the emperor, as well as the exhortations to offer oneself to the State on behalf of the Imperial throne.

The removal of emperor-centric Shinto elements from the public schools was a key element of the Occupation reforms. The Religions Division Chief William Bunce explained the rationale behind the Occupation policies as follows:

> Secularization is required not only by Article 20 of the Constitution, but by a long history of abuses and by occupation policy which calls for an end to those abuses. The complex religious situation in Japan, involving many sects of Shinto, Buddhism, and Christianity, renders impracticable any dissemination of religious knowledge with discrimination in favor of or against particular religious systems. There is no alternative but to keep religious education—sectarian and general—out of the public schools. *To fail to achieve secularization of public education is to fail to realize fully the mission of the occupation.*[18]

Although there were many religious leaders critical of this removal of religious and moral education from public institutions, Bunce reported that the process was "vitually complete" by November 1947.

The Shinto Directive declared that direct government support and administration of shrines would be ended, but Shinto shrines would be permitted to continue as voluntary religious associations. Two days after the Shinto Directive was issued, Kishimoto was asked to make a radio broadcast to explain to the public the main points of the new policy toward Shinto. Both Bunce and Warp joined him at the broadcasting office while he delivered his remarks on how the shrines had been transferred to the hands of the people (*kokumin no te ni utsuru jinja*).[19] That afternoon he visited Yasukuni Shrine again to confirm to those concerned that it had survived this initial crisis (Kishimoto 1963, 273).[20]

Although not one Shinto shrine was abolished as a result of the Shinto Directive, the future status and survival of Yasukuni and other state-protecting shrines was still uncertain. The directive assured "complete religious freedom" to the Japanese people, which included the practice of Shinto. It indicated, however, that certain conditions would need to be met: "Shrine Shinto, after having been divorced from the state and divested of its militaristic and ultranationalistic elements, will be recognized as a religion if its adherents so desire and will be granted the same protection as any other religion insofar as it may in fact be the philosophy or religion of Japanese people" (Woodard 1972, 298). Through these various reforms and the strict application of the separation of religion and state, Shinto was largely removed from the "public sphere." Shrines were allowed to continue in the "private sphere"—like other religious bodies (Buddhist, Christian, and New Religions)—only if militaristic and ultranationalistic elements were abandoned. Before the Occupation ended, even the most controversial state-protecting shrine, Yasukuni, had managed to transform itself into a "peaceful" institution and was approved as a religious corporation by the Religions Division, a process we will examine in more detail in the following chapter.

In addition to the Shinto Directive, SCAP abolished the 1939 Religious Organizations Law (*Shūkyō dantai hō*), which had authorized the State to disband any religious organization known for propagating "dangerous" thoughts (*kiken shisō*), that is, teachings in conflict with the "Imperial Way." This was initially replaced with a provisional Religious Corporation Ordinance (*Shūkyō hōjin rei*) in 1946, in order to allow religious groups to be officially registered with the government "without being subjected to government control or supervision" or required to pass the litmus test of "orthodoxy" (i.e., the Imperial Way).[21] The basic principles outlined in the post-defeat planning documents and the Shinto Directive also found their way into the postwar Constitution (1947), especially Articles 20 and 89, which clearly defined religious freedom and religion-state separation.

While it was relatively easy to end direct financial support from the government to the hierarchically ranked national shrines (*kokuheisha*) and imperial shrines (*kanpei taisha*), it was much more difficult to enforce strict separation at the level of local communities. One of the ongoing problems the Religions Division had to address was the steady stream of complaints from people across Japan about the continued solicitation of funds by neighborhood associations for the support and maintenance of local shrines and their festivals. It had been customary for people to be assessed and obligated to contribute to the support of shrines, but the Shinto Directive had clearly abolished this practice. According to SCAP, support for shrines should come from voluntary associations of worshipers (*ujiko*) not from "quasi-official" neighborhood associations that coerced all residents of an area to contribute whether or not they identified themselves as members of the shrine community.

To address this problem, SCAP and the Ministries of Education and Home Affairs issued instructions to all prefectural governors on 19 August 1946, which identified neighborhood associations as "public bodies" that were prohibited from engaging in the following activities:

> (1) the collection for the shrines of money substitutes for the offering of the first ears of rice (*o-hatsu-ho*), monthly dues, and contributions; (2) the payment of expenses for religious services or contributions out of the disbursements of towns or local communities, and (3) the distribution by the associations of the amulets (*shimpu*), paper charms (*mamori-fuda*), paper human figures (*katashiro*), etc. (Woodard 1972, 131)

These guidelines were publicized widely and distributed to local governments throughout the country, but they were hardly consistently followed.[22]

The Occupation archives provide extensive evidence of the tension and disagreement between SCAP's Religions Division and the Japanese Government's Religious Affairs Office over how some ritual activities should be categorized, which reveals serious Japanese resistance to the redefinition of Shinto practices. A report by W. K. Bunce (6 November 1947) on the "Violation of the Shinto Directive," for example, reveals that at least some of the staff of the Religious Affairs Office maintained the view that certain rites and practices did not constitute religion. According to the report, Makita and Fukuda "were brought in" by the Central Liaison Office in Tokyo to come up with clearer instructions to prefectural officials in order to "prevent future infractions" of the Shinto Directive. This was in response to the violation of the Directive by the governor of Fukui Prefecture who made a symbolic offering (*tamagushiryō*) at the dedication of a railway station. Mr.

Fukuda's explanations that it was not a Shinto or religious ceremony and that the official was acting in his "private capacity" were both rejected by the Religions Division:

> After a brief discussion, Mr. Fukuda and Mr. Makita were informed that so far as SCAP is concerned a presentation of a Tamagushi (symbolic offering to the gods) is considered a Shinto ceremony. They were also informed that the instruction should make clear the fact that this is prohibited.... They were further informed that the suggestion that the governor of Fukui Prefecture was acting in a private capacity is ridiculous.

Similar violations in Fukushima and Niigata were reportedly still under investigation, but the report clearly indicates that a serious gap in understanding existed between the Japanese staff and the SCAP Religions Division over what constituted religious rituals or ceremonies. In sum, the Religious Affairs Office was failing to provide clear instructions to public officials that Shinto-related rituals could no longer be promoted or paid for by those in political office.

SCAP was not persuaded that the Religious Affairs Office were up to the job. The next year the Religions Division issued a memo that identified a number of problems with the performance of this office, including "a tendency to violate the freedoms of religious groups by unnecessary inquisitions into their organization, doctrines, finances, and activities," "an interest in maintaining the status quo in the Japanese religious world," and "an inclination to 'whitewash' all alleged violations of occupation directives in the religious field." The problems were such that the 1948 memo recommended that "the Religious Affairs Section of the Secretariat, Ministry of Education, and the religions officials on the prefectural level be liquidated as of 1 April 1948 and that their functions be abolished."[23] This recommendation was never acted upon and the views held by Fukuda and others in the Japanese administration were never successfully eliminated.

THE PROMOTION OF CHRISTIANITY IN OCCUPIED JAPAN

The Religions Division pursued the strict application of the "separation of religion and state" with regards to Shinto and, at least Bunce, was very keen to enforce the same policy for all religious bodies in Japan, including

Christian churches. He was very aware that there would be a tendency for some within the Occupation Forces to become involved in religious activity and provide support for the Christian missionary enterprise. To address this concern, SCAP's Religions Division issued "Instructions to agencies of the Occupation Forces in the field of Japanese Religions" on 25 March 1946; this document reiterated the main points of the Shinto Directive, but added a section to clarify the relationship between the Occupation Forces and Christianity and cautioned personnel from actions that would be perceived as favoring one religion over the other, as elaborated under number 6:

> The propagation of Christianity is not one of the objectives of the occupation. Surveillance should, therefore, be exercised to see that
> a. Occupation personnel and facilities are not used to further the cause of Christianity over other religions.
> b. Christianity is treated in the same fashion as any other religion in Japan.
> c. Missionaries and Christian workers are shown no greater courtesies than are accorded to others of their nationalities.
> d. Active proselyting of Christianity by personnel attached to the Allied forces is discouraged.[24]

Two other documents provide additional support for the view that key leaders in the Religions Division emphasized that a clear separation of religion and state should be enforced with regard to all religions, including Christianity. A "Memorandum for the Record" regarding a "Talk to the Chaplains' Association" by Lt. W. K. Bunce on 14 May 1946, notes that Bunce not only reviewed the Occupation policy prohibiting the Japanese government from promoting or disseminating Shinto, but also cautioned the chaplains about using their position to promote Christianity in Japan beyond the spiritual care of the troops. Several passages are worth quoting here:

> b. It is not an objective of the occupation to propagate any particular brand of religion among the Japanese.
> 1. Religious liberty is guaranteed by the Potsdam Declaration.
> 2. Religious liberty implies a minimum of propagation, restraint, and interference on the part of civil authorities.

3. The occupation forces are in effect a "super-civil" authority.

4. The Japanese Government has been ordered to prohibit all sponsorship and support of Shinto and, by implication, of other religions as well.

5. For members of the occupation forces to propagate any religion among the Japanese would be to exercise a privilege denied to the Japanese Government, and, to the extent that occupation costs can be assessed against Japan, would be subsidization of a minority religion extracted from the pockets of a population of whom less than one-half of one percent are Christian.

c. Personnel attached to the occupation forces should, therefore, avoid the active promotion or propagation of any particular brand of religion among the Japanese people.[25]

Another Memorandum issued to all CIE personnel on the subject of "Participation in Religious Life of Japanese People" several months later (29 August 1946) reiterated the position outlined by Bunce in his talk to the Chaplains' Association.

> Freedom of religion implies a minimum of propagation, restraint, and interference on the part of the civil authority; it does not imply freedom on the part of the agents of civil authority to propagate the religion of their choice. In Japan, the occupation forces are in effect a civil authority, backed by the power and prestige of the Supreme Commander. Proselyting (sic) activity on the part of personnel attached to the occupation forces would tend to abridge freedom of religion.
>
> It is inadvisable for personnel—military or civilian—attached to the occupation forces to engage in proselyting (sic) activities among the Japanese people in behalf of particular religious creeds. *The task of proselyting (sic) is one for professionally trained missionaries who are being returned to Japan as rapidly as feasible and who, when they arrive in Japan, will operate independently of the occupation forces.*[26]

In spite of these directives and statements, many personnel attached to the occupation forces were not inclined to maintain neutrality or refrain from various forms of religious activity. The Supreme Commander himself, in fact, undermined the policy of the Religions Division by endorsing the promotion of Christianity. General MacArthur was convinced that the successful democratization of postwar Japan would require a new set of values based on the Christian religion and felt justified in disregarding the policies issued by the Religions Division to support postwar efforts for the Christianization of the Japanese people.

By 1947 it was obvious that it would be the Supreme Commander's views—rather than those of Bunce and the Religions Division—that would define and guide how Christianity would be supported during the Occupation. The year after Bunce had issued his instructions about "fairness" in the treatment of all religions, SCAP's Civil Censorship Detachment (CCD) was already monitoring and suppressing publications according to the General's standard. Although SCAP had issued a statement on "freedom of speech and press" (10 September 1945) in the early days of the occupation, declaring that any restrictions on speech would be kept at the minimum required to maintain "public tranquility," the Civil Intelligence Section (CIS) quickly organized a CCD, which monitored and censored the full range of print media—and even monitored personal correspondence and phone conversations—from early 1946 to late 1949. While we are concerned primarily with the suppression of religious views deemed problematic, this was only one aspect of the CCD's work. News reports that revealed misbehavior on the part of the Occupation troops were also censored extensively, though some were published before the censorship codes were strictly implemented.[27]

By early 1947, there were already over eight thousand staff involved in this operation. While there were a few hundred who were US military officers or War Department civilians in supervisory positions, the vast majority involved in the everyday censorship work were Japanese and Korean nationals who knew the language. Their translations of potentially problematic materials were reported to their superiors, who made the decision of what would be deleted, revised, or suppressed. Unlike censorship under the Japanese government until the 1930s, where publications retained marks (*fuseji*) indicating where material had been deleted, SCAP's "covert" approach made every effort to remove all "traces of censorship" before publication was permitted (Suzuki 2012, 10). Censorship was made "invisible" by only printing the final revised and corrected material to give the misleading impression that the Occupation authorities were protecting free press and free speech. According to Yamamoto (2013, 3), the censorship conducted by the CCD remained a "secret" operation, and its activities were largely hidden from most Japanese throughout the Occupation period.[28]

A review of the censored publications preserved in the Gordon Prange Collection reveals numerous examples of journals being suppressed, or unacceptable Shinto views being deleted prior to publication.[29] When public debates were being conducted about proposed revisions of the Constitution and the future of moral and religious education in public schools, for example, the following views in a pre-publication text of *Chōkoku* (May 1946) were disapproved because of their criticism of Occupation policy:

> To sweep out all things religious in school education, i.e., to remove religious materials out of textbooks, will bring about a great weakness to national education.... Especially to primary school children in the stage in which this spiritual happiness is most needed, the effect of this Constitution Draft will be great. From this point of view this article (of separating religious education from governmental and public schools) cannot but be blamed more or less as going too far. This point is regrettable.[30]

There are numerous other examples of censored passages from such journals as *Chōkoku* and *Fuji* for their views that were deemed to be "ultra-nationalisitic" and "anti-democratic" or regarded as "religious propaganda" due to their promotion of the "Imperial Way," militarism, and expression of devotion to the "most divine emperor." *Fuji*, for example, was a poetry magazine established by Kageyama Masaharu, which published *tanka* submitted by members of the Fuji Kadōkai from across the nation. Although it only had a print run of 3,000, even this small operation had its publication banned six times for violation of the press code, and there were at least 119 passages that required deletion prior to publication (Yamamoto 2013, 80–81, 173).

There are also many other examples that reveal a clear preference for Christianity in various examiners' comments, which clearly shaped what material would pass censorship and be published. Ishikawa Nobunari, a Japanese examiner employed by the CCD, for example, wrote the following comment on an article entitled "Faith of the Japanese People," scheduled to appear in the March issue of *Shūkyō kōron*: "According to the opinion of GHQ, the faith of the Japanese people is unpainted canvas, in other words, it is still wasteland and therefore it is necessitated to sow seed of pure faith.

General MacArthur considers that the doctrines of Christianity are those which are needed now for Japan."[31] No doubt followers of both Shinto and Buddhism would take issue with this characterization of Japanese faith as an "unpainted canvas" and a "wasteland."

In spite of the efforts of some staff in the Religions Division, the separation of religion and state was clearly undermined by General MacArthur and others in the Occupation through special treatment of Christian missionaries and their enterprise. The Civil Censorship Detachment provided support for General MacArthur's Christianization agenda by suppressing Shinto viewpoints and publications, and by promoting those in line with MacArthur's "spiritual revolution."

The problems generated by General MacArthur's strong support for the postwar Christian missionary enterprise have been well documented. Since he believed that Christianity provided the necessary foundation for Japan's postwar democratization, he was apparently untroubled by the possibility that his behavior violated the separation of religion and state. In spite of the statements issued by the Religions Division on impartiality, it should be noted that the Division itself had former missionaries on staff, working to facilitate the return of Christian missionaries to Japan and arranging for various forms of support, which was clearly not something other religious groups enjoyed. This was not lost on Shinto and Buddhist leaders. In short, the returning and new missionaries arriving—particularly those from the United States—were hardly operating "independently" of the "power and prestige of the Supreme Commander" or the resources of the Occupation Forces. General MacArthur was convinced that the successful democratization of postwar Japan would require a new set of values based on the Christian religion and felt justified in disregarding the policies issued by the Religions Division to support postwar efforts for the Christianization of the Japanese people.

A number of studies have drawn attention to the various forms of support given to the Christian missionary enterprise during the Occupation.[32] Here I can only highlight some of the more important examples to indicate how the stated principles and policies of the Religions Division were subverted through direct support of Christian mission and institutions by many individuals in positions of power and influence throughout this period.

First, the return of missionaries to Japan was encouraged by General MacArthur and facilitated by two former Japan missionaries (William Woodard, Charles Inglehart) assigned to the Religions Division staff and another (Russell Durgin) to the Political Advisor's office in MacArthur's Headquarters (Moore 2011, 36–37). An initial group of four representatives from American Protestant churches (Federal Council of Churches) arrived in Japan in October 1945 after receiving permission from MacArthur's office for travel to Japan. These religious leaders traveled from the United States for a portion of the journey on a military Air Transport Command plane, and the US Army provided their accommodations and domestic transportation within Japan. Russell Durgin, who had served years before as the Secretary of the YMCA in Japan, was already on the ground and assisting with arrangements for the group of four to meet with Japanese Christian leaders, General MacArthur, and even Emperor Hirohito. In meetings with MacArthur on 25 October and 4 November 1945, the four were warmly welcomed by the General and urged to send "one thousand missionaries" as soon as possible to "fill the spiritual vacuum" in Japan (Moore 2011, 40–41; Woodard 1972, 243).

MacArthur's assurance of support was not just for the Protestant missionary enterprise. In the first several months of the Occupation, he also met with two Catholic priests, Fr. Patrick J. Byrne (1888–1950), an American Maryknoll missionary, and Fr. Bruno Bitter, S. J. (1898–1987), a German Catholic priest who was part of the Jesuit community at Sophia University. Their conversations revolved around their common concern to promote Christianity in Japan. Two passages from Byrne's 31 December 1945 "Letter to Father General" about his meetings with the Supreme Commander attest to this shared interest and MacArthur's support for Christian missionary activity:

> I've had two conferences with MacArthur. He spoke with what I considered amazing frankness; and his attitude towards missioners was most encouraging. Catholics, not Protestants, are what this country needs, said he. They've lost Shintoism, with its ceremonies; and Protestantism, without any ceremonies, will not have for them the appeal that you have with your rich liturgical functions, your sacraments, etc. etc. "The country is now a religious vacuum, and you have the biggest opportunity that has been offered in hundreds of

years. The whole country is yours, if you'll come in and take it. Your missionaries should come in by carloads. If your missioners stick to religion, they'll have every cooperation from the army."

MacArthur's support for the Christian mission in occupied Japan is also clear in another passage: "I saw MacA. alone, for 45 minutes. He was most informal, kept the big pipe going, and handed out the smokes. With Marella, who saw him previously, there was Father Bitter, the rector of the University. Bitter asked him if the four Jesuits now in California could come out. 'Four,' said MacArthur, 'you ought to have four hundred coming out.'"[33]

The leadership of the Catholic Church and many Protestant denominations responded positively to MacArthur's enthusiastic vision and promise of support, and by 1950 over three thousand missionaries had been approved for work in Japan. With MacArthur's endorsement, Christian missionaries found they were able to receive permission to enter Japan without much difficulty and, as Moore (2011, 64) explains, after their arrival they received a great deal of assistance to deal with the difficult conditions of life in postwar Japan, including

> transportation from the port of arrival to their destination in Japan; shipment of baggage, household goods, automobiles and food supplies; use of Army postage privileges for American citizens and representative missionaries; use of Army and Air Force medical services and installations; use of the staff of the Religions and Cultural Resources Division for personal problems; use of transportation facilities and temporary billeting in Army quarters for incoming missionaries; use of military theatres; and use of military schools for missionary children.

Other religious groups struggling under the same difficult circumstances, of course, were not afforded similar forms of relief and support.

MacArthur not only paved the way for the return and support of missionaries, but also gave his personal endorsement for the printing and distribution of Bibles and Christian literature for use in their meetings across Japan. On behalf of the Pocket Testament League, for example, he wrote a letter of support for their efforts dated 4 April 1949, and also proposed that the print run and distribution be increased from one million to ten million portions of Scripture for distribution among the Japanese (Okazaki 2012, 268–270).[34]

These forms of support were clearly limited to the Christian missionary enterprise. Moore (2011, 63) points out that Ruth Sasaki, an American Buddhist, sought entry to Japan for missionary work and translation of Buddhist literature into English in 1946, but was denied assistance by the same Religions Division. The special treatment accorded Christian missionaries was obviously a sore spot for Shinto and Buddhist leaders who regularly raised the issue with the Religions Division staff.

The plan to establish a new Christian university—what was to become International Christian University (ICU)—was also endorsed by MacArthur. He not only served as the honorary chair of the fundraising drive, but also intervened with the Japanese government when possible sites for the campus were being considered. One area designated as farmland by the Department of Agriculture was identified as a possible site for the ICU campus, and it was reclassified by the Japanese government in response to an order from MacArthur's office, which allowed it to be used for that purpose (Okazaki 2012, 284–290; Moore 2011, 128–134).

Christian missionaries enjoyed special-status treatment during this period due to the quasi-official support provided by SCAP. There is some evidence that missionaries also took advantage of their privileged position and engaged in activities that clearly crossed the line of religion-state separation. The Woodard Collection contains files with reports about missionaries on the island of Shikoku who visited public schools for religious services during school assemblies, including the First Prefectural Marugame High School, the Second Middle School, and the Fujii Girls' High School in Marugame, and another school in Tokushima in February 1950. The missionaries distributed copies of the New Testament and, with the assistance of an interpreter, spoke about the Christian faith in the school assemblies on several occasions. These "incidents" were reported in the *Akahata*, the newspaper of the Japanese Communist Party, and it was noted that a "Mr. Yuasa warned the interpreter that they were violating the Fundamental Education law by such religious work" (Article 9 of the Fundamental Law of Education "forbids religious education in public schools").[35]

Finally, we should also note that the status of Christianity was enhanced by close connections with the Imperial Household during this period.[36] Some leading Christians, such as Kagawa Toyohiko and William Merrill Vories, expressed strong support for the emperor and indicated that there was considerable interest in Christianity among members of the Imperial Household. Bible studies were actually conducted by Kagawa for the emperor in 1946 and the two of them were seen together in public touring some sites of war-torn Japan. The empress and her daughters also received instruction in the Christian faith from Reverend Uemura Tamaki in regular religious gatherings that included Bible studies and the singing of hymns. These meetings continued for five years and were occasionally attended by the emperor until they ended abruptly at the end of the Occupation. One additional Christian influence on the Imperial Household was the appointment of the Quaker teacher Elizabeth Vining to the role of tutor to the crown prince, a position that lasted four years. Given these positive connections between the Imperial Household and Christianity, General MacArthur apparently believed that Japan could very well be transformed into a Christian nation. In hindsight, of course, this was clearly an unfounded and overly optimistic vision.

With the support of the Occupation infrastructure, missionaries and the resources of their denominations back home were channeled into Japan throughout this period. As Wittner (1971, 96) notes: "The American churches did not limit themselves to funding missionaries, but earmarked millions of dollars for schools, churches, and other religious facilities in war-torn Japan. By 1951 Americans had financed the rebuilding of 243 Japanese churches and seventy-two religious schools at a cost of several million dollars." In spite of the unusual support and special advantages received from the Occupation authorities, it is widely recognized that the effort to "Christianize" Japan was largely a failure. While churches had recovered from the membership losses of the difficult wartime years and increased slightly by the end of the Occupation, the number of Japanese Christians remained under one percent of the population.

CONCLUSION

As we have seen, Shinto institutions survived the Occupation, but faced a rather strict application of the "separation" principle and were monitored closely.[37] The role of Shinto in public life and institutions—particularly educational institutions—was dramatically reduced through the policies SCAP implemented, which accelerated the process of secularization. The views of Shinto leaders on issues of public concern—such as constitutional revision, moral and religious education in schools—were often suppressed by the CCD. Institutional survival also required a degree of self-censorship and a reshaping of rituals and practices in order to pass screening by the CIE Religions Division.

Although Bunce and some colleagues in the Religions Division sought to apply the same principles of separation to all religious groups, General MacArthur essentially undermined these efforts due to his conviction that the democratization of Japan would require Christianization. Under MacArthur's direction, official support of Christianity by the Occupation Forces and US government essentially replaced the official support that Shinto had received from the Japanese government from the early Meiji period until 1945. As a growing gap emerged between the stated "ideals" of the Occupation and actual "practice" of many on the ground, numerous problems were created for the staff of the Religions Division. Without denying that the Occupation brought with it a new level of religious freedom for the Japanese people and many different religious groups—particularly New Religions and Christian churches, the record shows that the "separation of religion and state" was a principle not so easily achieved.

Given the strong support of MacArthur and the mobilization of the US government Occupation resources on behalf of the Christian missionary enterprise, Moore (2011, 139) argues that "*imposing* its religion on other peoples was an established policy of American imperialism." This seems to me an overstatement given that the "quasi official" support for Christianity did not involve "coercion" or forced participation in religious rituals at Christian churches. It is undeniable that the resources of the Occupation were used to "promote" Christianity, and the principle of separation outlined in the Shinto Directive and incorporated in Articles 20 and 89 of the 1947 Constitution was conveniently ignored by many. It could have been much worse, however. As Takahashi Tetsuya (2004, 53–54) has observed, the Allied Occupation of Japan could have adopted the kind of policies that the Japanese government did when it colonized and occupied Korea, which included forced shrine visits and the adoption of the Japanese language and names. In other words, the Occupation authorities could have abandoned the notion of religious freedom and required membership and attendance at Christian churches and forced the adoption of English as the official language of Japan. If such extreme measures had been taken, then Moore's conclusion would be justified. In any case, the evidence from both the periods of Japanese and American empires indicates that religious freedom always has some limits, and the interpretation of the principle of separation depends on the interests of those holding political power.

2

Shinto Responses
to the Occupation

Privatization and Deprivatization

As we have seen, the Allied Occupation redefined the legal and political context that shaped all religious institutions in new ways. While the new policies represented an improvement of conditions for some religious groups—especially New Religions and Christian churches—for Shinto institutions they created a crisis situation. In this chapter, I will briefly review how Shinto shrines were transformed from "public" into "private" institutions and joined the ranks of other religious organizations—Buddhist, Christian, and New Religions. The adaptations required varied from shrine to shrine, and some observers thought it would be unlikely for the military, or "state-protecting," shrines (*gokoku jinja*) to survive. The most dramatic transformation occurred at Yasukuni Shrine, which we will examine in some detail. This case study will reveal the dramatic changes made by shrine priests to ensure survival during this difficult period.

Privatization and adaptation for survival is only part of the story of the early postwar period. As soon as the Occupation ended, Shinto leaders quickly adopted a new orientation and reverse course that involved policies for "deprivatization." It was the Shinto experience of marginalization—the result of unfair treatment by the policies of the Supreme Commander of Allied Powers (SCAP)—that planted the seeds of discontent and a determination to recover and restore the role of Shinto in public life and institutions. Once foreign and self-censorship was no longer required, religious and political leaders were able to openly discuss how they might repair the damage caused by the foreign occupation and promote their restorationist agenda. Given that SCAP's policies with regard to religion had found their way into the Constitution—Articles 20 and 89—meant that there would be serious constraints on this movement.

RESPONSES DURING THE OCCUPATION

The situation of all Shinto institutions was precarious in the early months of the occupation. In this fluid situation there were many behind the scenes meetings between priests, scholars, and government officials, as efforts were made to find a path for survival in response to the Shinto Directive issued in December 1945. The termination of financial support for Shinto shrines was significant, but for the vast majority of shrines it was business as usual.[1] Most shrines had survived on their own with only the support of local parishioners throughout the war years, and many priests found it necessary to supplement their meager incomes by working in agriculture, as teachers in public schools, or as staff in local government offices (Sakamoto 1994a, 363). In addition to the financial challenges shrines faced in occupied Japan, it was clear that shrines would also be required to make serious adjustments in their ritual life and calendar in order to signal to the authorities that their institution was compatible with the policies issued by SCAP.

Negotiating the Survival of Shrine Shinto. Although Shinto shrines were not abolished as a result of the Shinto Directive, they were required to register with the government under the Religious Corporation Ordinance (*Shūkyō hōjin rei*), issued first on 28 December 1945 with some urgency and in amended form on 2 February 1946. This ordinance permitted shrines to reorganize themselves as private voluntary associations, that is, supported by members who joined and maintained the shrines with personal funds. As Mark Teeuwen (1996, 178) rightly points out, "it is obvious that the change of Shinto shrines from public institutions to private juridical persons (*shihōjin*) was, at least in the case of the major shrines, not voluntary."

This, however, was the only choice for Shinto shrines if they were to continue for the duration of the Occupation.

The vast majority of shrines joined the National Association of Shrines (Jinja Honchō, NAS).[2] This was a new entity that had been created as a result of discussions and negotiations between representatives from three older Shinto organizations during the first several months of the Occupation, and registered according to the new system on 3 February 1946.[3] According to a 1950 report by the NAS, the total number of shrines was reduced by roughly 15 percent in the transition from management by the State to the system of registration as religious juridical persons.[4] Some shrines were simply too small and without the necessary resources to pursue the registration process. By 1950, nevertheless, the NAS claimed 88,132 shrines in its membership and some 1,340 shrines had registered independently and were outside of its jurisdiction. The ultimate fate of Yasukuni Shrine, which was one central shrine that had been allowed to register as a separate religious corporation, was still pending and undecided due to its close association with the military.[5]

As far as the doctrines of Shrine Shinto are concerned, the report states that the NAS's teaching had been "made to conform" to the requirements of the Shinto Directive, which meant it had distanced itself from the prohibited "militaristic and ultranationalistic ideologies."[6] This constituted a much more difficult challenge for Yasukuni Shrine, which was known as a military shrine and had been under the administration of the Army and Navy. The other military shrines located in prefectures across the country; namely, the state-protecting shrines and shrines dedicated to the war dead (shōkonsha) were grouped with Yasukuni and similarly investigated and monitored in the early years of the occupation.[7]

The Case of Yasukuni Shrine. The Shinto Directive assured "complete religious freedom" to the Japanese people, which included the practice of Shinto. It indicated, however, that certain conditions would need to be met: "Shrine Shinto, after having been divorced from the state and divested of its militaristic and ultranationalistic elements, will be recognized as a religion if its adherents so desire and will be granted the same protection as any other religion insofar as it may in fact be the philosophy or religion of

Japanese people."[8] Although Yasukuni Shrine had been allowed to register as a religious corporation in 1946, it was clearly regarded as a more problematic case due to its military orientation and close association with the emperor. How it survived is a more complicated story that involved the intervention of Japanese scholars, a period of "probation," and substantial changes in the shrine's calendar and ritual life, which allowed it to continue.

The Directive concluded with instructions to the Imperial Japanese government to "submit a comprehensive report to this Headquarters no later than 15 March 1946 describing in detail all action taken to comply with all provisions of this directive." According to Woodard (1972, 160), Bunce pursued a cautious approach and deferred any final decision about Yasukuni Shrine until it was possible to gather adequate information that would "permit the formulation of a prudent and equitable policy." While Bunce had been convinced that the shrine was "religious," he was uncertain if its "militaristic and ultra-nationalistic elements" could actually be

Yasukuni Shrine in wartime Japan. Photo provided from the personal files of William K. Bunce by his son Peter Bunce. No date.

removed. It was also unclear if it would be able to survive as a voluntary organization after state control and financial support was eliminated.

The fact that Yasukuni's fate was still not decided is clear from other actions taken by the Religions Division after issuing the Shinto Directive. One is related to the role of William Woodard, whose first assignment after joining the Religions Division in the summer of 1946 was to conduct a study of Yasukuni and other state-protecting shrines to address the question "whether their evident militaristic uses during the previous decades was inherent or the result of the use made of them by the extremists" (Woodard 1972, 161). This assignment is just one indicator that the shrine's status and fate remained ambiguous. Conducted with the assistance of Sakamoto Sadao, a Yasukuni Shrine assistant priest (*shuten*), the investigation of the shrines was a two-year project and was in part an effort to see to what extent the shrines had complied with the demands of the Shinto Directive. On 6 January 1947, after only six months into the project, Woodard (1947) communicated his views to Bunce in a confidential memo and

Yasukuni Shrine in wartime Japan. Photo provided from the personal files of William K. Bunce by his son Peter Bunce. No date.

recommended that "the shrine should be allowed to continue to exist. Its elimination would accomplish very little and would create additional problems." In spite of this recommendation, Woodard (1972, 163) later reported that no consensus had been reached about the final disposition of these shrines even after two years of investigation and deliberation.

A second indicator that the final adjudication on Yasukuni and the state-protecting shrines was still pending may be seen in the 13 November 1946 "Disposition of State-Owned Land Currently Used by Religious Institutions," prepared by Lt. Col. D. R. Nugent and issued by SCAP. Referred to in Japanese as the *Shaji kokuyū kyōnaichi no shobun hōan*, this directive returned to Shinto shrines and Buddhist temples land that had been appropriated by the Meiji government, but it was not universally applied. In fact, the document clearly stated that "the provisions for the transfer to religious institutions of land title *shall not apply in the case of military shrines (Yasukuni Jinja, Gokoku Jinja, Shōkonsha)*."[9] Many observers understandably assumed that this meant that the Occupation authorities were still leaning towards the abolishment of these shrines. This was certainly the view of some staff in the Ministry of Education's Religions Bureau (Shūmuka) as well as of Shinto leaders who later became a part of the NAS. Shortly after this SCAP action, for example, Fukuda Shigeru visited Bunce on both 19 and 21 November to discuss the implications of this decision. Yasukuni and state-protecting shrines were excluded, Bunce explained, because it was still unclear whether the military aspects of these shrines could actually be removed.[10]

Kishimoto's account also supports this interpretation. Although not one shrine was closed down as a result of the Shinto Directive, Yasukuni and the state-protecting shrines were still regarded as problematic, and the leaders of these shrines knew that their situation was precarious. According to Kishimoto (1963, 280), this is why the Yasukuni priests discussed one proposal after another with the Religions Division, which bought them some time, and eventually instituted changes that made the shrines acceptable to the Occupation authorities. In this sense, the shrine priests became responsible—at least in part—for their own survival until the end of the Occupation. Several more years of investigation and monitoring would be required before the Religions Division was convinced that appropriate actions had been taken to reform Yasukuni Shrine and transform it from a "military shrine" under the administrative control of the Army and Navy into a voluntary religious organization and "peaceful" shrine of the people.

The Transformation of Yasukuni Shrine. Yasukuni leaders were already thinking about what might be required in order to maintain the shrine under the Occupation administration even before the Shinto Directive was issued. In the October meeting with Kishimoto, Takahara, the first priest to take the initiative, suggested various changes that could be made. His successor, Yokoi Tokitsune, who took up his appointment as associate head priest (*gon gūji*) on 16 November 1945, wasted no time in pursuing these and other possibilities. It was under Yokoi's leadership that most of the changes that made it possible for Yasukuni to survive were instituted.

Yokoi broached the subject of plans for the future of Yasukuni—including a possible name change—when Kishimoto visited the shrine on 21 November, the day after the Special Grand Festival (*Rinji taisai*).[11] He followed up on these conversations with a visit to the CIE Religions Division office on 26 November to meet with Bunce, where he was accompanied by Professors Miyaji and Kishimoto, as well as Sakamoto Sadao.[12] Yokoi met a further time with Bunce on 21 January 1946, accompanied again by Kishimoto and Sakamoto, for additional discussions of the Yasukuni Shrine "problem."[13] At this meeting Yokoi indicated that he was prepared to introduce many changes and intended to register the shrine as a religious corporation under the new Religious Corporation Ordinance. Also discussed were plans to organize the worshipers from the bereaved families into groups that would select their own representatives, which would mark the beginning of the shrine's new form of existence as a voluntary religious organization.[14]

The conversation with Bunce on this occasion also revealed Yokoi's intention to shift the shrine away from its military associations, including plans to transform the Yūshūkan—the museum on the shrine precincts that usually displayed weapons and war-related materials—into a facility for entertainment and recreation. "Henceforth," he explained to Bunce, "everything will be changed, and we hope to set up an amusement center with roller-skating, ping-pong, merry-go-rounds, etc., and a movie theater." When Bunce inquired if there were plans to restore the "carnivals" of Yasukuni, which had been suspended, Yokoi replied: "The principles of Shinto lie in laughter. We like to accommodate the worshipers who come from survivor families by making them as happy as possible. If there is an approval, we would like to establish a pleasure center though there will be things which will not be too refined."[15]

It is worth recalling here that festival days at Yasukuni had for decades been lively and entertaining and often included horse races, sumo tournaments, and circus and monkey shows, as well as the usual food stalls that lined the streets to the shrine.[16] As the war intensified, however, the military administration began to restrict activities for entertainment and amusement on the shrine precincts. A new policy aimed at creating a more solemn and dignified atmosphere, in fact, was initiated from the Special Grand Festival in the spring of 1939.[17] Following the meeting with Bunce, Yokoi provided the leadership for implementing the systematic changes that would distance the shrine from its military associations and restore the more festive atmosphere that had once characterized it. As it turns out, plans for the "amusement center" never materialized, and the Yūshūkan was rented out to an insurance company as office space from November 1946 (Yasukuni Jinja 1987, 491).[18]

Yokoi's plan to register Yasukuni Shrine as a religious corporation became possible less than two weeks after this meeting with Bunce. The Religious Corporation Ordinance issued at the end of December 1945, which had initially applied only to those religious bodies (Buddhist, Christian, and Sect Shinto groups) that had been registered under the wartime Religious Organizations Law, was revised on 2 February 1946 to include Shinto shrines. These had been under the administration of the Home Ministry's Shrine Board and not treated as "religious" bodies by the government. With the revision of this ordinance and the abolishment of the Shrine Board, Yasukuni and other shrines were allowed to register as religious organizations. Yasukuni prepared the necessary documents and became recognized officially as a religious corporation on 7 September 1946.[19]

Since it was no longer under state control or the administration of the Army and Navy, it became possible to institute a number of changes rather quickly. The most immediate change, which symbolized the fundamental reorientation, was the appointment of a new head priest (*gūji*) to replace

Suzuki Takao, who had served in that capacity since 1938, following various appointments in the Army. His successor, Tsukuba Fujimaro (1905–1978), who served as head priest until his death in 1978, was without military connections.[20] Even the change in the name of a building reflected the new orientation. The National Defense Hall (Kokubō Kaikan), built in the shrine precincts in 1933, was renamed Yasukuni Hall (Yasukuni Kaikan) on 4 September 1946 and henceforth was dedicated to cultural activities and providing temporary accommodations for family members of the war dead when they came to worship at the shrine (Yasukuni Jinja 1987, 488–489).

The most profound change was the removal from the annual shrine calendar of rituals and events that had military or national significance. This was clearly in response to the Shinto Directive. The shrine eliminated rituals associated with State Shinto and the Imperial Household, such as *Kigensetsu*, which celebrated the accession of Emperor Jinmu, and the rites for "reverencing from afar" (*yōhai shiki*) the tombs of Emperor Jinmu and Emperor Taishō. The regular public enshrinement services (*gōshisai*) were also stopped in 1947 in response to GHQ's instructions, though the shrine continued them as unpublicized private services.[21]

This ritual vacuum was filled with the addition of a number of rites and ceremonies more closely related to the everyday religious life of the Japanese people (see TABLE 1).[22] Various annual events were also rescheduled. The dates for the Spring and Fall Festivals (*Shunki reitaisai, Shūki reitaisai*), for example, had been set in the Taishō period for 30 April and 23 October to commemorate military victories of the Army and Navy in the Russo-Japanese War of 1904–1905. These festivals were redefined in relation to widely performed rites for ancestral spirits (*sorei saishi*), traditionally celebrated during the spring and autumn equinoctial weeks, and the dates changed to 21 April and 18 October (Yasukuni Jinja 1987, 490; Moriya 1973, 178–180).

Over the course of several years, Yasukuni also added popular annual celebrations and life-cycle rites that typically were observed at many other shrines throughout the country, including the traditional Doll Festival (*Hina matsuri*) and Boy's Festival (*Tango matsuri*), and the more recent Seven-Five-Three (*Shichi go san*), and Coming-of-Age Day (*Seijin no hi*).

Year	Rescheduled Rituals/Ceremonies	New Rituals/Ceremonies
1946	Spring Festival (21 April) Fall Festival (18 October)	
1947		Spirit Festival (13–16 July) Seven-Five-Three (15 November)
1948		Doll Festival (3 March) Boy's Festival (5 May)
1949		Coming-of-Age Day (15 January)
1950		Special Memorial Services

TABLE 1. New Rituals and Ceremonies at Yasukuni Shrine, 1946–1950.

Probably the most important addition to the ritual life of the shrine was the Spirit Festival (*Mitama matsuri*). This development is said to have been inspired by Yanagita Kunio (1875–1962), the well-known scholar of folklore studies.[23] In 1946, Yanagita had given a number of lectures dealing with the theme "Ujigami to ujiko" (tutelary deities and their parishioners) as part of the new *Yasukuni bunka kōza*, a lecture series launched to provide a "correct" approach to Japanese culture suitable for postwar Japanese society (Yasukuni Jinja 1987, 488).[24] According to Tokoro Isao (2007, 70; 116), Yanagita's lectures expressed the view that the spirits of the fallen soldiers should be comforted by the traditional practices associated with the care of ancestral spirits, and he encouraged the shrine to begin holding the Spirit Festival. The fact that a gathering of *Bon odori* folk dance groups from Nagano prefecture was held at the shrine in July, even before Yanagita began his lecture series, indicates that there probably were other sources of influence and inspiration—if less famous—for the development of rituals and dances on behalf of the enshrined spirits and the inauguration of the Spirit Festival. In any case, the shrine officially began the four-day festival in July the following year, and it has been held ever since to comfort the spirits of the fallen war heroes (*eirei o nagusameru*; Yasukuni Jinja 1987, 487–488).

In addition to the development of this important annual festival, the shrine also responded to individual requests from bereaved families to hold some sort of service on the death anniversary (*meinichi*) of their family member. In October 1950, the shrine established a new system whereby interested families could request a special memorial service (*Eitai kagura sai*), which consisted of an offering of traditional music and dance to the enshrined kami. This effort to remake Yasukuni into "a shrine of the people" clearly addressed a need felt by many families, and the shrine reports that over thirty-eight thousand such memorial services had been held by 1985 (Yasukuni Jinja 1987, 513). The addition of this memorial service to Yasukuni Shrine rituals is not surprising given the experience many Japanese have with the ritual care long-provided by Buddhist priests and temples on the death anniversaries of deceased family members.

One final change that should be mentioned is the transformation of the shrine from a state institution into a self-supporting voluntary religious organization. Given the shrine's change of status and the elimination of government support, Yokoi was forced to explore new sources of revenue to maintain the shrine and provide the priests and staff with a means of livelihood. The rental of the Yūshūkan as office space is just one example. Yokoi even briefly explored the possibility of the shrine sustaining itself by sending the shrine staff to farm on former military land in Miura Peninsula in Kanagawa Prefecture (Nakamura 2007, 208–210). During the shrine's first year as a religious corporation, he and several other priests traveled widely across Japan to explain Yasukuni's new circumstances and to develop groups of supporters from among the bereaved families. Drawing on this natural membership base, Yokoi and other staff began organizing voluntary associations or confraternities (kō), first locally in the Kudan area around the shrine and then more widely across the country. By 1949, Yasukuni Shrine could report that forty-nine such associations had been formed, including ten groups in Tokyo and the rest scattered across ten different prefectures (see TABLE 2). Membership fees of ten to thirty yen per person were collected, and each confraternity donated approximately half of the funds to support the shrine. In addition to financial support, these associations became the base for a variety of group activities, offerings, and service to the shrine throughout the year.[25] The development of these new associations must be seen within the larger context of a radical decline in the number of worshipers attending the regular Spring and Fall Festivals and other events throughout the year. Over the New Year holidays in 1944, for example, visitors to the shrine numbered some 730,000, but three years later had dropped to just 30,000 (Nakamura 2007, 211).

Year Founded	Number of Confraternities	Number of Members
1946	0	0
1947	13	12,877
1948	36	7,909
Total	49	20,786

TABLE 2. The Development of Yasukuni Shrine Confraternities, 1946–1948, based on Information Reported in Yasukuni Jinja 1983–1984, vol. 2, 77–78.

All of these significant changes were systematically laid out in the head priest's report to the Religions Division in 1949 and presented as evidence that Yasukuni had been fundamentally transformed from a military shrine to a peaceful institution and shrine of the people. The changes were explained in terms of a "recovery of the founding spirit" and a shift away from the shrine's wartime militaristic orientation. Instead of focusing on the celebration of the military exploits of war heroes (*eirei kenshō*), the shrine was again devoted to the consolation and pacification of the spirits of the war dead (*eirei anchin*). This new policy is clearly recorded in the official Yasukuni accounts (Yasukuni Jinja 1983–1984, vol. 2, 75). According to Shibukawa (1967, 204–205), this shift in orientation was hardly "voluntary," but was simply an accommodation that the shrine was forced to make in order to survive under the Occupation administration. Given that the earlier emphasis on honoring war heroes was quickly restored to ritual life—as well as to exhibits in the Yūshūkan—in the post-Occupation period, Shibukawa's interpretation is probably correct. A case could also be made, however, that at least some of the adaptations and additions made during the Occupation reflected the genuine desire of priests to cultivate a richer religious life, which had not been possible while the shrine was under the administration of the military.

The demilitarization of Yasukuni Shrine and its transformation into a peaceful institution finally persuaded the Religions Division to reach a definitive decision on the shrine's status. A directive finally issued on 28 August 1951 concluded "that no repressive action would be taken and that those shrines located on state-owned land should be permitted to purchase their precincts on the same basis as other religious institutions similarly situated" (Woodard 1972, 163). The Religions Division had waited until just days before the San Francisco Peace Treaty was signed (8 September 1951) to recognize the shrine under the same terms and conditions as other religious organizations. By this time, the US military and the Occupation authorities were more concerned about the war in Korea than any lingering potential problems associated with Yasukuni Shrine.[26]

While the Religions Division would take no further actions with regard to the shrine, Woodard prepared two final memorandum in 1951 in which he anticipated some of the issues that would surround the shrine throughout the postwar period, including official visits (*kōshiki sanpai*, Prime Minister Yoshida was already planning to attend services in October), the redefinition of Yasukuni as a special "nonreligious" shrine that deserved state support, and the possible return of shrine visits (*jinja sanpai*) as a requirement in the public schools if Yasukuni were restored as a state institution. Woodard was opposed to these potential developments, but realized that it would be up to the Japanese people and their elected officials to determine the shape of the post-Occupation social order.

In the end, Yasukuni owed its survival to the fact that the Religions Division—in consultation with Japanese scholars—recognized the shrine's "religious" nature. Given this interpretation and US policy statements about establishing the free practice of religion, a cautious approach was taken, and the Shinto Directive ordered no shrines closed. The continued existence of Yasukuni, however, was clearly conditional and depended on whether its militaristic and ultranationalistic elements and associations could actually be removed. Although many observers thought this was unlikely to occur, Yasukuni's own historical records reveal that at least some priests embraced their "religious" identity and took concrete measures to distance the shrine from its wartime orientation. The shrine also was able to transform itself into a voluntary religious organization, supported by lay confraternities and groups of bereaved families. Nurturing these bases of support, Yasukuni was able to survive the difficult immediate postwar period without financial support from the government.

Shrine Shinto—including this most controversial shrine—survived the difficult foreign occupation, but leaders were already thinking about how to recover their losses and restore Shinto to its rightful place in public life and institutions. Shibukawa (1993, 519) a journalist for *Jinja shinpō*, the newspaper published by the Association of Shinto Shrines, reports on a meeting in the fall of 1951 between Shinto leaders and several Religions Division staff members (Bunce, Walter Nichols, and Woodard). According to his account, Bunce explained to those gathered that Japan was about to become an independent nation again and would be free to make changes according to the wishes of the Japanese people. He also stated his hope that they would not revive or restore *Kigensetsu*—the holiday commemorating the enthronement of Emperor Jinmu—because this would be a clear indication that the Japanese people had not learned anything from the Shinto Directive. The Shinto leaders at this meeting, however, felt that it was in fact their duty to restore *Kigensetsu*, as well as many other aspects of Japanese life that had been eliminated by Occupation policies.

THE SHINTO RESPONSE AS DEPRIVATIZATION

In view of the foregoing analysis, it is apparent that the privatization of Shinto occurred not as a result of modernization per se, which is the ideal typical pattern in other contexts, but due to its forced removal from the public sphere as a result of the directives issued by the Supreme Commander of Allied Powers and implemented by the Japanese government. The termination of financial support of some shrines, the removal of Shinto altars (*kamidana*) from public schools, the elimination of shrine visits from public school curriculum, the replacement of the Imperial Rescript on Education (*Kyōiku chokugo*) with an education law that removed patriotism and loyalty to the emperor as its central goals, were all changes that dramatically reduced and restricted the range of Shinto influence on the larger society. While certain aspects of the prewar Shinto were secularized and privatized, this process did not extend to the secularization of consciousness—at least for many key Shinto leaders. Their views on the public role of Shinto, expressions of loyalty to the emperor, and the need to preserve moral education in the public school system may have been effectively censored for the duration of the Occupation, but efforts by religious and political leaders were quickly launched to restore Shinto to public life and institutions as soon as the interlopers departed.

What is it that motivates and mobilizes religious groups to re-engage the public sphere? Under the circumstances, it is not surprising that the process of deprivatization in the postwar period is closely connected to the Shinto-related neonationalistic response to the imposition of a foreign social order on Japan. As Nakano Tsuyoshi (2004, 119) has observed, it was the "foreign coercive power" (*gaiteki kyōsei ryoku*) that accomplished secularization during the Occupation rather than a process driven by native or domestic reforms. This, he argues, became a causal factor for the emergence of movements to "recover" or "restore" Japanese tradition in the post-Occupation period. In *Public Religions in the Modern World*, José Casanova's (1994, 227) comparative sociological studies revealed that what seems to precipitate the involvement of religious groups in public life "are different types of state intervention and administrative colonization of the life world and the private sphere." Protestant fundamentalists in the United States became politically mobilized, for example, in response "to state rulings coming from the Supreme Court, the Internal Revenue Service, and Congress." In the Japanese context, we can similarly observe that mobilization of people in a variety of Shinto-related movements in postwar Japan was precipitated by the "intervention and administrative colonization" by the Allied Occupation and the perceived (and actual) loss of influence in the public sphere.

Ueda Kenji (1979, 303–304), the late Shinto scholar, clearly supported this interpretation. The overall consequence of these Occupation reforms, he argued, was that "*the public character of the Shinto shrine came to an end.*" For those who identified with the State Shinto tradition and institutions, the forced secularization brought about by the Occupation policies was hard to accept. Ueda points out, in fact, that as soon as the San Francisco Peace Treaty was concluded in 1952, the NAS began to work actively on numerous fronts to "restore Shinto to its lost status and to revitalize the old tradition" (Ueda 1979, 304–305). While the association had initially been organized in early 1946 to enable Shinto shrines to survive as religious organizations during the Occupation, leaders quickly abandoned its policy of accommodation and stance of privatization, redefining itself as a force for deprivatization.

In *War Memory and Social Politics in Japan, 1945–2005*, Franziska Sera-phim (2006, 41, 53) identified the NAS as a conservative rightwing organi-zation defined by its "politics of essentialism," which identified the emperor as "the locus of Japan's 'essence'" and his relationship to the Japanese people as constituting the "spiritual core" of Japan as a nation. According to the association, it is only Shinto—Japan's indigenous religion—which is in a position to provide "a non-negotiable essence relevant to all Japanese" (Seraphim 2006, 59). While the emperor-centric vision is the foundation of this essentialism, there is also a cluster of core beliefs and a political agenda aimed at "resurrecting aspects of the wartime system that occupation poli-cies had dismantled" (Seraphim 2006, 10–11). We now turn to consider the Shinto response to the Occupation that led to the emergence of a religio-political restoration movement.

CRITICAL RESPONSES OF SHINTO LEADERS TO THE ALLIED OCCUPATION

Standard postwar Shinto accounts of the Occupation paint a rather gloomy picture and a narrative of loss and marginalization. The initial twenty-year history of the NAS draws attention to the damage caused by the policies enacted by the Occupation across Japanese society (Okada 1966, 18–19). It caused confusion by changing laws, the national calendar, and removing religious and moral education from public schools, which fundamentally undermined the emperor-centric national polity (*kokutai*) that had integrated Japanese society. While acknowledging that scholars tend to consider Shrine Shinto as a "religion," that is, one religion alongside many others, this account claims that Shinto nevertheless deserved some special legal consideration given its role throughout Japanese history, par-ticularly such shrines as Ise and Yasukuni, which had such significant place in national and public life (Okada 1966, 272–273). Furthermore, the nature of the Shinto tradition had been completely distorted by the requirements of the Shinto Directive. It was much more than just a "personal" or "indi-vidual" faith, which was how it was accepted under the new religious cor-poration law. Shinto's character as a religion of the people (*minzoku sei*), its public nature (*kōkyōsei*), and its national character (*kokkasei*) were removed or destroyed by the Occupation policies. These fundamental aspects of Shinto's nature must be recovered and restored (Okada 1966, 984–987).

This volume also maintains that Article 20 of the postwar Constitution was unreasonable and unfairly restricted the role of religion in society by prohibiting government support of religious rituals in public life and removing religious and moral education from public schools—a strict application of religion-state separation, he observes, not required in many other countries where religious freedom is guaranteed (Okada 1966, 990). Okada recognizes the special character of Yasukuni Shrine as a national institution that deserves government support and recommends that its status be changed from that of a religious corporation to a special category corporation (*tokubetsu hōjin*), which would permit financial support to be restored. Not only should the government provide financial support to the shrine, but it is also the responsibility of prime ministers and other government representatives to make official visits to the shrine to memorialize and honor the war dead (1966, 994). These issues surrounding Yasukuni Shrine become the focus of recurring public debates throughout the postwar decades and can be expected to continue for the foreseeable future.

The Jinja Shinpōsha (1971) account of the early postwar period, *Shintō shirei to sengo no Shintō*, provides a similarly critical perspective on the Occupation particularly focused on the impact of the Shinto Directive and early efforts to reverse the damage. According to this account, many in the Shinto world experienced both shock and discomfort (*iwakan*) by the many changes brought about by SCAP, but there was initially little resistance to the Occupation policies and reforms implemented by the Japanese government. The priests and shrines associated with NAS were essentially loyal to the emperor, which meant that they followed his example and complied with the new social order and regulations. When the Occupation came to an end, however, many Shinto leaders found it impossible to passively accept the new order of things, which presupposed the destruction of ancient Japanese traditions, and began to initiate efforts to restore what had been destroyed by the Occupation (Jinja Shinpōsha 1971, 97).

This account emphasizes the primary concern of the association in the postwar period has been to "wipe away" (*fusshoku suru*) the lingering influences of the Shinto Directive and revive and restore the role of Shinto in national and public life (Jinja Shinpōsha 1971, 104). It provides an overview of the first two decades of these restoration efforts. When the San Francisco Peace Treaty came into effect on 29 April 1952, the occupation officially ended and Japan once again became an independent nation. This new situation meant that Shinto leaders were free to become more active and were keen on reversing the impact of the Shinto Directive on Japanese society. While the Shinto Directive no longer had any official status, the purpose and intent of the Directive had been institutionalized in the postwar Constitution and various laws, such as the religious organizations law, which meant that actually reversing the changes initiated by the Shinto Directive would be difficult.

Although the one aim of the Shinto Directive had been to establish religious freedom, we have seen that it, in fact, limited free religious expression of those belonging to Shinto shrines both by censoring Shinto viewpoints on issues of public concern and by requiring the revision of prayers and liturgies to eliminate problematic references to the emperor, the Imperial Household, and the State. Once independence was regained, the leaders within NAS began to review these liturgical resources and prepare new materials that would reflect their core concerns. A document entitled "Agenda for a life of kami worship" (*Keishin seikatsu no kōryō*) was drafted in 1956, which placed the emperor and Imperial Household back to a central place in Shinto prayers and liturgies (Jinja Shinpōsha 1971, 106; Breen and Teeuwen 2010, 200). Making these changes within the NAS would prove to be much easier than the restoration of the role of Shinto in the public sphere given the constraints of Articles 20 and 89, which were widely interpreted as requiring a strict religion-state separation not usually found in many other modern democracies.[27]

The Beginnings of a Restoration Movement. One of the first initiatives launched to restore the former order of things was with regard to Yasukuni Shrine, the site for the care of the war dead, which remained a prominent concern of many Japanese families. The shrine had been restricted from conducting a number of enshrinements and memorial rites for the public for the duration of the Occupation. Various actors and groups have been involved in the efforts to renationalize and promote Yasukuni Shrine in the postwar period, but the movement was initially launched with a resolution passed at the 1952 Annual Convention of the Japan Association of War-bereaved Families (Nihon Izokukai) to seek government funding to cover the costs related to the enshrinement of the war dead and the ongoing rites and memorial services (Nakano 2004, 121).

Debate regarding the future of the shrine began in the Diet from the mid-1950s. Politicians from the Liberal Democratic Party (LDP), with the support of the Japan Association of War-bereaved Families, and many from the Shinto world, proposed that Yasukuni and other state-protecting shrines be designated as "nonreligious" institutions again and government support be restored. One key figure involved in these discussions was Kanemori Tokujirō (1886–1959), who served as chief librarian of the Diet Library and in the first cabinet of Prime Minister Yoshida Shigeru. He argued that the new Constitution's articles on religion-state separation could only permit restoration of government support to Yasukuni if the religious elements of the shrine were removed. In the committee's debates and discussion, many of his opponents maintained the prewar view that the shrine was essentially a "nonreligious" patriotic site. Kanemori maintained that this view was no longer a tenable one since the shrine had registered as a religious corporation and had spent over a decade emphasizing its "religious character" (Jinja Shinpōsha 1971, 158; Haruyama 2006, 65).

The early proposal debated in the Diet required the secularization of the shrine as a condition for securing state support, and was opposed by both Shinto leaders and the Japan Association of War-bereaved Families. This opposition was expressed in a resolution passed by the priests from the state-protecting shrines at a special meeting held on 9 March 1956, which stated that the traditional Shinto rites could not be abandoned. In short, a "nonreligious" (or religiously neutral) memorial site for the war dead was viewed as unacceptable (Jinja Shinpōsha 1971, 158).[28] Due to the lack of consensus in these early debates, the issue of Yasukuni Shrine was pushed to the side for over a decade.

In the meantime, the NAS expanded its restorationist agenda to other issues and worked closely with other conservatives in the development of a number of affiliated groups, such as the Association for the Reestablishment of National Foundation Day (1957), the League Promoting Ties between Politics and Shinto (Shintō Seiji Renmei, 1969), the Association for Rectification of the Relationship between Religion and State (Seikyō Kankei o Tadasu Kai, 1971), and the Association to Preserve Japan (Nihon o Mamoru Kai, 1974), which collaborated initially in more realistic reform initiatives. It is the League Promoting Ties between Politics and Shinto that became the central organization within NAS used to mobilize political leaders to support their restorationist agenda, which deserves more focused consideration here.[29]

Shinseiren. The political arm of the NAS was at one time known as the League Promoting Ties between Politics and Shinto, but is better known today as the Shinseiren (Shinto Association of Spiritual Leadership). It began within the Tokyo headquarters of the NAS, but over the course of several years established branch offices in some forty-four cities and towns across Japan (Ōhara 2010b, 96). These offices organized and hosted a number of study meetings (*kenshūkai*) and lectures to educate local constituencies about the key issues of concern to Shinseiren. In 1974, a youth association (*seinentai*) was formed within Shinseiren, which was aimed at nurturing future leadership from among the younger priests.

As explained on the homepage and in numerous publications, "the Shinto spirit" provides the foundation for Shinseiren's political vision and activities. The central aims of Shinseiren are 1) to nurture support for the Imperial Household and to guard its dignity or majesty (*kōshitsu no songen goji*); 2) to work for a revised Constitution that will be the pride of the Japanese people; 3) to reestablish as a "national rite" the care of the Shōwa martyrs enshrined in Yasukuni Shrine; and 4) to put in place an education system that will cultivate the heart of young people and give them hope for the future (this is elaborated in various places in terms of a restoration of moral and patriotic education, which resembles the moral training (*shūshin*) curriculum of the prewar period). This particular political agenda is rooted in key beliefs and values that shaped Japan from the early Meiji period until the end of the Second World War.

Over the years, Shinseiren has worked especially closely with the LDP in order to gain national attention for their concerns and to bring their agenda and various initiatives to the central government for action. Its strategy, in fact, is related closely to its efforts to recruit Diet members to join its "debating club" known as the Shintō Seiji Renmei Kokkai Giin Kondankai, which seeks to mobilize Diet members to support the political agenda of Shinseiren. This is essentially a round-table discussion group for Diet members, which supports the broad goal of restoring the public role of Shinto. Shinseiren began endorsing candidates who supported their agenda from 1970, and their successes in this initiative brought some recognition that it had become a politically significant organization by 1974 (Ōhara 2010b, 96–97). In spite of their recruitment efforts, however, only 44 Diet members had been persuaded to join over the following decade (Shintō Seiji Renmei 1984, 151–152). In addition to efforts to influence the National Diet, the branch offices in prefectures and towns across Japan have similarly sought to shape the representatives elected for prefectural and local assemblies. As we will see in the next chapter, the fortunes of this organization would improve dramatically in post-disaster Japan.

According to the history of this political group, in 1984 there were some 945 shrines scattered across all the country's prefectures included in the list of supporting institutions (Shintō Seiji Renmei 1984, 167–184). This number represented less than 2 percent of the some 80,000 shrines that were a part of the NAS at the time. Although a current list of supporting shrines is unavailable, a close relationship remains between Shinseiren and a number of shrines affiliated with the association. The NAS provides office space in Tokyo for the group and for its local branches in affiliated prefectural headquarters throughout Japan. A link to the Shinseiren homepage is also maintained on the NAS's website.[30]

In the early decades after the end of the Occupation, the NAS and other restorationist groups worked closely with the LDP to bring their concerns and various initiatives to the Diet for action. Two early efforts that met with success were the movements to restore National Foundation Day (*Kenkoku kinen no hi*; *Kigensetsu* in the prewar period), which was finally re-established in 1966, and the reign-name legalization movement, which was achieved with the passing of the Reign-Name Law (*Gengō hō*) in 1979, which restored the Japanese calendar based on the reign of the emperor (Jinja Shinpōsha 1971, 98–101, 111).[31] Ruoff (2001, 158–201) provided a detailed treatment of these two successful campaigns, which he interpreted primarily as the restoration of the "cultural symbols of the Monarchy." This buttressed, of course, the essentialist vision of NAS, which was centered on the emperor.

In spite of these achievements, there were a number of equally important goals that were not achieved during this same period. Central among them were the attempts to renationalize Yasukuni Shrine. Efforts to renationalize the shrine were resumed in the late 1960s. Leaders of the LDP presented six bills (*Yasukuni jinja hōan*) to the Diet from 1969 to 1974 in an effort to restore direct government support to the shrine (Shintō Seiji Renmei 1984, 45–56). Proponents of the bills maintained that the shrine is a national site for remembering the war dead and should not be regarded as "religious."[32] They argued, furthermore, that "official visits" by government representatives and officials should be fully supported and recognized as a matter of civic duty and an example of patriotism. Critics of these bills, on the other hand, claimed that Yasukuni Shrine was clearly a "religious" site that was monopolized by the priests of one religious tradition—Shinto.[33] Any direct support, they argued, would violate the constitutional separation of religion and state. The bills promoting the restoration of state support to Yasukuni Shrine were defeated each time and faced strong opposition from various Buddhist, Christian, and secular groups, who shared the common concern to preserve the freedom guaranteed by the postwar Constitution.

The failed attempts to renationalize Yasukuni Shrine represents just one of the unfulfilled goals of the post-Occupation "restorationists." Other initiatives promoted by Shinseiren include movements to reclaim the ideals of the Imperial Rescript on Education and thereby restore proper moral and patriotic education in the public schools, the creation of new textbooks that would support such a curriculum, promotion of the use of the national flag and anthem for official ceremonies in public schools, and revision of the Constitution (Shintō Seiji Renmei 1984, 66–78). The NAS, Shinseiren, and other affiliated groups, however, "stood far to the right of the mainstream," Ruoff (2001, 187) explains, which is why "many of their campaigns have failed." These were to become the focus of renewed efforts in the wake of the disasters of 1995 and 2011, when some new actors—political and religious—joined the NAS and Shinseiren to form a coalition with a growing number of LDP Diet members to promote their neonationalistic agenda.

3

Disasters and Social Crisis

The Mobilization of a Restoration Movement

Since the mid-1990s, Japanese society has been shaken by a series of both "natural" and "man-made" disasters. Here I am referring specifically to the "double disaster" of 1995 and the "triple disaster" of 2011. First was the devastating Hanshin-Awaji earthquake that struck the Osaka-Kobe area on January 17, which caused major damage in the city of Kobe and surrounding areas. Over 5,000 residents died as a result of this disaster and over 30,000 were injured. In addition, 300,000 people had to evacuate their homes and move into temporary housing facilities as they sought safety from the aftershocks and fires, which destroyed over 100,000 buildings.[1] This was followed on March 20 by the sarin gas attack on several lines of the Tokyo subway system by members of Aum Shinrikyō, a new religious movement that had only been in existence for a decade. The sarin gas killed 12 people, but injured thousands more—many still suffering from permanent health problems as a result of exposure to the gas.

The scale of this "double disaster" pales in comparison with the "triple disaster" of 11 March 2011. The earthquake, tsunami, and nuclear accident at the Fukushima Daiichi plant brought unimaginable devastation to the Tohoku region and shocked the nation. Five years after this disaster, over 2,500 people were still reported as missing and 15,894 were confirmed dead as a result of the earthquake and powerful tsunami waves that had swept through coastal communities (Oskin 2017). Thousands were injured and over three hundred thousand people were displaced from their homes. Ever since the explosion and meltdown of the Daiichi nuclear plant, many residents across Japan—but especially in the areas near Fukushima—have been worried about the potential effects of radiation levels on food safety and human health. In addition to the human costs of the disaster years, the economic impact has been profound both in terms of rebuilding costs and the number of business enterprises destroyed.

The focus of this chapter is on the Japanese responses to these crisis events, particularly the steady growth of a broader coalition of religious and political actors united behind the neonationalistic agenda promoted by the National Association of Shrines (Jinja Honchō; NAS) since the early post-Occupation period. The significance of "social crisis" for nationalism has been noted for some time. Ivan I. Morris (1960, 164), in his now classic study, *Nationalism and the Right Wing in Japan*, observed that the "re-emergent rightists" in the early postwar period "would invariably begin and end by stressing the *crisis* with which Japan was faced on the political, economic, and international levels—a crisis to which, needless to say, they alone could provide a solution." In order to address this crisis, they claimed it was necessary "to restore a sense of national pride among the people and, for this purpose, to revive traditional national virtues." This chapter will provide evidence to show how the "restoration movement" Morris observed in the early postwar period has grown in post-disaster Japan.

Almost two decades ago, Matsudo Yukio (2001, 163) alerted me to this kind of "nativist response" to more recent moments of national crisis, which he framed as a return to "invented tradition." A number of other scholars have also observed this link between the neonationalist resurgence and the collective sense of social crisis (see, for example, Seraphim 2006, 27; Yoda 2006, 20–25; Harootunian 2006, 103). This crisis situation, I will argue, emboldened neonationalistic leaders and created an environment that allowed their concerns and initiatives to gain traction and achieve a degree of success that had been impossible in the preceding years. As we will document below, the restorationist movement, which had been languishing since it succeeded in passing the Reign-Name Law (*Gengō hō*) in 1979, found new life and relevance to many more Japanese in the post-disaster context.

THE 1995 SOCIAL CRISIS AND RESURGENCE OF NATIONALISM

A new opening for neonationalists and their initiatives began to emerge in the wake of the 1995 disasters. People across the nation were understandably shaken after months of non-stop media coverage of the earthquake devastation and the arrests, trials, and debates about the human suffering caused by Aum's efforts to bring about its apocalyptic vision. The disorienting events of early 1995, as Yoda Tomiko (2006, 20–25) has observed, raised serious concerns about established institutions: the disaster in the Osaka-Kobe area revealed the government's "ineptitude in crisis management" and the disturbing attack on the Tokyo subway system by some of Asahara Shōkō's closest disciples indicated that the police were unable to protect the public from deviant religious movements. Given that the sense of social order and stability was undermined in this way, it is not surprising that political and religious leaders, as well as the general public, were challenged to think more seriously about the nature of postwar Japanese society. The fact that 1995 was the year that marked the fiftieth anniversary of the end of World War II, also encouraged national reflection and debate about how Japan's military history should be remembered, celebrated, and mourned. As it turns out, it was a year that began decades of more serious debate and conflict over the meaning of the war, the nature of postwar Japanese society, and its future direction.

The government's initial response to the Aum crisis included the Diet's approval—in less than a year—of changes in the law governing all religious bodies in Japan (*shūkyō hōjin hō*) as well as new legislation that would allow the authorities to monitor Aum and its successor groups more closely.[2] In view of the tragic deaths, injuries, and widespread sense of insecurity that followed the Aum Shinrikyō gas attack, it is understandable that many Japanese expected the government to do more to protect them from dangerous religious groups. The Diet's hurried revision of the religious corporation law on 8 December 1995, sought to address these public concerns. Helen Hardacre (2003, 152) has suggested that the revision of this law may eventually be seen as a watershed moment: "Future researchers may come to regard the liberal period of 1945 to 1995 as a brief, foreign-dictated abnormality in Japan's long history of state monitoring of religion." Following the revision

of the religious corporation law, political leaders moved beyond the immediate concern to "protect" society from deviant religious movements and
expressed a broader interest in the problematic nature of postwar Japanese
society that allowed such a movement to emerge and attract young people
in the first place.[3]

While the "Aum Affair" seemed to confirm for some that society would
be better off without religion, these various incidents inspired others to
think more seriously about the need for religious and moral education.
The response of Umehara Takeshi, the well-known philosopher, public
intellectual, and popular author, provides a helpful illustration of this perspective. He was so shaken by the Aum affair that he found himself forced
to reevaluate the whole educational philosophy and system that had guided
postwar Japan. Within seven months of the Aum subway gas attack, Umehara (1995) wrote and published a volume in which he critically examines
the failure of both schools and families—including himself as a father and
teacher—to provide the ethical teaching and religious education that young
people so clearly needed. It was this system of education, Umehara claims,
which provided no moral education (*kokoro no kyōiku*) that nurtured the
young people who joined Aum and eventually committed the sarin gas
attack and other acts of violence. For that reason, he concludes, it is not just
these young people who bear the responsibility for this terrible crime: "We
must also reflect deeply on our own culpability" (Umehara 1995, 138–142).[4]

The concerns expressed by Umehara in late 1995, of course, were not
entirely new. For some years the news media had been bombarding view-
ers with almost daily reports regarding widespread social problems that
reflected a fundamental moral deficiency in young people: a steady increase
in the number of children refusing to attend school, the problem of bully-
ing in schools across the nation, the increase in suicides by children, and
the problem of *enjo kōsai* (teenage girls engaging in sex with older men for
compensation). The master narrative promoted by some conservative commentators and Liberal Democratic Party (LDP) politicians in the aftermath
of the Aum incident was that the involvement of Japanese youth in such a
group was the result of the individualistic and amoral education system that
had been in place during the postwar period. The restoration of moral education and patriotism in public schools—something that had been removed

by the Occupation policy of forced secularization—was clearly needed to keep young people loyal and committed to the "system" and to vaccinate them against deviant religious groups like Aum in the future. This concern for "morality" was often expressed by politicians who were unable to recognize (or denied) the ethical concerns and problems related to Japan's earlier history of empire-building and colonization. Among these concerns are the outstanding claims of some Asian neighbors for official recognition and compensation for their suffering at the hands of the Japanese military, particularly with regard to forced labor and the sexual exploitation of "comfort women" (*ianfu*) in the service of the troops. Several political leaders did in fact acknowledge Japan's responsibility in the mid-1990s for the pain and suffering inflicted on its neighbors, which only contributed to the resurgence of neonationalism in post-disaster Japan.

Although Umehara provides a useful example of the widespread sense of crisis brought about by Aum, it is Kobayashi Yoshinori, the manga artist and author, who reveals most clearly the link between this crisis and resurgent nationalism. Kobayashi's best-selling book series *Gōmanizumu sengen*—variously rendered in English as "My Arrogant Declarations" or "The Arrogant-ism Proclamations"—shows an increasingly nationalistic orientation after his engagement with Aum. Kobayashi was one of the few public figures brave enough to criticize Asahara and Aum long before the sarin subway gas attack and before their criminal activity had been actually confirmed by police investigation.

In *Shin gōmanizumu sengen* (1996), Kobayashi gives considerable attention to his conflict with Aum, which began in 1994 in connection with his public criticisms of the group and speculation about the fate of the lawyer Sakamoto and his family, who had disappeared in 1989 under suspicious circumstances (some observers suspected that the family had been eliminated by Aum operatives because of legal actions Sakamoto was pursuing against the group). The volume includes many unfavorable depictions of Asahara, critical references to an "irresponsible" religious studies scholar Shimada Hiromi who appeared to defend Aum as a legitimate religion, and also mentions the alleged assassination plan that targeted Kobayashi for his critical stance towards the movement. There is also a section devoted to a conversation between Kobayashi and Egawa Shōko, a journalist who was also actively investigating Aum and writing about the group before their crimes were fully known.[5]

Kobayashi admits that the Aum crisis had a serious impact on his orientation and subsequent work. In fact, he made a direct connection between his shift to the right and Aum Shinrikyō when interviewed by John Nathan (2004, 133) and asked why he had become such an ardent nationalist from 1996:

> Their guru, Shoko Aashara, taught a false history, which included an apocalypse that was due to arrive in 1999. In doing that, he created a discontinuity with history, and that disconnection allowed his followers to turn into monsters. It occurred to me that the rest of us Japanese are no different—we are all living in a present that is disconnected from history because we've been conditioned and brainwashed into reviling and rejecting our own past.[6]

Given this new self-understanding, it is not surprising to find that Kobayashi's manga since then have celebrated Japan's imperial past and provided an alternative account of many controversial issues surrounding the war, Yasukuni Shrine, the Imperial Household, and moral education. His popular volumes include, for example, *Sensōron* (1998), *Shin gōmanizumu sensōron* (2) (2001), *Yasukuniron* (2005), *Iwayuru A kyū senpan* (2006), *Shōwa Tennō ron* (2010), and *Shūshinron* (2010). Kobayashi's influence has not been restricted to popular culture and manga, however. In 1996, he became a core member of the Society for the Creation of New History Textbooks (Atarashii Rekishi Kyōkasho o Tsukuru Kai), a group which grew out of the Study Group for a Liberal View of History (Jiyūshugi Shikan Kenkyūkai), which had been organized the year before by Fujioka Nobukatsu, a University of Tokyo education professor, and Nishio Kanji, a specialist in German literature. Their primary concern was to provide textbooks that would cultivate in students a sense of national pride and patriotism and counter the "masochistic" historical narratives that were critical of Japan, which they felt had dominated postwar education (Saaler 2006, 15).[7] Although Kobayashi subsequently left this group, his wide-ranging activities as a manga artist and public intellectual since 1995 clearly reveals the close connection between the sense of social crisis precipitated by Aum's violence and his embrace and advocacy of a neonationalistic agenda.

While the Hanshin-Awaji earthquake and Aum incident may have been the precipitating events that led to the neonationalistic resurgence, the timing is also related to some profound economic and political changes during the preceding few years. First, the traumatic events of 1995 followed a decade of steady economic decline. Japan had been lauded as "Number One" for its successful rebuilding of the postwar economy and rapid growth into the 1980s, but the "bubble economy" burst in the early 1990s and the nation faced a rapid decline of stock prices and land values. While Japan was riding high there had been limited time or interest in nationalistic concerns, but the crisis generated by the long recession and events of 1995 forced many Japanese to face these fundamental questions again. In *Japan Unbound*, John Nathan (2004, 119) has captured this situation as follows:

> During the 1970s and 1980s, while Japan's economy was flourishing, *identity was not an issue*. People were secure in their jobs; hard work led to affluence.... Since 1990, when the high-flying economy crashed, confidence and pride and even sense of purpose have been eroded as the recession deepens.... *What remains is a deeply unsettling emptiness that has produced, yet again, an urgent need to feel identified. Japan's new nationalism is a manifestation of the need and a response to it.*

Japan's economic problems have only worsened over the past decade, and today it faces even larger challenges: rebuilding the Tohoku region after the 11 March 2011 earthquake and tsunami, and coping with the nuclear disaster in Fukushima.

Also contributing to the neonationalistic reaction were certain developments in the world of Japanese politics in the several years leading up to the fiftieth anniversary of the end of the war. It was during the brief three-year interlude (1993–1996) to the postwar domination by the LDP that several leaders of the coalition government initiated "apology diplomacy" and made significant efforts to actually improve diplomatic relations through the public acknowledgment of Japan's imperial past. Chief Cabinet Secretary Kōno Yōhei began this initiative with his statement and apology in response to the study on the "comfort women" issue on 4 August 1993. Prime Ministers Hosokawa Morihiro and Murayama Tomiichi both struggled to address calls for an official apology from the government in acknowledgment for the pain and suffering caused by Japan's military aggression and colonial rule. Shortly after becoming the head of the coalition government, Hosokawa publicly admitted in a speech to the National Diet on 23 August that Japan bore responsibility as the aggressor (*kagaisha*) for the invasion and colonization of its neighbors in Asia. This was followed two years later by a similar statement from Prime Minister Murayama on 15 August 1995, who apologized for the pain and suffering caused by Japan's military aggression and colonial rule.[8] Doi Takako (2007), the former leader of the Socialist Party, who herself had pushed for an official apology for some years, has argued that these admissions of guilt by representatives of Japan's government were more than the conservative politicians and rightwing groups could endure, which contributed to the rightwing reaction and neonationalistic response that followed.[9]

This public recognition of Japan's responsibility as the aggressor towards its neighbors in Asia represented a significant shift in orientation among some political leaders. Such an admission clearly challenged the revisionist narrative of Japan's imperial past celebrated at Yasukuni Shrine and promoted by Yūshūkan, the shrine's military museum, as a glorious effort to "liberate Asia" from Western imperialism. Reflecting on these official apologies, for example, Ishihara Shintarō, the ardent nationalist and former Governor of Tokyo, expressed how appalled he was by these public statements:

> Hosokawa was a horrible prime minister who got in on a fluke and only lasted a year. But what I can't forgive is the ignorance of history that allowed him to declare that our war in the Pacific was a war of aggression. As if the imperialism that drove Europe and the United States to colonize the rest of the world was acceptable and only our war was evil. I believe that the worst offense a government leader can commit is to sell his own country down the river. Hosokawa's remarks, and Murayama's sentimentalism about "painful repentance and heartfelt apologies," amounted to a desecration of our nation's history. I can't forgive that. (Nathan 2004, 170)[10]

This brief conciliatory period ended with Murayama's resignation and the start of a new phase of neonationalism that was symbolically marked by Prime Minister Hashimoto Ryūtarō's official visit to Yasukuni Shrine in 1996.

NEONATIONALISM IN THE POST-DISASTER CONTEXT

The period since the initial 1995 social crisis has been a busy one for those embracing the restorationist vision of the religio-political rightwing in Japan (see TABLE 3). A coalition of religious and political leaders quickly emerged that shared the "politics of essentialism" and began to work together in order to realize their neonationalistic agenda. The coalition I refer to here, of course, has it roots in the early efforts in cooperation in the late 1970s between the NAS, Shinseiren (Shinto Association of Spiritual Leadership), Japan Association of War-bereaved Families, Nihon o Mamoru Kai, and leaders and activists from the rightwing Seichō no Ie, a New Religion (Ruoff 2001, 161; Tsukada 2017, 54). This coalition has been strengthened by the revitalization and expansion of the older Shinto political organization, Shinseiren, and the formation of the Japan Conference (Nippon Kaigi), a new organization established in 1997, which is essentially providing a broader base of support for the central concerns and agenda that have been pursued by the NAS for decades.

Year	Movements and Activities
1995	Study Group for a Liberal View of History organized by Fujioka Nobukatsu and Nishio Kanji.
1996	Society for the Creation of New History Textbooks formed in association with the Study Group for a Liberal View of History.
1997	The Japan Conference established building on two earlier groups, Nihon o Mamoru Kai and Nihon o Mamoru Kokumin Kaigi.
1998	Publication of Kobayashi Yoshinori's *Sensōron*.
1999	Legal recognition of national flag (Hinomaru) and anthem (Kimigayo). Ministry of Education issues guidelines and instructions for all public schools to sing the national anthem and use the flag for official events, such as entrance and graduation ceremonies.
2000	Prime Minister Mori Yoshirō's 15 May address at the celebration of the thirtieth anniversary of the League Promoting Ties between Politics and Shinto (Shintō Seiji Renmei) refers to Japan as a "divine nation" (*kami no kuni*) centered on the emperor.
2001	Prime Minister Koizumi Jun'ichirō participates in rituals at Yasukuni Shrine (which he did a number of times between 2001 and 2006). Revisionist history textbook prepared by the Society for the Creation of New History Textbooks approved by Ministry of Education for junior high schools in 2001, but less than 1 percent of junior high schools adopted the new history textbooks in 2001 and 2005.

Year	Movements and Activities
2002	*Kokoro no nōto*, patriotic moral education texts distributed to elementary and junior high schools by Ministry of Education.
2003	Under the direction of Tokyo Governor Ishihara Shintarō, the Tokyo Education Committee issues an order for all teachers and staff in the public schools to participate in leading students in singing the Kimigayo for entrance and graduation ceremonies or face disciplinary action (23 October).
2004	Disciplinary action taken against 180 teachers of the Tokyo public schools in March 2004 for failure to sing the national anthem and properly guide their students in official ceremonies before the national flag.
2005	LDP draft proposal for a New Constitution made public. Publication of Kobayashi Yoshinori's *Yasukuniron*.
2006	Revision of Fundamental Education Law (*Kyōiku kihon hō*).
2007	Pro-Yasukuni anime DVD entitled *Hokori* (Pride), produced by Nihon Seinen Kaigisho for the Ministry of Education, distributed for viewing in 93 locations across Japan.
2008	Regulation banning school visits to Yasukuni Shrine and state-protecting shrines ruled no longer valid by Minister of Education (27 March). Ministry of Education provides orientation on new policy allowing school visits (June and July).
2011	On May 30, the Supreme Court ruled that it was constitutional for a principal to instruct teachers and staff to stand and sing the Kimigayo in front of the national flag at school ceremonies.
2012	On 4 August, the City of Yokohama Education Committee announces that from 2012 textbooks prepared by the Society for the Creation of New History Textbooks will be used in 149 schools with an approximate student population of 80,000 students. On 5 June, the Osaka Prefectural Assembly passed the *Kimigayo jōrei*, an ordinance that requires all teachers and staff employed by public schools in its jurisdiction to stand for the singing of the Kimigayo at all official school ceremonies. Additional action by the Assembly in September defined in more detail the punishment facing those employees who fail to comply. LDP revised draft proposal for new Constitution made public in April.
2013	On 1 May, Prime Minister Abe makes public his plan to target Article 96 for initial revision to ease the process of amending the Constitution. Osaka Education Committee informs public schools in September that principals have been instructed to check if teachers are fulfilling their duties and properly singing the national anthem at entrance and graduation ceremonies.
2014	On 1 July, Prime Minister Abe and his Cabinet announce their reinterpretation of Article 9, which would allow Japan's military to engage in collective self-defense and aid allied forces.
2015	At a 16 June meeting of National Universities held in Tokyo, the Ministry of Education informs some 86 universities that it expects the flag and anthem to be used for graduation and entrance ceremonies.
2016	Ministry of Health, Labor, and Welfare issues guidelines for nursery schools (*hoikusho*) to incorporate opportunities and activities for children age three and above to become familiar with the flag and anthem.

Year	Movements and Activities
2017	In May, Prime Minister Abe announces plan to complete revision of the Constitution by 2020.
2018	On 11 December, Prime Minister Abe reaffirms his intention to pursue revision of the Constitution by the 2020 target, but postpones submission of proposal until next Diet session.

TABLE 3. Neonationalist Movements and Restoration Initiatives, 1995–2018.

Both Shinseiren and the Japan Conference have effectively entered into a symbiotic relationship with the rightwing of the LDP, including several prime ministers, and draw their membership from a shared base of support, which includes a number of organized religions. This has enabled them to achieve several legislative victories over the past two decades. As Nakano Kōichi (2016, 23) reminds us, the LDP began as a "broad church" when it was launched in the mid-1950s. It included both liberals and a faction of rightwing nationalists who maintained close ties with Shinto shrines and were sympathetic to the political agenda of the NAS. Given wartime devastation and the widespread concern for rebuilding the country, however, this nationalistic agenda was pushed to the sidelines and the policies of the more moderate wing of the party focused on economic development and recovery (Toyoda and Tanaka 2002, 278–280). However, there has been a steady movement of the rightwing from the sidelines to the center of the party over the past several decades. Nakano (2016, 24) sees this rightward shift as an "elite-driven" process, which has steadily increased in successive waves over several decades. Each shift to the right is related to reactions to the left—the Murayama government in the 1990s and the Democratic Party of Japan (DPJ) government between 2009 and 2012—and the crises provoked by the disasters of 1995 and 2011.[11] A brief review of these key political and religious actors and their achievements is in order.

THE NAS AND POLITICS IN POST-DISASTER JAPAN

As documented in the previous chapter, the NAS began to reorganize itself as a force for deprivatization as soon as the Occupation ended. This became particularly apparent after it established the League Promoting

Ties between Politics and Shinto (Shintō Seiji Renmei) in 1969—which later became the Shinseiren—and began to recruit Diet members to support its restorationist agenda. The number of LDP politicians affiliated with Shinseiren's debating club for Diet members (Shintō Seiji Renmei Kokkai Giin Kondankai) has increased significantly in post-disaster Japan. In 1984, there were only 44 Diet members claimed by this association, but this grew to 204 by late 2013, and to 268 in 2014. This number has steadily increased under Shinseiren's chairperson, Prime Minister Abe, and reached 295 at the end of 2018, which represents 41 percent of the Diet membership of 722.[12]

How does this close relationship between the NAS, Shinseiren, and the LDP actually manifest itself in the course of political life? This can be illustrated with several concrete examples. The first is provided by Yamatani Eriko, one of the darlings of Shinseiren and a person who represents the far right of the LDP. Yamatani is a popular speaker and regularly appears at Shinseiren study meetings and gatherings held across the country. She has also served as the chief secretary of a group of Diet members who support Yasukuni Shrine and is a strong advocate of "official visits" (kōshiki sanpai) to the shrine by the prime minister.[13] She is also a strong supporter of the Imperial Household and has recently been promoting group tours and pilgrimages to Ise Shrine in order to cultivate a deeper appreciation for the Imperial Household, gratitude for Japanese identity, and worship of Amaterasu, the ultimate source of the nation.[14] Finally, the fact that she has maintained a re-election office within the shrine precincts of Katori Shrine, in Katori City, Chiba Prefecture—with her campaign posters prominently displayed there—indicate how closely Shrine Shinto is linked to Shinseiren politicians.[15] What makes Yamatani a particularly interesting example is that she is also well known as a Catholic and a regular contributor to a Catholic radio broadcast. Although a Catholic, she clearly holds to the view of Shinto shrines as "nonreligious" civic institutions, a view the Catholic Church adopted under duress from 1932 to 1945. This puts her at odds with the critical stance of the Japan Catholic Bishops' Conference in recent decades, which we will consider later with reference to patriotic education and Yasukuni Shrine, but her position clearly illustrates the widely held view that the ideas and practices associated with the emperor and shrines are "essential" to authentic Japanese identity, and transcend the category of "religion" and individual religious commitment to a particular denomination.

Another example may be seen in the statements and bold actions of some prime ministers from the LDP. In a speech to Diet members at a Shinto-related (Shinseiren) political gathering on 15 May 2000, for example, Prime Minister Mori Yoshirō gave full expression to the civil religious vision and agenda that drives the NAS and other restorationist groups, stating that "Japan was a divine nation centered on the emperor" (*kami no kuni*). This statement was interpreted by many observers to be in fundamental tension with the postwar Constitution, which placed power and authority with the people and defined the emperor as a "symbol"—i.e., without political power.[16]

After his remarks were widely circulated by the media, Mori found himself in a difficult press conference in which he was forced to clarify his position. Mori affirmed the freedom of religion as guaranteed by the Constitution and claimed that he had no interest in restoring Shinto as the State religion. His statement, *Tennō o chūshin to suru kami no kuni* [the nation with the emperor at its heart in the land of deities], he explained, was made "in the context of describing the activities of the Council of the Shinto Political Federation of Diet Members" (that is, Shinseiren). After apologizing for causing such a misunderstanding, he concluded with a very revealing statement:

> What I most intended to express in my statement at the Council of the Shinto Political Federation of Diet Members meeting was that, as we have seen again and again criminal cases committed by youths in which it is clear that they pay little regard to human life, we must educate our children to understand the invaluable importance of human life, while deepening their *natural religiousness*.[17]

This statement clearly reveals that Mori and the Shinseiren have a religious agenda for public institutions. While Mori apologized for the misunderstanding caused by his statement, he refused to retract it.

It seems apparent—notwithstanding claims to the contrary—that it is this civil religious vision at the foundation for the restoration initiatives and educational reforms aimed at nurturing patriotism and morality. Mori's concluding statement is another example of the widespread understanding of Shinto as something "nonreligious" (in the sectarian sense, that is), but still regarded as something that is essential for defining what it means to be Japanese. This perspective, which Thal (2002, 112) notes "pervaded public discourse until at least 1945," has clearly been revived and cultivated in the postwar period and is central to the postwar initiatives of Shinseiren.

A third example may be seen in the response of Shinseiren to the return of the LDP to power in December 2012. The "triple disaster" in March 2011 overwhelmed the leadership of the governing DPJ. The DPJ was already in trouble, but the scale of this disaster and inadequate responses by the national government paved the way for the return of the LDP. After the three-year hiatus under the leadership of three successive DPJ prime ministers, the LDP made a comeback in December 2012, and Abe Shinzō began his second tenure as prime minister. Gotō Toshihiko, the chairperson of Shinseiren, heralded the return of Abe and the LDP in the organization's monthly magazine, *Kokoro*, and expressed his hope that there was, at last, the leadership needed for the rebirth and restoration of Japan.[18] While Gotō acknowledged that the victory of the LDP in December was due more to the utter failure of the DPJ and disappointment of the people than to a genuine trust and hope in the LDP, he noted that Abe—as a leading member of the Shintō Seiji Renmei Kokkai Giin Kondankai—truly shared the values of the Shinto world and would work for their restoration in public life.

While several hundred LDP politicians are now affiliated with Shinseiren, it is important to recognize that the political agenda promoted by the head office of the NAS through Shinseiren actually has rather limited support from local shrine priests and parishioners. As noted earlier, there were only 945 shrines identified as supporters of Shinseiren in 1984. Tsukada (2017, 374–375) estimates that less than 10 percent of NAS shrines actually support Shinseiren today, and these would be the larger and wealthier shrines. Most priests are preoccupied with survival issues at most smaller local shrines and are largely uninvolved in the political activities.

Some years ago, John Nelson (2000, 246) observed that not all shrines support the vision and priorities of NAS, but they were in a weak position to openly criticize given the authority of the head office to certify and appoint priests at member shrines. At many shrines "one finds a cautious acceptance at best," he explained, "and often a real resistance to these totalizing themes and agendas." The head priest of Kamigamo Shrine, the site of Nelson's ethnographic study, was reluctant to support the nationalistic rhetoric coming out from the headquarters, explaining: "'I'm old enough to remember that this kind of road leads nowhere,' he said. 'People like me have to set an example for others who did not experience directly those years leading up to the war'" (Nelson 2000, 247).

Since Nelson documented this quiet internal resistance to the political agenda of NAS almost two decades ago, some very public criticisms of the NAS, as well as the Japan Conference have begun to appear—though still uncommon—from within the Shinto world. Miwa Takahiro, the resident priest of Hiyoshi Shrine in Nagoya, is one of these critics and his views have appeared in weekly magazines, online reports, and personal blog posts since 2016. Miwa claims that the NAS and Japan Conference essentially share the same ideology and understanding of what constitutes Japanese identity and tradition. Their views and agenda are shared by Prime Minister Abe and are currently shaping the direction of Japan. In an interview for a special issue of the weekly magazine *Shūkan kinyōbi* (27 May 2016), which focused on the Japan Conference and its close relationship with the NAS, Miwa explained that these organizations shared a mistaken view of what constituted authentic Japanese "tradition," claiming that it was defined by the strong bonds between the Imperial Household and the Japanese people. This so-called "tradition," however, was only created in the recent past as a result of the Meiji Restoration. Miwa maintains that a much older and pervasive Japanese tradition was, in fact, characterized by the predominance of shrines that focused on their own local tutelary deity (*ujigami*), rather than on the Imperial Household and Ise Shrine, and that these shrines were often a part of a shared site with Buddhist temples and a combinatory form of religious practice (*shinbutsu shūgō*). The Meiji government was in fact the "destroyer" (*hakaisha*) of this older religious culture and created state Shinto with its new system of national rites and one unified value system centered on the emperor, which was used to control the people. This particular version of Japanese tradition, he argues, only appeared in the last century and hardly represents the older plural Shinto traditions that preceded it for much of Japanese history. He regards the restorationist vision and political agenda of NAS and the Japan Conference as an expression of fundamentalism (*genri shugi*) and authoritarianism (*ken'i shugi*).[19]

It is not just a matter of relatively low support among shrine priests. Most parishioners have little interest in the political agenda of NAS headquarters. Although the NAS officially reports over 87 million followers nationwide, Tsukada (2017, 374) claims that most shrines struggle along without many "true believers" or dedicated parishioners who actually support their local shrine, and few of them are mobilized for political action. Survey research over the past few decades supports this interpretation. National surveys of participation in organized religions consistently found that people visited shrines for festivals and rites of passage, and only a small percentage of respondents indicated that they participated in the political activities of religious institutions: 1979→2.0 percent, 1984→2.2 percent, and 1989→2.4 percent. Another study conducted in 2000 asked respondents what they thought about organized religions being involved in political activities and elections, and only 5.4 percent replied that it was not an issue of concern while the majority—67.7 percent—regarded it as problematic. Other surveys conducted in 1999 and 2004 asked respondents about the religious activities they had participated in over a two to three year period, and participation in the political activities of an organized religion was the least common activity for both years at 0.7 percent for 1999 and 1.6 percent for 2004.[20] So the vast majority of Japanese avoid personal involvement in the political activities of organized religions. In addition, as Roemer (2012, 38–39) has observed in his review of Japanese data reported in the Asian Values Survey (2001) and World Values Survey (2005), some 80.91 percent (AVS) of Japanese respondents thought that "religious leaders should not try to influence politics." Similarly, the World Values Survey found that 71.20 percent of the Japanese sample agreed that religious leaders should not influence "government decisions," and 74.74 percent agreed that "religious leaders should not influence how people vote."

These findings from national and international surveys, which indicate a general lack of interest and involvement in political activities promoted by organized religions, are consistent with the results of a 2007 NAS survey that found most parishioners or visitors to shrines were oblivious to its political agenda and activities. Reporting on the results of this survey,

Breen and Teeuwen (2010, 203–204) observed that most visited shrines for the first visit of the New Year (*hatsumōde*, 62 percent), rites of passage for children (53 percent), or to pray for health and well being of family members (37 percent). What is striking is that "no respondents cited imperial, patriotic themes as a reason for visiting their local shrine, a fact that brings into relief an important slippage between the NAS understanding and that of the common man or woman."

While Ruoff (2001, 200) has suggested that the NAS provides a popular base of support for the rightwing political movements much like the Christian coalition has for rightwing causes in the United States (i.e., the Moral Majority movement), it appears that there is only minimal popular support provided by parishioners, and the NAS and Shinseiren is primarily a top-down elitist movement guided by Shinto leaders in the head office. This is certainly the view of Tsukada (2017, 366–367), one scholar who has looked at this most closely. The NAS has effectively mobilized Diet members through Shinseiren in support of their political agenda, but it has failed to attract widespread support at the local level. The actual number of parishioners across the country who could be mobilized for political action by the shrines appears to be rather limited. Nevertheless, even without widespread support of the masses, it has met with considerable success in pushing forward its political agenda over the past two decades, but this is due in large part to collaboration with the Japan Conference.

THE JAPAN CONFERENCE

The Japan Conference, which was formed through a 1997 merger of Nippon o Mamoru Kai with another nationalistic group, Nippon o Mamoru Kokumin Kaigi, has become a key coalition partner with the NAS, Shinseiren, and the LDP in the post-disaster period. Although it has been active for over two decades, its role in contemporary politics only became a serious focus of media attention during the last several years. While the newspaper of the Japanese Communist Party, the *Akahata*, began to regularly report on the Japan Conference and its activities from 2005, other media coverage was minimal for at least the first decade of its existence. A few more detailed articles began to appear in 2007, which sketched the early development of the Japan Conference and its relationship to rightwing religious organizations and political leaders (Fuwa 2007; Uesugi 2007; Tawara 2013).[21] It was 2014 before the mainstream press began to give more serious attention to the Japan Conference and its role in shaping and supporting the rightwing of the LDP. According to Yamazaki's (2016, 52–56) review, it was on 31 July 2014 that the *Tokyo shinbun* published a piece, which identified the Japan Conference as "the largest rightwing organization in Japan" (*Nihon saidai no uha soshiki*). This was followed the next day by an article in the *Asahi shinbun* (1 August), which highlighted the close relationship between the organization and the Abe administration, and the active role played by assembly members in local districts. Weekly magazines, such as *AERA* and *Friday*, began to publish about the Japan Conference the same year, but broadcasts on NHK—the mainstream television outlet—still had not seriously reported on the significance of this relationship.

The situation changed dramatically from 2015, when one book after another appeared in succession, which examined the Japan Conference in more depth, particularly its role as a support base for Prime Minister Abe and his political agenda (Yamazaki 2015; 2016; Aogi 2016; Sugano 2016; Tawara 2016; Uesugi 2016).[22] These studies provide considerable background and information on the history, membership, and relationship with organized religions, as well as some analysis of the political strategies of the Japan Conference.[23] They also tend to be very critical in their assessment of the organization and its vision for the future. Uesugi (2016), for example, likens it to a "cult" organization that is pushing to revise the Peace Constitution, while Yamazaki (2015) regards it as a part of a larger movement to restore the social order of the prewar period (*senzen kaiki*), which indicates that some Japanese have relapsed or caught another case of the "great imperial Japan illness" (*Dai Nipponbyō*). This negative interpretation, of course, is in sharp contrast with how the Japan Conference understands and presents itself.

According to the group's publications and homepage, its mission is to rebuild a beautiful and independent Japan, which necessarily includes restoring proper respect for the emperor and Japanese traditions, patriotic education, revision of the Constitution, and support for official visits to Yasukuni Shrine. It claims a nationwide network of some 100,000 members, including some hundred Diet members who are associated with branches in local towns and communities from Hokkaido to Okinawa. Some four hundred members serve at the Central Office and another 3,100 on the prefectural and city boards across the country. It also boasts the ability to attract some 500,000 signatures in support of its causes.[24] According to Tawara (2016, 109–110), the Japan Conference began to make considerable efforts to organize branches across the country from the year 2000 and now has close to 300 nationwide. These are seen as important new bases to promote revision of the Constitution and counter the expansion and influence of the Article 9 Association (Kyūjō no Kai), which was launched in 2004 in an effort to increase popular support for the preservation of the Peace Constitution. It has now expanded to over 7,500 branch associations across the country, so the Japan Conference still has some catching-up to do.

The Japan Conference hosts symposia and study groups on Constitutional revision, patriotic education and new history textbooks, and is especially effective in raising support for its causes at the prefectural and local levels of government through its Local Assembly Members League (Nippon Kaigi Chihō Giin Renmei). According to Tawara's (2016, 111) recent survey, there were some 1,632 individuals belonging to this League, which included one governor, thirty-one mayors, 795 prefectural assembly members, and 805 heads of local governments. Their representation on a number of prefectural assemblies has grown substantially; it claims over 70 percent of the assembly members for Yamaguchi Prefecture, the home prefecture of Prime Minister Abe, over 60 percent for Yamagata, Ibaraki, and Ehime prefectures, over 50 percent for Miyagi, Nagasaki, and Kumamoto prefectures, and over 40 percent for Akita, Gunma, Saitama, Chiba, Gifu, Shizuoka, Okayama, Fukuoka, Miyazaki and Kagoshima prefectures, and both the Tokyo and Kyoto municipal governments. As a result, many local governments and school boards are increasingly under pressure to adopt the Japan Conference policy positions with regard to patriotic education, required use of flag and anthem, adoption of revisionist textbooks, and Constitutional revision.[25] These efforts at the local level extend to signature campaigns calling for the revision of the Constitution, which have also led to concrete actions taken by local and prefectural governments. In February

2014, for example, the assembly of Ishikawa Prefecture passed a resolution to call on the National Diet to revise the Constitution. This action prompted more serious efforts to gain support for the revisionist initiative, and the Japan Conference managed to get another thirty-five prefectures and twenty-five local governments to adopt the same resolution before the end of the year (Sugano 2016, 100).

Here it must be recognized that the Japan Conference is essentially providing a broader base of support for the central concerns and agenda that have been pursued for decades by the NAS through Shinseiren and its supporters in the LDP. As Tsukada (2015, 65) has observed, the interests of these organizations are so closely aligned that it is virtually impossible to identify any distinguishing features that separate them. They share the same "essentialist" understanding of Japan—the emperor-centric vision promoted by the NAS and the notion of "nonreligious Shinto" institutions, which ideally should be supported by the state.[26] Many LDP politicians, in fact, are affiliated with both organizations, and the same religious groups line up in support of their common political agenda. Shinto priests actively involved in Shinseiren are often strong backers of Japan Conference activities in their communities. This comes out clearly in Aogi's (2016, 127–139) interview with Ishikawa Masahito, the resident priest of Morooka Kumano Shrine in Yokohama City, and head of Shinseiren for Kanagawa Prefecture, who estimates that some 15 to 20 percent of priests in the prefecture support the Japan Conference and its initiatives. The overlapping membership of leaders in both the NAS and the Japan Conference supports the interpretation that the organizations today are simply a part of a larger coalition of rightwing religions, political activists, and Diet members.

Although the Japan Conference is not a "religious" organization per se, its leadership draws heavily on representatives from a variety of religious groups that share the same ideology and political agenda. It has attracted the support of leaders from many spheres of Japanese society—academic, legal, business, and religious—but the leaders of the Shinto world have a particularly prominent place, including representatives from the NAS, Shinseiren, Yasukuni Shrine, and Meiji Shrine. As may be seen in TABLE 4, the religious representation on the Japan Conference Board extends beyond Shrine Shinto and includes individuals from Buddhist institutions and

New Religions. Of the forty-seven board members, twenty are associated with a religious organization or NGO founded by a religion (42.5 percent), and of that number 10 are Shinto-related and affiliated with Shinseiren, the NAS, and other well-known Shinto institutions (see TABLE 4).[27] The role and influence of Shinto leaders on the Japan Conference board is also reflected in the number of Shinto institutions that provide various forms of support for its activities across the country, including fourteen prefectural offices of the NAS and another ninety-six individual shrines.[28]

In addition to the New Religions represented on the board, the organization has also received support from other religious groups, such as Reiyūkai, Sūkyō Mahikari, Gedatsukai, and Kurozumikyō.[29] Even the Christian group Genshi Fukuin—also known as Makuya—is among the supporters.[30] This "ecumenical" association suggests that the ideals and activities of the Japan Conference transcend all sectarian forms of religion and represent what is regarded as indispensable for the nation (for at least some members of these diverse religious groups).[31] In short, representatives

Group	Position
Shinto	President, National Association of Shrines Head Priest, Ise Shrine Director, National Association of Shrines President, League Promoting Ties between Politics and Shinto Head Priest, Atsuta Shrine President, Tokyo Branch of the National Association of Shrines Priest, Yasukuni Shrine Associate Head Priest, Ise Shrine Head Priest, Meiji Shrine Chairperson, Meiji Shrine Sūkeikai
Buddhist	Board Representative, Hieizan Enryakuji (Tendaishū)
New Religions	Chief Advisor, Shinsei Bukkyō Kyōdan Senior Leader, Gedatsukai Master Teacher, Nenhō Shinkyō Chairperson, Bussho Gonenkai Kyōdan Management Head, Sūkyō Mahikari Director General, OISCA (The Organization for Industrial, Spiritual, and Cultural Advancement International, Ananaikyō) President, Institute of Moralogy Head, Daiwa Kyōdan Board Chairperson, Ethics Research Institute (Rinri Kenkyūsho)

TABLE 4. Religious Advisors and Members of the Japan Conference Board, 2017.

of a variety of religions still embrace the emperor-centric vision of the "politics of essentialism" and the restorationist agenda promoted by both the Japan Conference and Shinseiren.

While the support for the Japan Conference from organized religions is substantial, it should not be exaggerated. It is important to recognize that most religious organizations are in serious decline and are unlikely to provide a long-term popular base of support in the mobilization of human and financial resources in support of the restorationist political movement. As Tsukada (2017, 370–371) has observed, some of the key New Religions known for their strong support—Gedatsukai, Bussho Gonenkai Kyōdan, and Reiyukai—have all declined dramatically in the two decades between 1994 and 2014: Gedatsukai from 224,302 to 99,325 (-56 percent), Bussho Gonenkai from 2,190,591 to 1,167,960 (-46.6 percent), and Reiyukai from 3,072,780 to 1,340,703 (-56 percent).

The situation of the NAS is similarly gloomy. In recent years, it has attracted unwanted media coverage of a number of conflicts between the head office and local shrines over finances, leadership succession, and priestly appointments. In addition to these tensions, the number of shrines struggling for mere survival is increasing and the shortage of priests becomes more critical each year. A decade ago, Breen and Teeuwen (2010, 219) observed that there were only "some 20,000 priests and 1,900 priestesses" responsible for some 80,000 shrines across the country. The situation has only continued to deteriorate. The declining birthrate and steady movement of the population from rural to urban areas over the postwar decades is clearly taking its toll on many shrines. In many localities across Japan the population is shrinking to such an extent that a number of established religious institutions are unlikely to survive. Ishii Kenji, an established researcher on contemporary Shinto, has reviewed recent demographic studies that project some 49.9 percent of municipalities across the country could disappear by 2040. According to Ishii's analysis, some 35.6 percent of all religious corporations are located in these precarious municipalities. If local governments cannot be sustained due to population decline, it is likely that religious institutions will also collapse. Ishii indicates that this would include 41 percent of the shrines (31,184 of 76,030) that belong to the NAS.[32]

What is important to recognize here is that the growing prominence and role of rightwing religious organizations in the public sphere in post-disaster Japan—what has been referred to as deprivatization—is actually occurring at a time when almost all organized religions are in the midst of secularization or institutional decline. These demographic realities indicate there will likely be a continued shrinking of the religious base available to support the restorationist political agenda in the future.

It is not just a matter of the organizational decline of the religious base of support, however. Seichō no Ie, a New Religion that once provided strong support for nationalistic causes, recently made a radical shift in orientation and has abandoned the Japan Conference and its support for Prime Minister Abe's administration and political agenda. Under the leadership of founder Taniguchi Masaharu (1893–1985), whose emperor-centric vision included a call to restore the Meiji Constitution in the post-Occupation period, many Seichō no Ie members were mobilized for political engagement through its political alliance, Seichō no Ie Seiji Rengō, organized in 1964. Members were subsequently involved in the rightwing anti-communist student movement, Nippon Seinen Kyōgi Kai (1970), and restoration initiatives through Nihon o Mamoru Kai (1974), and eventually became a core of support for the Japan Conference when it was formed in 1997 (Yamazaki 2016, 68–71; 87–89; Tsukada 2015, 49–57).

This history of involvement in nationalistic political activity and support for the Japan Conference has recently ended under the third president, Taniguchi Masanobu, who assumed leadership of Seichō no Ie in 2009. A conversion (*tenkō*) of sorts has occurred and in November 2012 the organization officially announced that it had reversed course under this new leadership. In 2013, it moved its head office from downtown Tokyo (Harajuku) to the town of Fuefuki, Yamanashi Prefecture, where it has built a solar power complex as a part of its "Office in the Forest." Given the challenges facing the world today, particularly the destruction of the environment, Taniguchi was convinced that a religious reformation was desperately needed and the move out of Tokyo and into the countryside symbolized their new religious vision. In his book, *Shūkyō wa naze tokai o hanareru ka?* (2014, 30), Taniguchi explained the organization's radical change in orientation in terms of a fundamental shift from a concern for "the spiritual protection of the state" (*chingo kokka*) to a focus on "world peace." It is now developing spiritual practices that are consistent with their new ecological concerns and international vision. In his recent New Year's Greeting, for example, he highlighted practices that constitute the path for implementing this new vision in everyday life, including a vegetarian, low-carbon dietary life, and leisure activities with a low carbon footprint.[33]

Seichō no Ie has made a clear break with the Japan Conference and withdrawn its support for the ruling LDP government and Prime Minister Abe's agenda. On 4 October 2017, it issued a statement that urged its members to make political decisions that were consistent with its new vision of environmentalism and urged its members not to support ruling party candidates in the upcoming election.[34] The statement also expresses opposition to Abe's plan to revise Article 9, reaffirms the principle of constitutional democracy which limits political power, and raises serious concerns about the prime minister's authoritarian style, which is undermining this principle. The statement goes on to explain that Seichō no Ie is now seeking to contribute to world peace through international exchange and dialogue, and working for peaceful co-existence in a world of religious pluralism and cultural diversity. It seeks to focus its efforts on solving problems related to the environment. It is opposed to the restart of Japan's nuclear facilities as well as the current policy of the Abe government to export nuclear technology for economic development, urging the government to export Japanese technology and expertise to help other nations address pressing environmental concerns, and in this way contribute to world peace.

THE GROWING INFLUENCE OF THE RELIGIO-POLITICAL RIGHTWING UNDER PRIME MINISTER ABE

Over the course of LDP administrations since 1995, one can document a renewed effort to pass legislation to restore and strengthen patriotic education in public schools, to promote "official" Yasukuni Shrine visits, and to revise the Constitution of Japan. As may be seen in TABLE 5,[35] a number of the key concerns advanced by Shinseiren for several decades and more recently promoted by the Japan Conference have received renewed attention and support by prime ministers and many members in the Diet. When considered in isolation, some of these developments may appear unrelated to religion, and they probably are without religious significance for many individuals whose lives are shaped by the new policies (in public schools, for example). However, when taken all together and seen in relation to the political agenda and goals of the NAS and Shinseiren, they are clearly a part of a civil religious vision for Japanese society. Patriotic education, for example, may indeed be based on nonreligious foundations. In the case of Prime Minister Abe Shinzō, however, an active member and chairperson of Shinseiren, it is clearly rooted in the religious beliefs and values promoted by NAS, a body registered as a religious corporation. This connection is obvious to religious minorities who have been in opposition to these recent developments.

With the growing strength of the Shinseiren and Japan Conference in post-disaster Japan, LDP Diet members and prime ministers have become emboldened in the public support of the shared neonationalistic agenda. This has been demonstrated by both symbolic actions—promotion of Yasukuni Shrine visits—and through legislation passed by the Diet to achieve significant restoration goals in the first decade after the Aum-related crisis. While Yasukuni Shrine remains a controversial site—both domestically and internationally—and efforts to revise the Constitution have only been restarted since the return of the LDP and Prime Minister Abe to power in late 2012, some restoration goals related to patriotic education have already been achieved through legislation passed by the Diet. Under Prime Minister Obuchi Keizō, the Diet was finally able to pass a bill to provide official recognition of the flag and anthem in 1999. Like Abe, Obuchi was a strong supporter of Yasukuni Shrine who similarly appointed members to his Cabinet that represented Shinseiren and other conservative groups (Nelson 2003, 462). During Prime Minister Abe's first term in 2006, he successfully pushed through the revision of the Fundamental Education Law (*Kyōiku kihon hō*), which provided legal support for the compulsory use of the flag and anthem in official ceremonies in public schools as a part of the new push for patriotic education.

Name	Term in Office	Initiative/Legislation Promoted or Passed
Obuchi Keizō (1937–2000)	30 July 1998– 5 April 2000	Diet passed a bill to provide official and legal recognition of the national flag and anthem in 1999. Ministry of Education issues guidelines and instructions for all public schools to sing the national anthem and use the flag for official events, such as entrance and graduation ceremonies. On 5 April 2001—the last day of Obuchi's term and first day of Mori's term—the Ministry of Education approves the new revisionist textbook for junior high schools, which was prepared by the Society for the Creation of New History Textbooks.
Mori Yoshirō (1937–)	5 April 2000– 26 April 2001	Prime Minister Mori Yoshirō's address at the celebration of the thirtieth anniversary of the League Promoting Ties between Politics and Shinto refers to Japan as a "divine nation" centered on the emperor (15 May 2000).
Koizumi Jun'ichirō (1942–)	26 April 2001– 26 September 2005	Fulfilling his promise to supporters that he would visit Yasukuni if elected as prime minister, Koizumi participates in official visits on a number of occasions between 2001 and 2005. *Kokoro no nōto*, patriotic moral education texts, distributed to elementary and junior high schools by Ministry of Education (2002). LDP makes public draft proposal for new Constitution, including revisions to articles 20 and 89 that pertain to religion, which would clearly weaken the clear separation of religion and state.
Abe Shinzō (1954–)	26 September 2005– 26 September 2007	Revision of Fundamental Education Law (2006). Pro-Yasukuni anime DVD *Hokori* (Pride), produced by Nihon Seinen Kaigisho for the Ministry of Education, distributed for viewing in 93 locations across Japan (2007).
Fukuda Yasuo (1936–)	26 September 2007– 24 September 2008	Regulation banning school visits to Yasukuni Shrine and state-protecting shrines ruled no longer valid by Minister of Education (27 March 2008). Ministry of Education provides orientation of new policy allowing school visits to shrines during the summer of 2008.
Asō Tarō (1940–)	24 September, 2008– 16 September, 2009	On his personal homepage Asō promotes a proposal to make Yasukuni Shrine a special category organization, eliminating its current status as religious corporation, which would allow direct financial support by the government.

Name	Term in Office	Initiative/Legislation Promoted or Passed
Abe Shinzō (1954–)	26 December 2012–	Abe renews call to revise the Constitution and on 1 May 2013 proposes revision of Article 96 to allow amendments to be passed by simple majority in the Diet rather than a two-thirds majority. Reiterates his stance that a revision of the Constitution is indispensable for true liberation from the postwar regime. Initially avoids visiting Yasukuni Shrine as prime minister, but makes offerings for the Spring Festival and 15 August; indicates that whether or not Cabinet members participate in Yasukuni Shrine rites should be decided by the individuals concerned; makes official visit on 26 December 2013. On 1 July 2014, Abe and his Cabinet members announce their reinterpretation of Article 9, which would allow for Japan's military to engage in collective self-defense activities overseas. Lower House of the National Diet passes new security bills based on reinterpretation of Article 9 on 16 July followed by the Upper House on 19 September 2015. In May 2017 Abe announces plan to complete revision of the Constitution by 2020. On 11 December 2018, Abe reaffirms his intention to pursue revision of the Constitution by the 2020 target, but postpones submission of proposal until next Diet session.

TABLE 5. LDP Prime Ministers and Restoration Initiatives, 1998–2018.

The influence of Shinseiren and the Japan Conference has steadily increased since Abe's return to power in 2012. As noted earlier, the number of Diet members affiliated with Shinseiren reached 295 at the end of 2018, and this is reflected in their increased presence in the composition of successive Cabinet memberships under Abe. The percentage of Shinseiren members in the Abe Cabinet in 2012 reached fourteen (73.7 percent), and increased again to sixteen out of nineteen members (84.2 percent) in 2015.[36] This shift to the right has increased yet again and may be seen in the full range of nationalistic affiliations of Abe's Cabinet members in 2012 and 2018 (see TABLE 6).[37] Only one member of the current Cabinet, Ishii Keiichi, a Diet member from the LDP coalition partner Kōmeitō, belongs to neither Shinseiren nor the Japan Conference. In its critical coverage of the

Neonationalistic Memberships and Affiliations	2012	2018
Shinseiren	14 (73.7%)	18 (94.7%)
The Japan Conference	13 (68.4%)	14 (73.7%)
Diet Member Alliance for Promoting the Assessment of a New Constitution (Kenpō Chōsa Suishin Giin Renmei), organized in 1997 to promote revision of the Constitution, especially Article 9.	12 (63.2 %)	8 (42.1%)
Association of Diet Members for Worshiping at Yasukuni Shrine Together (Minna de Yasukuni Jinja ni Sanpai suru Giin no Kai), established in 1981.	15 (78.9%)	18 (94.7%)
Diet Member Group for Considering Japan's Future and History Textbooks (Nippon no Zento to Rekishi Kyōkasho o Kangaeru Giin no Kai)	9 (47.4%)	6 (31.5%)

TABLE 6. Affiliation of Abe Cabinet Members with Neonationalistic Associations, 2012 and 2018.

steady rightward shift of the government and its support of the Yasukuni Shrine, patriotic education, and revision of the Peace Constitution, the Communist Party's newspaper *Akahata* has identified the Abe Cabinet both as the "war hawks" sect (*taka ha*) and "Yasukuni sect."[38]

As noted in TABLE 5, shortly after Abe returned to office in 2012, he proposed a revision of Article 96 to allow amendments to be passed by simple majority in the Diet rather than a two-thirds majority. This proposal faced considerable opposition and criticism, and Abe was forced to withdraw it from consideration. The overwhelming victory of the LDP in the July 2013 elections, however, meant that Abe would have another opportunity to push through his agenda of constitutional revision. Abe renewed the call for revision of the Constitution on 1 May 2013 and again on 11 December 2018. In preparation for his planned push for constitutional revision, he has surrounded himself with close to half of the Diet membership and a large majority of his Cabinet who belong to either or both Shinseiren and the Japan Conference. Given the impact of legalization of the flag and anthem in 1999 and the revision of the Fundamental Education Law in 2006, religious minorities are particularly concerned about possible revision of Articles 20 and 89, which clearly define and protect religious freedom and the separation of religion and state.

FROM "POLITICS OF ESSENTIALISM" TO "POLITICS OF INCLUSION"

As we have seen, the number of religious and political actors embracing the "politics of essentialism" has increased in post-disaster Japan. Their restorationist agenda, which aims at shaping public life and institutions for all Japanese, has also met with some success during this period. Many critics claim that "coercion" has been brought back into public institutions as a result of the coalition's legislative victories. It is apparent that the sociologic of the "politics of essentialism" has given birth to a "politics of inclusion." Here I am not referring to policies and strategies to give all people a voice in the democratic process; rather, the phrase is used here to indicate that ideological "orthodoxy" (essential beliefs) and "orthopraxy" (appropriate behaviors) are being forced on all people who identify themselves as Japanese. This interpretation of the "politics of inclusion" is drawn from the work of Peter van der Veer (1994), which appears in his treatment of Hindu nationalism and the Vishva Hindu Parishad (VHP) movement's effort to "bring tribals and untouchables within the Hindu fold." In sharp contrast to Ghandi's vision of pluralism, Veer explains, the VHP practices a "politics of inclusion rather than a tolerance of difference." The legislative efforts that have accompanied the restorationist movement in Japan are similarly producing a politics of inclusion and "an intolerance for those who do not want to be included" (Veer 1994, 559–660). In sum, the effort to restore aspects of the social order that existed prior to the Occupation is putting in place coercive policies that require conformity, which is already leading to an erosion of individual rights and civil liberties in public institutions.

The restorationist agenda has met with some critical resistance both from the secular left as well as from a range of religious groups. While religious groups do not clearly line up one way or another on issues surrounding patriotic education, official statements by many organized religions do tend to divide along pro- or anti- positions with regard to Constitutional revision and Yasukuni Shrine (see TABLE 7).

In spite of official statements, however, it is important to recognize that religious organizations tend to be deeply divided on these political matters regardless of what "official" position statements might be issued. Over the past three decades, for example, the Catholic Bishops' Conference of Japan

Groups Opposed to Revision of the Constitution, Renationalization of Yasukuni Shrine, and Official Visits	Groups in Support of Revision of the Constitution, Renationalization of Yasukuni Shrine, and Official Visits
Religious Organizations Japan Buddhist Federation (to which 102 Buddhist sects and 90 percent of temples belong) Jōdo Shinshū Sōka Gakkai Federation of New Religious Organizations of Japan (Shin Nihon Shūkyō Dantai Rengōkai, 40 New Religions, including Risshō Kōsei Kai) Seichō no Ie (from 2012) Roman Catholic Church Anglican-Episcopal Church United Church of Christ in Japan (Nihon Kirisuto Kyōdan), other Protestant churches *Other Groups* Kirisutosha Izokukai Heiwa Izokukai Shinshū Izokukai Article 9 Associations	*Religious Organizations* National Association of Shrines (NAS) Seichō no Ie (until 2012) Sekai Kyūseikyō Bussho Gonenkai Kyōdan Reiyūkai Kirisuto no Makuya (Genshi Fukuin) *Other Groups* League Promoting Ties between Politics and Shinto (and later the Shinseiren) Japan Association of War-bereaved Families Japan Conference (previously, Nihon o Mamoru Kokumin Kaigi) Group for Correct Government (Seikyō Kankei o Tadasu Kai) Society for the Creation of New History Textbooks

TABLE 7. Religious Groups and Voluntary Associations on Constitutional Revision and Yasukuni Shrine.

and Japan Catholic Council on Peace and Justice have issued numerous statements of protest to the government regarding efforts to renationalize Yasukuni Shrine and to promote official visits by the prime minister and government officials. They have also opposed more recent legalization on the national flag and national anthem, approval of revisionist history textbooks for public schools, revision of the Fundamental Education Law, and the proposal of the LDP to revise the Constitution (particularly Articles 20 and 89).[39] Pastoral letters addressing these issues have also been distributed widely to the faithful as the bishops are concerned that the Church be careful not to embrace the government's agenda as it did in the 1930s and 1940s. Their stance today is based on critical self-reflection and a belief that the Church failed to perform its prophetic task during the difficult circumstances of the wartime period.

Notwithstanding the "official statements" issued by the Catholic Bishops' Conference, Japanese Catholics remain deeply divided over these public issues.[40] Some members hold to a pietistic or apolitical faith and frown on the political engagement by Church representatives, while others actually support the agenda of the LDP and neonationalists considered above. Some of the best-known Japanese Catholics and political figures, in fact, include two LDP Diet members—former Prime Minister Asō Tarō and Yamatani Eriko—who both fully support the current government's position on patriotic education, constitutional revision, and Yasukuni Shrine. The well-known Catholic novelist and writer, Sono Ayako, and her husband, Miura Shumon, are also strong supporters of the LDP government's position on patriotic education and Yasukuni Shrine.[41] These public figures could very well have more influence than the prophetic Japanese Bishops, who these days tend to offer a critical perspective on these controversial issues that is closer to the position of many Protestant leaders. This observation on the divided nature of the Catholic Church holds true for many other organized religions in this line-up.

With this caveat in mind, we now turn to examine in some detail the critical response of religious actors, particularly religious minorities, to the "politics of inclusion." The following chapter considers key issues surrounding Yasukuni Shrine with a focus on the controversy over postwar enshrinements of the war dead without permission of the families concerned. The sixth chapter turns to consider public schools and the debate over the role of flag and anthem in patriotic education. Both are institutional sites known historically as the key carriers of State Shinto in the wartime period, which involved obligatory participation in patriotic rituals—a requirement that many religious minorities fear is being reconstituted by the current government and its rightwing supporters. The seventh chapter examines the proposed revisions to Articles 20 and 89 of the Constitution and considers why religious minorities in particular are concerned about their fate if the proposed changes are made.

PART TWO

The Neonationalist Agenda Contested

4

The Politics of Yasukuni Shrine

Official Visits and Postwar Enshrinements

Yasukuni Shrine, a sacred site in Tokyo's Kudan district—
only a short distance from the Imperial Palace—has been
an important part of Japan's religious landscape since the late nineteenth
century. Initially established in Kyoto by Emperor Meiji in 1868 as Shōkonsha, it was relocated to Tokyo the following year. Although it began as
a shrine dedicated to those who had sacrificed their lives in the Boshin
War (1868–1869) on behalf of the emperor, it quickly became the central
shrine for memorializing all of Japan's war dead for the next century. It was
renamed Yasukuni or "peaceful country" in 1879, and the following year

The Torii Entrance to Yasukuni Shrine's Main Hall (photo by author, 11 May 2013).

was given a special rank (*bekkaku kanpeisha*) in the new system of national shrines established by the Meiji government. Yasukuni Shrine—along with other "state-protecting shrines" (*gokoku jinja*)—was central to what came to be known as "State Shinto."

Yasukuni Shrine was under the direct administration of the Ministries of the Army and Navy and financially supported by the government until the end of World War II. Although Shinto priests conducted rites of deification and pacification of the deceased, the government defined these ceremonies as "nonreligious" patriotic or civil ceremonies and clearly distinguished them from the "religious" rituals conducted by followers of Buddhism, Christianity, and various New Religions. By defining what went on at Yasukuni and other Shinto shrines as "nonreligious," the government was able to require all of its citizens to participate in such ceremonies as a part of their patriotic duty. In this way, sacred sites such as Yasukuni Shrine became the symbolic focus of a new Japanese identity based on the ideal of self-sacrifice for the nation and emperor. It is this understanding of the shrine that the coalition of neonationalists—Liberal Democratic Party (LDP) politicians, the National Association of Shrines (Jinja Honchō; NAS), Shinseiren (Shinto Association of Spiritual Leadership), and the Japan Conference (Nippon Kaigi)—seek to restore in contemporary Japan.[1]

The NAS regards the Grand Shrine of Ise as the highest ranking shrine—it enshrines Amaterasu, the ancestral deity of the Imperial Household—and it encourages the distribution of Ise Shrine's amulets throughout its 80,000 affiliated shrines across Japan. Notwithstanding the prominent position of Ise in the Shinto world, however, it has been Yasukuni Shrine that has often functioned as the symbolic center for the restoration movement's central concerns, which include renationalization of Shinto, patriotic education, and promotion of historical revisionism. Yasukuni Shrine is registered as an independent religious corporation (*shūkyō hōjin*) and does not belong to the NAS; however, it is backed solidly by the NAS leadership. Although both shrines have attracted state patronage and visits by prime ministers and other government officials since the end of the occupation period, it is those to Yasukuni Shrine that have generated the most controversy and public debate.

Why is it that this particular shrine—which represents itself today as the foundation for a "peaceful nation"—has been such a source of social conflict and the focus of legal battles in postwar Japan? At least two developments at Yasukuni Shrine in the postwar decades have made it the focus of critical attention. First, in 1979 it became known that Yasukuni Shrine had "secretly" enshrined B and C-class war criminals in 1959, and had extended enshrinement to fourteen class-A war criminals in 1978 under the direction of Chief Priest Matsudaira Nagayoshi.[2] Many observers felt that the shrine had legitimized the worst aspects of Japanese imperialism and militarism by conducting these enshrinements, which constituted a transformation of "war criminals" into "deities to be worshiped." This constituted a symbolic rejection of the judgments of the Tokyo War Crimes Tribunal, which many viewed as a form of "victor's justice," and was something that Matsudaira sought to "discredit" by these enshrinements (Takenaka 2007, 5). Serious consequences followed these revelations, in any case. Emperor Hirohito never made another personal visit to the shrine after revelations of the 1978 enshrinements, nor has his successor, Akihito. The April 2007 diary account of Urabe Ryōgo, Chamberlain to the emperor for some two decades, revealed that the late Emperor Hirohito disapproved of the enshrinement of class-A war criminals, which is why he did not visit the shrine after 1975 (Breen 2008, 3).[3] As we will see below, this has become a serious issue of concern for the Japan Association of War-bereaved Families (Nihon Izokukai).

The second development has to do with the fact that the shrine hosts the Yūshūkan, a war museum, restored and expanded in the post-Occupation period, which contains a highly contested account of Japan's history from the Meiji Restoration to the end of World War II. As historian John Breen has shown, the museum promotes a rather "selective memory" about the past, one that tends to glorify or sanitize the wars of Japan's modern century. "The exhibits are all designed to proclaim the glory of dying for the emperor and country," Breen explains. "There is no encouragement to dwell on the evils of militarism; and no room to consider that lives lost were lives wasted" (Breen 2004, 91–92). Given this account and legitimation of Japanese imperialism, it is not surprising that Japan's neighbors are incensed when the prime minister or other political leaders visit the shrine and provide symbolic support and implicitly accord Yūshūkan's account of the war a kind of "official status." This is a version at odds with what many Chinese, Koreans, and Okinawans experienced, and one that glosses over some well-documented atrocities by Japan's military as well as the brutal exploitation of laborers—including "comfort women" (*ianfu*)—who were forced to provide sexual services to officers and troops in the expanding empire.

Ise Shrine, by contrast, does not share such negative associations and has largely avoided controversy in the postwar period. This probably explains why in May 2016 Prime Minister Abe felt that it was possible to include a tour of Ise for international leaders as a part of the G7 Summit. While Ise is clearly less controversial than Yasukuni, some religious minorities did issue statements criticizing the government's plan to guide the G7 foreign guests to this site, regarding it as a political use of religion and an effort to promote Shinto, which would lend support to the movement to restore State Shinto (*kokka Shintō no fukken*). Such criticisms, however, did not discourage Prime Minister Abe from making a return visit to Ise on 4 January 2017.

Yasukuni Shrine has become the focus of public concern and debate on a number of occasions during the postwar period. As already noted in a previous chapter, from 1969 to 1974, the first major controversy surrounded the efforts of the LDP to pass the *Yasukuni Jinja hōan*, a bill to renationalize the shrine and provide direct government support, which provoked widespread protest. In spite of strong support from the NAS, the Japan Association of War-Bereaved Families, and other rightwing religious groups, these efforts all failed. The focus of this chapter is on two other issues that have mobilized critics of Yasukuni Shrine: "official visits" (*kōshiki sanpai*) by prime ministers and enshrinements (*gōshi*) of the war dead. These have become political and legal problems in the postwar period due to the fact that Yasukuni Shrine was registered as a "religious" institution in 1946, and the postwar Constitution (1947) clearly defined the relationship between the state and religion as one of "separation" and established the rights of individuals to freely practice (or not) a religion of their choice (Articles 20 and 89).

The controversies and legal battles surrounding Yasukuni Shrine today are related to claims that either the principle of separation has been violated or the rights of individuals have been constrained or violated in some way. Postwar enshrinements, in particular, are closely related to our concern over the "politics of inclusion" and the situation of religious minorities. The vast majority of over two million war dead enshrinements occurred after the new Constitution was passed and enacted by the Diet, and some bereaved families have appealed for protection from the shrine's unilateral enshrinement of their deceased family members without permission or regard for their religious faith. Our treatment of these issues will highlight the responses and critical perspectives of Buddhist and Christian public intellectuals and religious leaders to the pro-Yasukuni stance.

"OFFICIAL VISITS" TO YASUKUNI SHRINE

Prime Ministerial visits to Yasukuni Shrine resumed shortly after the Treaty of Peace with Japan was signed in San Francisco (8 September 1951). Yoshida Shigeru, in fact, visited on 19 October 1951, almost six months before the Occupation officially ended. While many prime ministers visited over the following decades, they usually explained that their visits were conducted in a "private" capacity (*shijin no shikaku*) or avoided clearly indicating whether the visits had been personal or official. Conservative leaders within the LDP, however, were adamant that official visits be resumed and fully recognized as such. This issue was finally addressed head on during the period Nakasone served as the prime minister (1982–1987). Prime Minister Nakasone Yasuhiro visited the shrine on 15 August 1983 and the following year, but whether these visits were made as a "private citizen" or as a "public official" remained ambiguous (although he did sign the shrine's registry as prime minister).

It was in this context that in August 1984 Chief Cabinet Secretary Fujinami Takao convened a private Advisory Committee to gather information from a range of experts on how Japanese people viewed the shrine and to address the lingering problem of whether or not official shrine visits by the prime minister and cabinet members constituted a violation of the Constitution.[4] The composition of the fifteen-member advisory committee was diverse and included public intellectuals, a company president, lawyers, a former Supreme Court judge, professors of constitutional law and philosophy, a literary critic, and a novelist.

The committee met some twenty-one times over the course of a year to deliberate these issues. Given the make-up of the committee, it is not surprising that a consensus was never reached. While some firmly argued that such "official visits" would be a violation of religion-state separation and offered other reasons why such visits were inadvisable, the majority opinion submitted to Fujinami in the final report endorsed the view that these visits constituted legitimate behavior on the part of government representatives.[5] On 14 August 1985, Fujinami issued a public statement that presented the majority opinion—and the government's preferred view—that visits to the shrine by prime ministers and cabinet members would not constitute a violation of the constitutional separation of religion and state if these visits were simply to pay respect to the war dead and without religious significance. This could be achieved, he explained, by avoiding the Shinto rituals usually performed on such visits.[6]

The majority position and final recommendation of Fujinami's committee was based in part on a consideration of the 1977 Supreme Court Decision (13 July) on whether the use of municipal funds for the Tsu City grounds purification rite (*jichinsai*) in 1965 constituted a violation of Article 20 of the Constitution. The Supreme Court ruled that if the purpose of the activity (*kōi no mokuteki*) was not religious, and the action did not aim to support or promote one particular religion (*shūkyō ni taisuru enjo, jochō, sokushin*) or involve coercion or interference (*appaku, kanshō nado*) in the free practice of another religion, then the activity would not constitute a violation of Article 20. In short, the majority opinion and recommendation to Fujinami was based on the expansion of this judicial interpretation from grounds purification rites to include official visits.[7]

On 15 August, Prime Minister Nakasone visited Yasukuni Shrine and closely followed the approach recommended by Fujinami. He went directly to the main hall, bowed once, but did not observe the traditional Shinto protocol, which normally includes a purification ritual, an offering of a sprig of the *sasaki* tree, and the usual ritual process of two bows, clapping of the hands twice, and a final bow (*nirei, nihakushu, ichirei*). Rather than making a direct financial donation, Nakasone simply used public funds to purchase the flowers that were offered on the occasion of his visit. The general public may have been oblivious to these fine distinctions between "religious" and "nonreligious" observances and simply regarded Nakasone as a "pro-Yasukuni" nationalist when he made the visit accompanied by most of his Cabinet members. The head priest, Matsudaira Nagayoshi, however, was incensed that the traditional rites had been abandoned and regarded Nakasone's visit as a sign of disrespect to the kami enshrined there.[8]

In spite of the efforts by Fujinami and Nakasone to redefine "official visits" as civic and nonreligious and therefore constitutional, critics were hardly persuaded given the fact that the ritual respect accorded the war dead occurred in an institution registered with the government as a religious corporation. Many intellectuals and religious leaders expressed their strong opposition to the Prime Minister's initiative, and domestic lawsuits were launched against Nakasone and the government for violating the constitutional separation of religion and state. As it turns out, the two courts adjudicating these cases followed the reasoning of the justices in the 1977 Supreme Court Decision regarding the Tsu City grounds purification rite case mentioned above and ruled against the plaintiffs. In the decisions of both the Osaka District Court (November 1989) and the Fukuoka Court (December 1989) it was determined that Nakasone's actions had not violated Article 20 since the religious freedom of the plaintiffs had not been infringed upon in any way.[9]

CRITICAL PERSPECTIVES ON "OFFICIAL VISITS"

Several months after Prime Minister Nakasone's controversial visit, the "minority" perspectives of some advisory committee members were published in the November 1985 issue of *Jurist*, which was devoted to the problem of "official visits to Yasukuni Shrine." While their alternative views had been referred to in the report submitted to Chief Cabinet Secretary Fujinami, this publication provided a fuller treatment of their arguments against the "majority" recommendation that official visits to Yasukuni be resumed. Two responses by public intellectuals serving on Fujinami's committee—one Buddhist and one Catholic—provide us with the reasoning behind those opposed to Yasukuni visits and deserve consideration here. This special issue contained articles by two public intellectuals, the late Buddhist philosopher Umehara Takeshi (1925–2019) and Sono Ayako (1931–) a

Roman Catholic novelist, which explained their concerns about Yasukuni Shrine and government support for "official visits."[10] Although these two prominent figures are often regarded as "conservative" or "nationalistic," they both critically engaged the pro-Yasukuni Shrine position advanced by Prime Minister Nakasone's administration in the mid-1980s.[11] The positions of Umehara and Sono represented "minority opinions" at the time, but the concerns they raised have become a part of the public discourse in the debates over the past several decades.

Umehara, a graduate of Kyoto University, was a well-known Buddhist philosopher who has had a distinguished academic career, which has included faculty appointments at Ritsumeikan University and Kyoto City University of Arts, where he also served as president in the mid-1970s. He was the founding Director of the International Research Center for Japanese Studies, a position he held from 1987 to 1995. His collected works were published by Shogakukan (2002–2003) in a series of twenty volumes. His influence extends beyond the academic world. Many of his books are popular volumes aimed at a wider audience, and his public role is also evident from his numerous essays and editorials published in newspapers and magazines, and through his involvement as a leader in the Article 9 Association (Kyūjō no Kai), which he and some other prominent intellectuals organized in 2004.

The second figure, Sono Ayako, is a Roman Catholic and graduate of Sacred Heart University in Tokyo. She is widely known as the author of best-selling novels and volumes of essay collections, and as a regular columnist for conservative magazines and newspapers (such as *Sankei shinbun*). From 1996 to 2005 she served as chairperson of the Nippon Foundation, a philanthropic organization established by Sasakawa Ryōichi in 1962 to support a range of domestic and international humanitarian activities. She has had a close association with the LDP as an advisor for many years and served on the Ad Hoc Educational Committee of the Japanese Ministry of Education, and most recently on the education reform panel organized by Prime Minister Abe's administration in 2013.[12] Here I provide a brief synopsis of their positions.

Umehara Takeshi's Perspective. In his 1985 article entitled "The Merits and Demerits of Official Visits to Yasukuni Shrine," Umehara (1985, 10) offered a pragmatic approach to the issue and identified some key problems associated with shrine visits by government representatives. His essay begins with the acknowledgment that he and some of the other members of the Advisory Committee—along with most constitutional scholars—regarded "official visits" to Yasukuni Shrine as a clear violation of the separation of religion and state. One member of the committee, however, opposed the strong focus on the current Constitution—seen as a foreign imposition by General MacArthur—and argued that it should not be regarded as the basis for final arbitration of the issue; rather, in his view, the Constitution needed to be revised as soon as possible.[13] Umehara, however, expressed appreciation for the postwar Constitution—regardless of its "foreign" connections—since it brought about significant democratic reforms and helped to liberate Japan from a misguided nationalism. After expressing his opposition to any hasty revision of the Constitution, he focuses his attention on other reasons why official visits should either be "promoted" or "avoided," and argues that the "merits" and "demerits" for such visits should be reviewed and a decision made after the sum total is calculated. Although this was the approach he proposed to the Advisory Committee, the majority were not persuaded and the Committee's final recommendation, Umehara (1985, 11) explained, was based on the "mood" among the members after a rather "heated discussion."

Umehara then highlights two potential "merits" of prime ministerial visits to Yasukuni. First, if such visits were resumed it would satisfy the longing of many bereaved families for proper recognition of their deceased family members by the government. While Yasukuni Shrine has memorialized them as heroes (*eirei*), the fact the prime ministers in the postwar period have only been willing to visit the shrine in their "private capacity" is regarded as a slight by bereaved families who lost a family member in wars fought on behalf of the emperor and nation. A second possible merit he acknowledged—and one emphasized by a number the Committee members—was that national defense would be enhanced if official visits were resumed. If the government does not show proper respect, honor, and gratitude toward those who sacrificed their lives for the nation in the past, in other words, it was reasoned, one should not expect citizens to willingly offer their lives for their country in a future time of national emergency.

In Umehara's view, these "merits" are outnumbered by the "demerits," which he gives more detailed treatment. The first problem is the potential impact of official shrine visits on Japan's international relations. Writing at a time when Japan was in the midst of difficult trade negotiations and conflict with the United States and Europe, Umehara felt that maintaining friendly relations with Japan's closest neighbors—Korea and China—would be vitally important for economic stability in the future. Although one or two members of the committee shared his concerns, most were "utterly indifferent" to the possibility that prime ministerial visits would damage Japan's international relations. Given what Yasukuni Shrine represents to China and Korea, however, Umehara anticipated that official visits by prime ministers would lead to the negative reactions and diplomatic problems, which, in fact, did occur following Nakasone's August visit.

The second problem or demerit has to do with the particular form of Shinto institutionalized by Yasukuni Shrine, which he regards as a distortion of authentic Japanese tradition. Umehara (1985, 12) confesses that for several decades he struggled with the question of whether the ultranationalism of the wartime period was a natural and inevitable expression of Japan's spiritual heritage or based upon a misunderstanding of that spiritual tradition by rightwing thinkers. If it does, in fact, represent authentic Japanese tradition, then he worries whether it is possible to derive spiritual principles from this tradition that can provide the foundation for Japan to maintain a peaceful existence in the international world today.

Umehara explains that after three decades of research, he reached the conclusion that Yasukuni Shrine—its beliefs and practices—deviates from Japanese tradition in significant ways. For example, the exclusive memorialization of the war dead by Yasukuni Shrine—and only those who died on behalf of Japan—he views as a post-Meiji development that departs significantly from ancient Japanese tradition and practice. Prior to the formation of State Shinto under the influence of the Hirata School of Shinto, he argues, traditional care of the dead included both Shinto and Buddhist rites, the latter closely associated with both the care of the ancestors (*shirei no chinkon*) and the pacification of dangerous spirits (*onryō osame*).

While he acknowledges that Yasukuni Shrine provides some traditional Shinto rites for care of the dead, its monopoly over the war dead, which eliminates Buddhist ritual care, constitutes an abandonment of authentic Japanese tradition. He goes on to explain that the development of State Shinto from the early Meiji period was due to the influence of the Hirata School and its concern to purify native traditions from foreign influences. This shaped the government policies that abolished the place of Buddhism and led to the disintegration of the natural co-existence and reverence for both kami and buddhas, which he claims characterized life in pre-modern Japan.

According to Umehara, the development of State Shinto from the Meiji period not only damaged Buddhism, but also had negative repercussions for the Shinto tradition. The authority and control over shrines by priestly families was replaced by government administration. Furthermore, many local traditions and practices were often eliminated as Shinto was reorganized around Ise Shrine and the ancestral deities of the Imperial Household, Meiji Shrine and the kami of the Meiji Emperor, and Yasukuni Shrine, which enshrined the deified soldiers who gave their lives for the emperor and nation. Umehara argues that this *was not the structure of traditional Shinto*, but a new form reconstructed in relation to nationalism. The key "demerit" of "official visits," in short, is that it represents a tacit approval of a distorted version of Japanese tradition that will give people both inside and outside Japan the impression that the government is seeking to revive or resurrect the old wartime nationalism that was supported by State Shinto. The narrow nationalism supported by official visits to Yasukuni Shrine, he concludes, is misguided and inappropriate for Japan to function as a member of international society today (Umehara 1985, 15).

Two decades later, Umehara would provide a more detailed treatment of this criticism—that Yasukuni Shrine represents a distortion of authentic Japanese tradition—in his books *Kami koroshi no Nihon* (2006) and *Nihon no dentō to wa nani ka* (2010). The target of his criticism in these works is expanded to include the Imperial Rescript on Education (*Kyōiku chokugo*). In his view, misguided leaders have idealized this document as the basis for educational reform and the promotion of patriotism in contemporary Japan. Umehara rejects these attempts to revive key elements of what he refers to as Tennōkyō, which characterized wartime Japan. He argues that all of this was part of a manufactured system rooted in the narrow-minded and intolerant orientation of the Kokugaku movement that influenced the reshaping of Japanese tradition from the Meiji period (Umehara 2006, 34).

Given that Yasukuni Shrine represents a distortion of authentic Japanese spiritual tradition, Umehara proposed that a new memorial site (*matsuri no basho*) be established to honor the war dead as an alternative to Yasukuni Shrine. This would be a site where people of any religious affiliation could conduct memorial services according to their own faith tradition, and it would *exclude the war criminals* that Yasukuni Shrine arbitrarily enshrined (*katte ni gōshi shita*). He suggests that it could also serve as a memorial site for others who gave their lives in public service in the postwar period, including, for example, members of the Self-Defense Force (Umehara 1985, 16). While some might suggest that reform of the current war memorial site is possible, Umehara quotes a well-known biblical text—"new wine is put into fresh wineskins" (Matthew 9:17)—to conclude his argument that only an entirely new site unencumbered by the problems associated with Yasukuni Shrine will ever be regarded as an acceptable and legitimate memorial institution by the larger Japanese public and Japan's neighbors in Asia.

Sono Ayako's Perspective. Sono similarly argues that a new religiously neutral memorial site needs to be established as an alternative to Yasukuni, but for some other reasons not addressed by Umehara. At the outset, Sono makes it clear that she regards "official visits" by prime ministers and cabinet members to be a clear violation of the Constitution. Given that Yasukuni was registered as a religious corporation in 1946, and conducts its rituals according to Shinto tradition, it is impossible to argue that it is a religiously neutral site that simply observes the ancient Japanese custom of spirit pacification (*irei*). In her view, the notion that what goes on in the shrine precincts is either nonreligious or religiously neutral is something that will never be accepted from the international commonsense point of view (Sono 1985, 32).

Sono notes the argument made by some—that the only reason Yasukuni became a religious corporation and was clearly identified as a Shinto institution—was simply as a strategy to survive the particular circumstances of the Occupation. Sono reasons that if that is, in fact, the case, then the shrine administrators could end the Shinto monopoly and make arrangements so that all religions could conduct their own services within its precincts. If arrangements for equal access were guaranteed, she would not be opposed to the preservation of the sanctuary or Great Torii, as it stands, nor to the continued management of the facility by Shinto priests. The fact that this kind of change would never be accepted is clear evidence that the shrine is biased toward one particular religion (*akiraka ni tokutei shūkyō ni katayotteiru*), which means that "official visits" to the shrine as it operates today would violate the Constitution by giving support or endorsement to one particular religious tradition (Sono 1985, 32).

The normalization of such "official visits," she also fears, could lead to restrictions on religious freedom or the freedom to oppose participation in rites of any kind. If "official visits" are defined as the duty of all those holding public office, Sono reasons, it could lead to situations of coercion in which individuals with other religious convictions are required to participate in Shinto rites. While she believes that prime ministers and government officials should express their gratitude and remember those who gave their lives for the nation, Yasukuni Shrine remains a problematic site for this to be a duty of those holding public office.

To avoid these potential problems, Sono concludes that it is necessary to construct a new memorial site (*kinenbyo*) for the war dead. This would need to be a religiously neutral space where people and religious organizations could freely conduct memorial services according to their own tradition. It is only in such a place that government officials will be able to participate in official visits without impediments or controversy.[14]

POST-NAKASONE OFFICIAL VISITS

In spite of the efforts by Fujinami and Nakasone to redefine "official visits" as civic and nonreligious and, therefore, constitutional, critics were hardly persuaded given the fact the ritual respect accorded the war dead occurred in an institution registered with the government as a religious corporation. Within Japan many intellectuals and religious leaders expressed their strong opposition to the prime minister's initiative. International criticism also appeared in newspapers and media reports in China, North

Korea, South Korea, Singapore, and the Soviet Union. The negative press and reaction was such that Nakasone canceled his planned visit to the shrine the following year. As a result, "official" prime ministerial visits to the shrine were avoided for over a decade and the debate subsided. It would be eleven years before another prime minister—this time Hashimoto Ryūtarō—would visit the shrine in 1996. This was the year after the Hanshin-Awaji earthquake and the Aum Shinrikyō subway gas attack and, as argued earlier, marks the beginning of the surge in neonationalistic activity. As the former chairperson of the Japan Association of War-bereaved Families, Hashimoto was a well-known supporter of the shrine and, unlike Nakasone, followed the prescribed Shintō ritual on his one and only visit as prime minister on 29 July 1996. Hashimoto was forced to cancel plans for another visit due to strong criticism from China.

Prime Minister Koizumi Jun'ichirō reignited the public controversy by following through on a campaign promise he made in 2001 when running for the presidency of the ruling LDP that he would visit Yasukuni Shrine in his official capacity, which he did a number of times between 2001 and 2006. His visits were not particularly surprising given that he had been serving as Vice-President of the League Promoting Ties between Politics and Shinto (Shintō Seiji Renmei) in 2000 (Tsukada 2015, 47). There was considerable domestic opposition to Koizumi's visits, and eight different court cases were launched against him across the nation. Over 900 plaintiffs claimed that his behavior violated the constitutional separation of religion and state, caused them mental anguish, and demanded compensation. Although some district courts dismissed these lawsuits, both the Fukuoka District Court in April 2004 and the Osaka High Court in September the following year ruled that the Prime Minister's visits did violate the Constitution, but denied compensation for damages.

Koizumi's behavior also provoked widespread international concern. The governments of South Korea and the Peoples' Republic of China issued strong official statements and criticisms of his actions. It did not escape notice in the United States either. At a hearing before the House of Representatives Committee on International Relations on 14 September 2006, Republican Henry Hyde and Democratic member Tom Lantos, a holocaust survivor, both expressed their concerns about Japan's "historical amnesia." In their statements they urged future prime ministers to avoid visits to the shrine out of concern for peace in the region, and urged them to do something about Yūshūkan, the museum adjacent to the shrine, which promotes a revisionist history that especially disturbs Japan's nearest neighbors. "For the survivors of World War II in Asia and America," Lantos explained, "visits to the Yasukuni Shrine where fourteen class-A war criminals are interred would be the equivalent of laying a wreath at the graves of Himmler, Rudolph Hess and Herman Greer in Germany. My message to the incoming Japanese prime minister is very simple; paying one's respects to war criminals is morally bankrupt and unworthy of a great nation such as Japan. This practice must end." Both Hyde and Lantos are now deceased.[15] Because of the negative reaction to Koizumi's initiative, in any case, the LDP prime ministers who followed him—Abe Shinzō, Fukuda Yasuo, and Asō Tarō—avoided visiting Yasukuni Shrine during their brief tenures (though Abe would visit the shrine early in his second tenure). Asō had been a particularly outspoken supporter of Yasukuni over the years and in the February 2008 issue of *Shokun*, a popular rightwing publication, clearly stated his position that prime ministers "should" visit the shrine (Asō and Miyazaki 2008, 31).[16] Despite his strongly expressed views, he did not chance a visit during his short and difficult term, but tried to fulfill his obligation with an offering to the shrine during its Spring Festival in April 2009. Even this expression of support was picked up by the press and attracted critical attention prior to his China visit.

Some observers thought that the landslide victory of the Democratic Party (DPJ) in the August 2009 election, which essentially ended half a century of domination by the LDP, would have some significant implications for Yasukuni Shrine. Even before assuming the office of prime minister, Hatoyama Yukio made it clear that he thought it was inappropriate for government officials to visit Yasukuni and indicated that he was in favor of restarting discussions about the creation of an alternative memorial site, one that would be religiously neutral and unencumbered by the negative history and association with class-A war criminals.[17] Hatoyama was preoccupied with other matters during his brief time as prime minister and his successors, Kan Naoto and Noda Yoshihiko, were overwhelmed by the 11 March 2011 earthquake, tsunami, and nuclear disaster, which meant that the Yasukuni Shrine problem was essentially ignored during their administration.

With the return of the LDP and Abe Shinzō to power, however, Yasukuni Shrine became an issue again. Although Abe avoided Yasukuni visits during his first term as prime minister (2006–2007)—a decision he later regretted—he could resist no longer and made his way to the shrine for an official visit on 26 December 2013. There have already been some serious repercussions from this shrine visit—both internationally and domestically—as it drew strong condemnations from South Korea and China, and even the unexpected public expression of "disappointment" by the United States. In April 2014, two lawsuits were launched against the government by citizens' groups in Osaka and Tokyo, which together have some 800 plaintiffs bringing Abe's shrine visit before the court on grounds that it violated the constitutional separation of religion and state, and they are seeking compensation for the psychological stress it caused.[18] Since the lawsuits against Abe were initiated, both the lower and higher courts (2017 and 2018) rejected the claims of the plaintiffs for compensation and ruled that the Prime Minister's actions did not violate their religious freedom.

Under these circumstances, Abe has avoided another personal visit— though he has continued to make ritual offerings to the shrine for the Spring and Fall Festivals and on 15 August. His wife, Akie, has carried the banner on his behalf and visited the shrine again on 18 August (her earlier visit to the shrine and Yūshūkan on 20 May was shared with photos on her Facebook account).[19] Although the prime minister has been forced to exercise some self-restraint,[20] under his leadership there has been a continued shift to the right among Diet members and an increasing number making visits to Yasukuni Shrine on August 15 and during the Spring and Fall Festivals.

While Yasukuni Shrine was largely a domestic concern until the 1970s, controversies surrounding the shrine have increasingly taken on an international dimension. Supporters of Yasukuni Shrine have not remained silent in the face of these criticisms and what they regard as "foreign interference" in Japan's domestic affairs. Over the past few years numerous publications have appeared in support of the view that government officials have every right—and even a duty—to participate in the ritual care of the military war dead at Yasukuni Shrine. The shrine's supporters argue furthermore that such patriotic behavior should be encouraged on the part of all Japanese citizens. Japanese nationalists have appealed to foreign figures—like Fr. Bruno Bitter, the Catholic priest who intervened with General MacArthur in the early days of the Occupation, and Judge Radhabinod Pal, the Indian jurist who served on the International Tribunal for the Far East, for example, who concluded that the Tokyo War Crimes trials were unfair and an example of "victor's justice." In more recent years, the publications of Georgetown Professor Kevin Doak, who still embraces the 1936 position of the Catholic Church that encouraged the faithful to visit the shrine and fulfill their patriotic duty, are widely referred to by nationalist leaders to support their position on Yasukuni Shrine. It is not my concern here to engage the "use" or "abuse" (depending on one's point of view) of such foreign figures for contemporary ideological purposes, but simply note how they have become

Monument established to honor Judge Radhabinod Pal, located in the Yasukuni Shrine complex in front of the Yūshūkan War Memorial Museum (photo by the author, 11 May 2013).

a part of the domestic political conversation as international criticism towards pro-Yasukuni actions by Japanese politicians have increased.[21]

ENSHRINEMENT AS A RELIGIOUS AND LEGAL PROBLEM

The public interest and media coverage of Yasukuni Shrine has tended to focus on the question of prime ministerial visits or whether the government should restore direct financial support, but remained largely oblivious to the way in which the war dead have been unilaterally enshrined in the postwar period without regard for the wishes or feelings of many bereaved families. In addition to the highly critical statements issued by the governments of Japan's neighbors in response to shrine visits by prime ministers and other government officials, citizens of South Korea and Taiwan have also become involved in the debate by formally objecting to postwar enshrinements of their family members. Given the media preoccupation with politically significant figures, the more fundamental conflict over postwar enshrinements of the war dead has not received the attention it deserves. It is this particular problem that I want to consider in more detail here to draw attention to the problem of "coercion" that is the concomitant of the politics of inclusion. In cooperation with Japanese Buddhists and Christians, these foreigners have initiated lawsuits (gōshi torikeshi soshō) against Yasukuni Shrine and the Japanese government for this alleged violation of the Constitution, and have sought to have the names of their family dead removed from the shrine register.

It is hardly surprising that enshrinement would become a problem in the context of postwar Japan with its new "official" understanding of religion. In the early months of the Occupation, in fact, Miyaji Naokazu (1886–1949), a leading scholar who had occupied the Chair for Shinto Studies at the Imperial University in Tokyo, recognized that enshrinements could very well become a contentious issue. In a 1946 interview conducted soon after Yasukuni Shrine had been registered as a religious organization, Miyaji explained:

> Now that Yasukuni has become a religion, Buddhists and Christians may not want to be enshrined there. This is quite a natural phenomenon, for the shrine has become connected with religion. This problem will arise concerning

THE POLITICS OF YASUKUNI SHRINE | 135

Gokoku Shrines too. Those who fail to understand the fact that the shrine has become religion may feel unpleasant, due to misapprehension because of the existence of the Buddhists and Christians who refuse to be treated as kami of Yasukuni. (Hiyane 1966, 149)[22]

The phrase "Yasukuni has become a religion" should not be misunderstood here. Miyaji is referring to the fact that the shrine had become clearly defined as a religious corporation. He is not denying the shrine's "religious" character prior to this postwar change in legal status. Earlier in the same interview he stated: "In my opinion religion is intercourse between human beings and what is superhuman. Therefore, all shrines naturally fall into the category of religion.... The government did not negate the religious activities of the shrines even when it did not regard the shrines as religion" (Hiyane 1966, 143). This is a striking statement coming from someone who just a decade earlier had headed the Research Department of the Shrine Bureau of the Ministry of Home Affairs.

Although State Shinto was disestablished by the Occupation authorities at the end of the war, Yasukuni Shrine survived in the postwar period as a voluntary religious organization supported by the faithful and without direct financial aid from the government. In some respects, however, it has operated "as if" nothing had been changed by the Occupation policies or the postwar Constitution. Given the postwar legal framework defined by Articles 20 and 89, one might assume that those among the bereaved families who wished to have a family member enshrined would indicate this to Yasukuni and request that the ritual be conducted. In fact, however, Yasukuni Shrine officials contacted the Ministry of Health and Welfare— without consulting any families—to request assistance in the preparation of lists for all of the war dead so that enshrinement rituals could be completed.

After the war, this ministry was responsible for veterans' affairs, repatriation of Japanese from overseas, and Yasukuni Shrine, which had been managed by the Army and Navy. The paper trail revealing cooperation between Yasukuni Shrine and government offices stretches back to 1956. That year the Ministry of Health and Welfare sent instructions to city and prefecture offices to assist with Yasukuni Shrine's administrative needs related to enshrinement plans. At least twenty meetings between shrine representatives and government officials occurred over the years to discuss and arrange for the paperwork required. Extensive documentation that reveals the extent to which government offices were involved in assisting with this process is now preserved in the National Diet Library.[23]

While those who belong to the Japan Association of War-bereaved Families are strong supporters of Yasukuni and pleased about the enshrinements, there are many who belong to alternative associations of bereaved families—the Shinshū Izokukai (Buddhist) and Heiwa Izokukai (Christian), for example. They are appalled that their family members have been enshrined and deified, and are now worshiped as a "kami" (god) along with the class-A war criminals enshrined several decades ago. Over the years, a number of individuals have made personal visits to Yasukuni Shrine and requested that enshrinement be canceled and the names of their family dead be removed from the shrine register. In addition to appeals from Japanese families, there are also Koreans and Taiwanese who have been dismayed and angered to learn that Yasukuni's generous enshrinement policy extended even to individuals from former colonial domains who had been conscripted and mobilized for Japan's war efforts and later died "on behalf of the emperor and nation." While shrine representatives no doubt believe they are honoring their memory and sacrifice, these Korean and Taiwanese families feel they have been exploited by Japan in both life and death, with their ancestors still spiritually under "colonial rule" symbolized by enshrinement in Yasukuni.

In spite of their numerous personal appeals, Yasukuni priests have insisted that "de-enshrinement" is impossible. Families have never been consulted in advance, they explain, since all are enshrined according to the "will of the emperor" and the tradition established in the early Meiji period. It has nothing to do with the will or desires of the deceased or the bereaved families. Furthermore, as priests often explain to shrine visitors, the spirits of the war dead are like drops of water that have merged into a larger body of water and now share a collective spiritual identity as martyrs (eirei), which can no longer be separated into individual parts. For these reasons, Yasukuni continues to engage in "business as usual," and "usual" here means according to the norms established in the prewar period. The "will of the emperor," according to priestly interpretation at Yasukuni Shrine, still trumps individual choice and family religious tradition.

Much to the dismay of many Yasukuni supporters, as noted earlier, it was revealed in 2007 that Emperor Hirohito was not pleased with the shrine's handling of the war dead in the postwar decades and was opposed to the plan to enshrine class-A war criminals. No doubt nervous about being too closely associated with those held responsible for Japan's wars of aggression, he even stopped making visits to the shrine. While many Japanese may be offended that their relative has become part of such a questionable pantheon, those who belong to the alternative associations of bereaved families are opposed to all that Yasukuni Shrine stands for, particularly the glorification of so many tragic deaths and promotion of the view that Japan's past wars were all about liberating Asia from Western colonialism and oppression.

LEGAL ACTION AGAINST YASUKUNI AND THE JAPANESE GOVERNMENT

Since Yasukuni Shrine has been unwilling to comply with requests for cancellation of enshrinement and removal of names from the register, a number of individuals decided to pursue legal action against both Yasukuni Shrine and the Japanese government.[24] Several years ago lawsuits were launched almost simultaneously by three different groups and are now being processed by the courts in Tokyo, Osaka, and Okinawa. Unlike the issue of prime ministerial visits to Yasukuni, these court proceedings have received minimal media coverage. Here I turn to a brief review of the ruling handed down by the Osaka District Court on 26 February 2009.

The nine plaintiffs in the Osaka case are an ecumenical group of seniors—ages ranging from 64 to 82—and include several Buddhists and one Christian. Two have written extensively about their personal struggle with Yasukuni Shrine over the years. Sugahara Ryūken, a Jōdo Shinshū priest and head of the Shinshū Izokukai, provides a critical Shinshū perspective in his *Yasukuni to iu ori kara no kaihō* (2005). In the same vein, Nishiyama Toshihiko, a Catholic priest of the Osaka Archdiocese, records his unsuccessful efforts to have his father's enshrinement revoked in an interim report published in 2006. While their philosophical and theological reasons for opposing Yasukuni Shrine may differ, the plaintiffs are united in their view that ritual enshrinement without permission is a violation of their personal right to remember the deceased without interference from a third party. Individuals and families, the plaintiffs maintain, should be protected from actions and labeling that bring dishonor to a person's name and memory.

Although Buddhist and Catholic anti-Yasukuni activists are not that common, both Jōdo Shinshū denominations and the Catholic Church in Japan have issued critical statements for decades regarding the LDP efforts to renationalize Yasukuni and expressed strong opposition to prime-ministerial visits. In connection with this most recent Osaka court case, a representative of the Japan Catholic Council for Justice and Peace, Bishop Matsuura Gorō, also wrote a letter in 2006 to express support for Fr. Nishiyama and his legal struggle, which was published in *The Catholic Bishops' Conference of Japan Yearbook* (Katorikku Chūō Kyōgikai 2008, 108–110). In this document, Bishop Matsuura recognizes that Yasukuni Shrine—as an independent religious organization—has every right to conduct religious activities as long as it remains separate from the government. He also maintains, however, that "the unilateral enshrinement of people of other religions and creeds against their will is not proper conduct."

While the plaintiffs made it clear that they were opposed to their family members being "used" by Yasukuni Shrine to legitimize and beautify Japan's past wars of aggression, they were primarily concerned in this case with the actions Yasukuni took with regard to people who do not belong to the shrine. The plaintiffs demanded that the enshrinement be canceled and the names of the family members be erased from the shrine register. The judges regarded the plaintiffs' claim that the self-image and memory of the deceased was damaged by Yasukuni's actions to be too "subjective" and "abstract" to be taken seriously by the Court, and their demands for compensation were denied.

The plaintiffs also argued that the enshrinement of their relatives was an illegal action carried out with close cooperation between the government and Yasukuni Shrine, which is clearly prohibited by the postwar Constitution. In their view, the government violated their right to privacy and provided information to the shrine, which enabled it to proceed with the enshrinement ritual. The judges ruled, however, that the government could not be held responsible for the enshrinements, reasoning that the

The plaintiffs speak to reporters outside the Osaka District Court following the decision of the three judges on 26 February 2009 (photo by author).

Health and Welfare Ministry routinely provided information regarding the deceased to various parties (in connection with pension inquiries, for example), and it would have been discrimination against a religious organization if the government offices refused to provide the requested information to Yasukuni. Although the government did provide information, in the end the decision to enshrine was made by Yasukuni officials according to their accepted tradition and practice, and did not involve the government.[25]

The Osaka District Court dismissed the case as "groundless" and reduced it to the issue of religious freedom. In addressing this issue, the judges clearly followed the precedent established by the 1988 Supreme Court decision regarding a similar case, which involved the enshrinement of Nakaya Takafumi, a Self-Defense Force officer, in the Yamaguchi Prefecture Gokoku Jinja (state-protecting shrine) in 1972. The Self-Defense Force Veterans Association had the enshrinement conducted in spite of opposition from the surviving spouse, Nakaya Yasuko. Nakaya filed a civil law suit against the government for violating both her religious rights and Article 20 of the Constitution, which prohibits government involvement in religion. She also sought compensation "for mental damages allegedly caused by the enshrinement of her dead spouse." Although Nakaya won her case at the Yamaguchi District Court in 1979, and again at the Hiroshima High Court in 1982, these earlier decisions were overturned by the Supreme Court in 1988. The Court ruled that the Veterans Association was not a "state agency" and, therefore, no violation of the separation of religion and state could have occurred. Furthermore, Nakaya's religious rights had not been violated since she was not required to participate in the enshrinement ritual. Finally, the judges found no legal basis "for giving priority to a surviving spouse over surviving parents or children with regard to mourning and honoring the memory of the deceased." In the end, Nakaya was required to repay with interest the 1 million yen that had been awarded by the Yamaguchi Court.[26] Yokota Kōichi (1988, 13, 23), Kyūshū University law professor, captured the reasoning of the Supreme Court justices in his review of their ruling with the phrase "*Kan'yō naki shakai no kan'yōron*" (an argument for tolerance in an intolerant society), and noted how their decision revealed how difficult it must be for minorities to live in Japanese society.

Following the logic of the Supreme Court decision, the judges in the Osaka case concluded that the religious freedom of both parties—Yasukuni Shrine and bereaved families—must be protected. Yasukuni Shrine's "freedom" to remember and worship the dead according to their own tradition must be recognized. The Court is not in a position, they argued, to interfere with a religious organization and dictate what is appropriate belief and practice. While the judges conceded that it is clearly advisable to have the permission of the bereaved families, they concluded that the enshrinement did not violate their rights in any way since they were not forced to participate. Each party must allow the other to freely memorialize the dead in their own way and according to their respective faith tradition. Representatives of Yasukuni Shrine and the government were obviously pleased with the Court's decision, but the plaintiffs vowed to carry on their struggle to liberate their family members from the "cage" of Yasukuni Shrine.

Hishiki Masaharu, a Buddhist priest and scholar, and leader of the support group for the plaintiffs in the Osaka case, finds it ironic that Articles

20 and 89 of the postwar Constitution, which were meant to establish religious freedom and "protect" people from the coercive practices of State Shinto—such as forced shrine visits during the war—are today being used to "protect" the religious freedom of Yasukuni Shrine over the rights of individuals. In stark contrast to the judges' perspective and reasoning, Hishiki argues that religious organizations do not have unlimited freedom. The government can intervene without violating the constitutional separation of religion and state if a religious organization is involved in illegal activities. In fact, the courts have intervened in cases of tax evasion, fraudulent fund-raising activities, harassment of individuals through high-pressure membership recruitment activities, and when religious groups engage in acts of violence and murder (the most extreme example in recent Japanese history is the Tokyo subway gas attack by Aum Shinrikyō members in 1995, which was legitimized by religious doctrine). All of these cases reveal that the courts and the Japanese public recognize there are some "limits" to the freedom of religion. In spite of all this, Hishiki maintains that the courts have given Yasukuni Shrine a "free pass" to conduct business as usual even though their activities bring dishonor and shame to the name of the deceased and contribute to the suffering of the bereaved families concerned.[27] The "politics of inclusion" as practiced by Yasukuni Shrine reveals the limits of religious pluralism and represents a harsher reality that still faces individuals and minorities in contemporary Japan.

In spite of losing their legal battle in 2009, those involved in the de-enshrinement movement have continued to visit Yasukuni Shrine each year to reiterate their appeal.[28] The shrine has politely granted a half-hour meeting annually between five or six representatives of the group with the chief priest and his assistants, but there is no indication that the shrine will change its position. On a 18 September 2015 visit, Sugahara Ryūken led the small group to the meeting and submitted two documents: another appeal for de-enshrinement and a list of questions to press the shrine priests for clarification and to address some of their problems with the shrine's stance.[29]

One point raised in the second document with regard to the frequent comparisons made between Yasukuni and Arlington Cemetery in the United States deserves consideration here since it has been used so frequently in the polemics by all groups to justify official visits to the shrine.

One distinctive difference between these two memorial sites for the war dead noted is that in the case of Arlington Cemetery soldiers are buried and memorialized there according to the expressed will of the deceased or the wishes of the family. The religious freedom and choice of the individual or family is respected. By contrast, the enshrinements at Yasukuni have been conducted without consulting the families concerned and in many cases against their wishes. Given the postwar Constitution's protection of religious freedom, should Yasukuni Shrine not first consult with the families concerned and only proceed with enshrinements once consent is given? According to the document, the enshrinements as they stand are simply based on "authoritarian actions" (*kenryokuteki kōi*). Therefore, the shrine cannot be regarded as caring for the war dead in the same manner as Arlington Cemetery or other memorial sites around the world, which respect the wishes and rights of the individual families concerned.[30] This group plans to continue its appeal for de-enshrinement, but the position of Yasukuni Shrine is unlikely to change given the Court's ruling in the matter.

Although shrine representatives have insisted that de-enshrinement is impossible, there is evidence that at least one exception has been made in the past. According to the testimony of the late Onoda Kanrō, a former Second Lieutenant in the Imperial Japanese Army, he had been enshrined in Yasukuni after the war although he was still alive and living in the Philippines.[31] Although the war ended in 1945, this news had not reached Onoda, who spent almost another three decades on Lubangu Island searching for the enemy and gathering "intelligence information." He only made it back to Japan in 1974 and learned that he had been enshrined in Yasukuni. According to his testimony, however, he was "worshiped for fifteen years before he was removed from the shrine after it became clear he had returned alive from the battlefield.[32] This example suggests that there is a bit more flexibility about the treatment of spirits and the possibility of de-enshrinement than is stated in Yasukuni Shrine's official position.

Chapter and verse from a sacred Shinto text is never offered in support of Yasukuni's stance, though there are undoubtedly historical precedents for their interpretive traditions. The wider Shinto world, however, appears to include other viewpoints on the matter. Much to the consternation of Yasukuni Shrine priests, for example, Matsuhashi Teruo, the former head priest of Tōgō Shrine, a shrine dedicated to a former admiral of the Imperial Japanese Navy, offered to move the spirits of the problematic class-A war criminals to his shrine in Shibuya, and suggested that with them out of the way it might be possible for the emperor and government officials to visit the shrine without generating such international and domestic disputes. He first made this proposal during the time that Prime Minister Koizumi was attracting harsh criticisms from China and Korea for visiting Yasukuni Shrine in 2006, but found that it was causing "an inconvenience" (*meiwaku*) for some—i.e., Yasukuni officials—and decided not to push ahead at the time. Three years later, however, Matsuhashi went public and published a book that included his proposal about relocating the problematic spirits (Matsuhashi 2008, 15–31).[33]

According to the shrine, the human spirits (*jirei*) of the almost two and half million war dead enshrined in Yasukuni have been transformed into divine spirits (*shinrei*) through the rites of apotheosis and are now worshiped and pacified through rites of propitiation conducted each year at the Spring and Fall Festivals and the Spirit Festival (*Mitama matsuri*) in July. These rites were initiated according to the will of the emperor and promises were made by the state that those who made the ultimate sacrifice on behalf of the emperor and nation would be venerated in this way.[34] Yasukuni Shrine considers itself under moral obligation to protect and preserve this system of ritual care for the Shōwa martyrs. Accordingly, neither changes in the constitution nor familial appeals for de-enshrinement can void this obligation.

CONCLUSION

As we have seen, the pro-Yasukuni camp have come out ahead of the anti-Yasukuni forces as far as the courts and legal action are concerned. It would be a mistake, however, to think that all is well in the coalition of Yasukuni Shrine supporters. There are serious divisions emerging in the pro-Yasukuni camp, and the leadership of Yasukuni Shrine has recently become the focus of serious controversy due to statements by the chief priest.

Ever since Nakasone's official visit in 1985, it has been apparent that Yasukuni supporters are divided between those who simply want to remember the war dead with a "nonreligious" ritual of respect and those who insist that proper Shinto protocol be observed. Even within the membership of the Japan Association of War-bereaved Families, which is the primary base of support for Yasukuni Shrine across the nation, divisions have begun to appear in their ranks over the problem of class-A war criminals being enshrined along with the other war dead. In 2014 and 2015, some of the prefectural chapters in Fukuoka passed a resolution petitioning Yasukuni Shrine to remove the class-A war criminals, which they believe would make it possible for the emperor to once again visit the shrine and honor their enshrined family members. Most of the association remains opposed to this idea, however, and Yasukuni priests have declared numerous times that neither de-enshrinement or movement of the spirits is possible.

The most serious problem facing the pro-Yasukuni coalition is the ambivalent relationship between the emperor and the shrine. The strained relations became the focus of media attention in late 2018, when the chief priest of Yasukuni Shrine, Kobori Kunio, resigned his position after only eight months on the job due to the embarrassing leak of his "disrespectful" (*fukei*) words about the emperor made before ten staff during an in-house study meeting at the shrine: "His Majesty is seeking to shut down the shrine" (*Kinjō heika wa Yasukuni o tsubusō to shiteiru*), rather shocking words that appeared in the 12 October 2018 issue of *Shūkan posuto*.[35] In the December issue of *Bungei shunjū*, a widely read monthly magazine, Kobori (2018, 94–101) provided his own account of the incident that prompted his resignation and explained the context for his statement about the emperor's negative impact on the shrine. First, Kobori highlights the fact that Emperor Hirohito's last visit to the shrine was in 1975, three year before the enshrinement of the class-A war criminals. His successor, Emperor Akihito, has not visited the shrine once since his enthronement in 1989, which he is unlikely to do before the end of Heisei on 30 April 2019. Although an imperial envoy has delivered offerings to the shrine on the occasion of major festivals, the emperor has avoided personal visits to Yasukuni Shrine throughout his reign. At the same time, Kobori observes, the emperor has engaged in a number of trips (*irei no tabi*) to battlefields as far away as Saipan and the Philippines to pay his respects to the war dead. This avoidance of Yasukuni by the emperor represents a serious "crisis" for the shrine, which Kobori claims he was trying to communicate to the shrine staff by using such strong words.[36] The raison d'être for Yasukuni Shrine is being weakened by the emperor's behavior, he claims, and contributing to its increasing isolation in contemporary life, a process he terms the "gala-pagosization" (*garapagosuka*) of Yasukuni. He does not expect that relations between the Imperial Household and Yasukuni Shrine will improve once Crown Prince Naruhito becomes emperor, so this sense of "crisis" is unlikely to be resolved in the foreseeable future.

It is not just the pro-Yasukuni camp that is divided. Buddhists and Christians also hold diverse views about the shrine and some have established congenial relations with Yasukuni Shrine priests. While our treatment has focused on the Buddhist and Christian critics, there are certainly supporters within Buddhist and Christian institutions. The Japan Buddhist Federation—to which some 90 percent of all Buddhist denominations and Buddhist prefectural associations belong—has for many years expressed opposition to "official visits" and demanded that prime ministers and cabinet members avoid such public visits. While support for this critical stance is particularly strong among the Jōdo Shinshū organizations, there are individual Buddhist priests from some denominations clearly breaking with this position and participating in ritual activities at Yasukuni Shrine. On 9 November 2017, for example, Tendai and Shingon Buddhist priests conducted memorial services at both Yasukuni Shrine and Chidorigafuji National Cemetery, with some 130 participants from 13 different Buddhist and Shinto organizations. This was the third year such an ecumenical memorial service had been led by Buddhists at the shrine.[37] Similarly, there is a small lay Roman Catholic group that gathers for joint visits to Yasukuni Shrine each year on 15 August, where Catholic prayers are offered for the war dead.[38] It appears, therefore, that Yasukuni Shrine officials are taking a more flexible approach and allowing for at least some non-Shinto ritual elements within the shrine precincts, which is contributing to the normalization of the shrine for a least some Japanese.

Ikegami Yoshimasa has reminded us that Yasukuni Shrine has multiple meanings and for many Japanese the shrine is first and foremost a site to address personal and familial grief at the loss of a loved one (Ikegami, Sueki, and Shimazono 2006, 23–25; Ikegami 2019, 294–335). Those with strong ties to the shrine are primarily concerned with the rituals that address these concerns rather than the political issues that attract the most media attention each year. For many individuals, Ikegami explains, it is the personalized and individual relationship with the deceased family member that motivates and shapes involvement with the shrine, rather than the abstract notion of the nation's responsibility to memorialize the "war heroes." Expressions of familiarity dominate the conversation of bereaved families and the deceased are referred to in affectionate personal terms and those grieving as the "mothers of Kudan" (*kudan no haha*) or the "wives of Yasukuni" (*Yasukuni no tsuma*). For many families, it is the daily memorial services conducted on the individual death anniversaries (*kobetsu senshisha no meinichi*) of each soldier that is the most significant ritual activity attracting them to the shrine each year. While only attended by small groups of ten to thirty people—family members and friends—it is these memorial services that are most meaningful and not the major annual festivals and events that tend to attract the throngs of visitors.[39] For many grieving families, the shrine represents the sacred space for communion between the living and the dead and provides the ritual practices necessary to preserve the memory of the deceased.

While for some religious minorities the shrine represents a site of coercion and an expression of the politics of inclusion, for many more it remains a place of remembrance and comfort. As explained by John Nelson (2003, 464) some years ago:

> Until the individuals and organizations affiliated with Yasukuni Shrine discover alternatives of an equally empowering or emotionally satisfying scope, we should not be surprised that the shrine continues to provide solace and legitimacy through its seductive embrace of nation, social memory, and the moral certitude of ritual practices.

For these reasons, Yasukuni Shrine will not disappear nor will the conflict and controversy it attracts likely dissipate in the foreseeable future.

5

Patriotic Education

Civic Duties versus Religious Rights

According to the leaders of the restorationist movement, one of the critical problems facing contemporary Japan is the lack of patriotism among the postwar generations. This deficit was caused in large part by the Allied Occupation reforms that removed moral education from public schools and important national symbols—flag and anthem—from public life and institutions. The history textbooks used in public schools during the postwar decades also failed to properly represent Japan's past in a manner that cultivated patriotism and national pride. This chapter reviews some of the efforts to restore patriotism in public schools and examines the critical response of religious minorities to this agenda over the past two decades.

Our particular focus is on the response of Japanese Christians—both Protestant and Catholic church leaders and public school teachers—who have been the most outspoken religious critics of neonationalistic trends in public education, especially the reappearance of coercion in schools as a result of the reintroduction of civic rituals related to flag and anthem at official ceremonies. Legislation passed by the Diet in 1999 made the Kimigayo (national anthem) and Hinomaru (national flag) the "official" symbols of Japan, and this legal action provided the foundation for the Ministry of Education to issue new guidelines and instructions for how these symbols should be integrated into the calendar and curriculum of public schools. These policies were strictly enforced in two major metropolitan public school systems under the leadership of the nationalistic former governor of Tokyo, Ishihara Shintarō, and Hashimoto Tōru, mayor of Osaka.[1]

It is important to keep in mind that we are talking about a "minority within a minority" when we consider how Christians are critically engaging the government in the Japanese context. The total Christian population is small (less than 1 percent) and many members hold to a pietistic or apolitical faith. Also, the churches (both Protestant and Catholic) are deeply divided over these issues. The Catholic Bishops' Conference, which has been taking a critical stance on neonationalistic trends and government policies for several decades, regularly faces criticism from conservative priests and parishioners who are unhappy about their political activism and much prefer the accommodating stance of the Catholic Church in the 1930s. It is also worth remembering that there is a large network of Catholic and Protestant schools across the country, including some 85 elementary schools, 174 junior high schools, and 218 high schools, which employ many of the Japanese Christian teachers.[2] While not all teachers in these schools are Christian—in fact most of these schools continue to struggle with the shortage of Christian faculty—there are many Christian teachers in these private institutions, so the actual number of those facing the challenges in the public schools is relatively small.

THE REAPPEARANCE OF NATIONAL SYMBOLS IN PUBLIC LIFE

It is not surprising that following Japan's defeat and Occupation in August 1945, the use of the flag and anthem was restricted and discouraged. The Supreme Commander of Allied Powers (SCAP), in fact, issued a directive on 1 October that banned the official hoisting of the Hinomaru without special application and permission in advance. Although no prohibition was issued with regard to the Kimigayo, the general climate discouraged the public use of these symbols until January 1949, when SCAP rescinded the restriction and General MacArthur announced in his New Year message that the Japanese people could once again freely use the flag and anthem (Cripps 1996, 81). The following year, Amano Teiyū, the Minister of Education, issued a statement that encouraged schools to raise the flag and sing the anthem on national holidays. From that time, their use in schools and public life was promoted and their use began to slowly expand.

It was in 1958 that the Ministry of Education first instructed (*gakushū shidōyōryō*) public schools that it was "desirable" for the flag to be raised and the anthem sung at official school events (entrance and graduation ceremonies). Under these "soft" guidelines, however, compliance rates were not too impressive.[3] While the flag reappeared and was waved proudly in the 1964 Tokyo Olympics, considerable opposition remained in the schools and the teachers' union (Nikkyōso) and other critics argued that these symbols were unsuitable for use today. Many teachers refused to go along even after the Ministry of Education issued instructions in 1989, which made the rituals mandatory for school ceremonies.

Over the years conflicts erupted in many schools across Japan when school administrators attempted to enforce the Ministry of Education policy, but it was the suicide of a high school principal over the issue that focused the nation's attention and contributed in part to the government's effort to legalize these symbols. Ishikawa Toshihiro, Principal of Sera Senior High School in Hiroshima Prefecture, committed suicide by hanging himself on 28 February 1999; this was after difficult negotiations with teachers in an effort to persuade them to go along with the directives from the Ministry of Education and Prefectural Education Board to sing the Kimigayo at the graduation ceremony. Some political leaders reasoned that the problems surrounding use of these symbols could be resolved if they were "officially" recognized by passing legislation in the Diet.

Although widely accepted as Japan's national symbols from years of use, the Hinomaru and Kimigayo had never been officially approved as such by any government administration. In 1974, Prime Minister Tanaka Kakuei expressed an interest in legislation to officially recognize these national symbols, but it would take more than two decades before this would be achieved during the administration of Prime Minister Obuchi Keizō. In 1999, after considerable debate, the Diet finally approved the Kimigayo and Hinomaru as the official symbols of the nation.[4] At the time this legislation was being debated in the Diet, Prime Minister Obuchi clearly stated on 29 June that freedom of conscience would be protected and no coercion would ever be involved in public institutions if the bill passed.[5]

CRITICAL RESPONSES OF CHURCH LEADERS TO THE DIET LEGISLATION

In spite of such assurances, many religious leaders and public intellectuals raised serious concerns about this legislation. The Catholic Council on Justice and Peace, for example, sent a letter of appeal to Prime Minister Obuchi on 12 March 1999, which expressed opposition to the government's rushed efforts to legalize the flag and anthem. According to the Council's interpretation, the Hinomaru is a symbol of Japan's military aggression and invasion in Asia. Likewise, the lyrics of the Kimigayo express praise for the emperor as the ruler (*tōchisha*) of Japan, which violates Japan's postwar Constitution that placed the government clearly in the hands of the people. Rather than approving these as the symbols of the nation, the letter urges government representatives to consider a new flag and anthem that will reflect the principles of peace and democratic values that are foundational to Japan's Constitution.[6] Months later, just four days before the legislation was passed, the Japan Catholic Council on Justice and Peace and several Protestant bodies issued a joint declaration addressed to the prime minister and representatives of the Liberal Democratic Party (LDP) and Kōmeitō Party to express their strong opposition to the legalization initiative.[7] The declaration states that if the legislation is passed, it will undoubtedly lead to coercion and a violation of the individual rights and freedoms—thought, conscience, belief—that are protected by Articles 13, 19, and 20 of the Constitution.

> Article 13. All of the people shall be respected as individuals. Their right to life, liberty, and the pursuit of happiness shall, to the extent that it does not interfere with the public welfare, be the supreme consideration in legislation and in other governmental affairs.
>
> Article 19. Freedom of thought and conscience shall not be violated.
>
> Article 20. Freedom of religion is guaranteed to all. No religious organization shall receive any privileges from the State, nor exercise any political authority. No person shall be compelled to take part in any religious act, celebration, rite or practice. The State and its organs shall refrain from religious education or any other religious activity.

In particular, the declaration expressed concern for public school teachers who would undoubtedly be forced to provide leadership in the ritual use of the Hinomaru and Kimigayo against their will.

It turns out that these religious minorities had legitimate concerns. The action of the Diet strengthened the position of politicians and educators who felt it was their duty to have all teachers and staff lead students by example in singing the national anthem before the flag for important school ceremonies. Before the end of the year, the Ministry of Education reaffirmed its instructions to require all public schools to use the "legal symbols" for official events, such as entrance and graduation ceremonies, and worked closely with School Boards to see that the rules were enforced. Even before the intensification of "guidance" from the Ministry of Education, a number of teachers had already been disciplined for failing to comply with the 1989 guidelines.[8] The situation only became more difficult for teachers after 1999.[9] Initially, there were many protests against these policies by both teachers and students in various schools across the nation, but the widespread resistance quickly subsided. The strict enforcement of these new policies soon followed in two major metropolitan public school systems under the authoritarian leadership of Ishihara Shintarō, the former governor of Tokyo, and, more recently, Hashimoto Tōru, the former governor of Osaka and mayor of Osaka.

THE EMERGING RESISTANCE AND LEGAL ACTION

Although the vast majority of teachers and schools have fallen into line, a number of teachers have continued to refuse to stand or lead students in what they regard to be oppressive patriotic rituals that will recreate an educational environment that too closely resembles that of wartime Japan. Some members of the leftist teachers' union, Nikkyōso, argued that these symbols were unsuitable for use in the schools since they had been used for the mobilization of both teachers and students in wartime Japan. As Okada Akira (2013, 11) observes, many union members actively resisted the efforts to reintroduce the flag and anthem back into the public schools and rallied under the catch-phrase "we will not send our students to the battlefield." The pressure on teachers to comply was intensified in the Tokyo schools from 23 October 2003, when the Tokyo Metropolitan Board of Education issued an order for all teachers and staff to participate in leading students in singing the Kimigayo before the Hinomaru at official ceremonies or face disciplinary action (the Board, of course, was under the direction of the well-known nationalist and hardliner Governor Ishihara Shintarō at the time).

For those enforcing the Ministry of Education policy, the primary concern is to preserve the social harmony (*wa*) of the school community and promote patriotism and pride in country. Those teachers refusing to participate are viewed as selfish (*wagamama*) and excessively individualistic. For the small minority of teachers—whether members of the more critical left teachers union or Christians—the new policy is a clear sign of Japan's rightward shift and represents a return to the wartime educational policy of coercion. While those imposing the new patriotic rituals do not regard them as religious and some who participate may gain a sense of well-being and Japanese pride through the experience, others forced to participate regard them as oppressive and linked to the wartime policies that required public school teachers to participate in rituals of respect toward the Imperial Rescript of Education, singing of the national anthem, and shrine visits (*sanpai*).

Anticipating a range of disciplinary action for non-compliance to an educational policy and directive that they regarded as a violation of Article 19—freedom of conscience—228 teachers launched a preemptive lawsuit (*yobō soshō*) in January 2004 against the Tokyo Metropolitan Board of Education to protect themselves.[10] The lawsuit asked the court to 1) clearly state that teachers had no duty or obligation to sing the national anthem; 2) instruct the Board that they should not follow through with the disciplinary action threatened in the 23 October statement; and 3) confirm that music teachers could not be compelled to provide piano accompaniment for the anthem at school ceremonies (Okada Akira 2013, 17). The number of plaintiffs quickly grew to 401 teachers and their concerns were represented by a group of some 50 lawyers over the course of 14 hearings.

The teachers could clearly see what was coming under Ishihara's Board of Education. Just five months later, in March 2004, some 180 teachers in the Tokyo Public School system were reprimanded for failing to comply and properly guide their students in these patriotic events. Many teachers have since been disciplined, fined, suspended, or reassigned to schools that require a longer commute.[11] Over the past decade there have been over 700 plaintiffs (teachers or staff) at various stages of appeal with District Courts and the Supreme Court to either reverse or prevent future disciplinary action for non-compliance.

"CIVIC DUTIES" VERSUS "RELIGIOUS RIGHTS"

At least two Christian teachers were involved in this initial legal action and one (Okada Akira) was called to provide testimony as a person of faith for why he opposed and refused the order to lead students in the anthem. In addition to appealing to Article 10 of the Fundamental Education Law, which prohibits the political intervention into education, and Article 19 of the Constitution, which guarantees freedom of thought and conscience, he and other Christians regard forced participation as a violation of Article 20, which guarantees religious freedom and states that: "No person shall be compelled to take part in any religious act, celebration, rite or practice." For the Japanese Christian teachers opposed to these new school policies, the anthem cannot be dissociated from the larger system of State Shinto that dominated wartime Japan, so singing the anthem in praise of the emperor remains a "religious act" and would violate their personal faith.

Given the history of Christian churches in wartime Japan, these teachers are concerned that they are again being forced to compromise their faith through participation in the civil religious rites at schools. Takahashi Seiju (2004, 177), a teacher in the Tokyo Metropolitan school system, has reached back to the Tokugawa period to find another parallel, comparing this policy to the one used by the authorities centuries ago to force Kirishitan (Japanese Christians) to abandon their faith and conform to the government's expectations. Required participation in these patriotic rituals "is like forcing teachers and staff to step on a *fumie* [sacred object] before students," Takahashi explains, "and it is absolutely unforgivable." For these religious minorities, the use of the flag and anthem has become a humiliating public "test" of their identity and loyalty as Japanese.[12]

In response to developments in 2004, the Catholic Bishops' Committee for Social Concern published a letter to "All Our Brothers and Sisters" and raised its concerns again over coercion in the Tokyo Public School system since the Hinomaru and Kimigayo were made "official." The letter explains to the faithful that:

This year in the capital city of Tokyo, teachers who did not stand during the raising of the national (Red Sun) flag and the singing of the (You Are Eternal) national anthem, were given punishments, and those children who took the same actions were given a warning. In the Convention On the Rights of the Child, Article 12, it states, "the child who is capable of forming his or her own views (has) the right to express those views freely in all matters." In Article 13, "the right to freedom of expression," in Article 14, "freedom of thought, conscience and religion," are praised. It can be said that these latest responses by the Tokyo Government put unjust pressure on the children, are a tightening of management control, and are an infringement of their human rights. The forced use of the "Red Sun" flag and the "You Are Eternal" anthem directly affects the identity of multicultural children and those children with a foreign nationality, (same Treaty Article 8), and is a serious problem that cannot help but cause divisions in the classroom.[13]

In the same year, the National Christian Council in Japan, which includes representatives from thirty-three different churches and Christian organizations, also issued a rather detailed position statement in 2004, entitled "We Oppose the Compulsory Use of Hinomaru and Kimigayo," which included the following harsh criticism of the implementation carried out in Tokyo:

After the national anthem and flag law was put forth in August 1999, the Tokyo Metropolitan Board of Education issued protocols for the Hinomaru and the Kimigayo at public school ceremonies in October 2003. In April 2004, it punished teachers who refused to sing and play the piano for the Kimigayo at the graduation ceremony of public schools in Tokyo. It even punished teachers whose students did not stand up to sing the Kimigayo.

These acts of the Tokyo Metropolitan Government contradict the word of late-Prime Minister Keizo Obuchi who clarified that the national anthem and flag law will not be carried out by force. They violate freedom of thought and freedom of conscience (Article 19) and the freedom of religion (Article 20) as guaranteed in the Constitution.

They are also violating the Article 14—freedom of thought, conscience and religion—of the Convention on the Rights of the Child, which was adopted in 1989 and ratified by Japan in 1994. In an environment like this, we cannot expect that there will be respect for uniqueness of each child at school, which is essential for the growth of children. Punishment of teachers is oppressive and affects the children who are developing their own ideas about the anthem and flag.[14]

REVISION OF THE FUNDAMENTAL EDUCATION LAW

In 2006, a decision of the Tokyo District Court gave the teachers involved in the initial lawsuit some temporary reassurance that their rights would be protected by the Constitution. On 21 September, presiding Judge Namba Kōichi found that the Tokyo School Board's directive was invalid. As Lawrence Repeta's (2007, 3) helpful review of this case notes, Namba acknowledged that the flag and anthem had been used in the recent past as a "spiritual support" for Japanese imperialism and militarism and these symbols have not yet "attained a status of political and religious neutrality among the people." In this context, he concluded, it would be a violation of freedom of thought and conscience to force a teacher to sing or provide musical accompaniment for the anthem against their will.

It is not surprising that Governor Ishihara and the Tokyo School Board appealed the 2006 Tokyo District Court decision that supported the teachers. To the dismay of the plaintiffs, the Supreme Court ruled on 30 May 2011 that it was not a violation of the Constitution for a principal to instruct and require teachers and staff to stand and sing the Kimigayo in front of the national flag at school ceremonies. This Supreme Court decision is undoubtedly related to the revision of the Fundamental Education Law (*Kyōiku kihon hō*) by the Diet in 2006, which "restored" patriotic moral education as a central component of public education and legitimized the use of the flag and anthem in public schools.

The movement to revise the education law can be traced back to discussions that began in the 1960s, but it was Prime Minister Abe Shinzō, a well-known nationalistic leader and member of both Shinseiren (Shinto Association of Spiritual Leadership) and the Japan Conference (Nippon Kaigi) (at the time, twelve of the eighteen members of Abe's Cabinet were also members of the latter group), who finally pushed the legislation through the Diet.[15] His tactics alienated many, however. In an effort to raise public support for revisions of the education law, for example, the government collected opinions and comments from both specialists and citizens at large, and even organized "town meetings" to discuss the proposed revision. It turns out that this was not really "democracy" in action. As Hardacre (2011, 207–208) reports:

When it emerged in late 2006 that the government had paid agents to speak in support of the revision proposal at these Town Meetings, Prime Minister Abe and others in his cabinet apologized and returned their salaries to the public purse. The Prime Minister declared, however, that the revision itself was not the problem, and the government pressed on to promulgate it.

Abe's demise was not just because he overreached and used less than above-board tactics in promoting reforms, but also due to unexpected problems related to the national pension program that came to light during this year.

In spite of his downfall and resignation in September 2007 due to a series of scandals, corruption allegations, and ineffective cabinet reshuffles, Abe nevertheless achieved significant results during his term in office and left behind a more regulated school system with a particular type of moral and patriotic education in place. Of course, the revision of the Fundamental Education Law was only one part of his larger vision for Japan that he laid out in a book entitled *Utsukushii kuni e* (2006), a popular volume published just three months after the revised law was passed by the Diet.[16] Even though the plan to revise the Constitution was temporarily derailed—or at least put on the back burner for the time being—the revision of the Fundamental Education Law alone is having a serious social impact.

While Abe and his supporters firmly believe that this has laid the foundation for a "beautiful" Japan, the Catholic Bishops' Conference argues that the individual rights guaranteed by the Constitution are being violated by the strict enforcement of the revised Fundamental Education Law. In fact, they point out that the revised law has provided the basis for a radical shift in the educational system from one that seeks to nurture individual character to one aimed at cultivating individuals who will comply with the policies of the state.[17] In response to the government's promotion of the new education law, Catholic leaders raised additional concerns closely related to the demographic changes experienced by the Church in Japan due to immigration trends and the arrival of migrant workers over the past several decades.

Since the late 1980s, the number of foreign workers arriving in Japan has steadily increased to partially make up for the shrinking Japanese workforce and shortage of laborers needed for the less attractive jobs widely known as the three Ks—*kiken* (dangerous), *kitanai* (dirty), and *kitsui* (demanding)— usually associated with factory work, construction, and domestic jobs. The highest concentrations of these migrant workers are in Yokohama, Nagoya, Tokyo, Saitama, Kyoto, and Osaka, which are also the areas where many Catholic parishes have suddenly found themselves with many new non-Japanese parishioners.

The Catholic Bishops' Conference in Japan has not included this influx of non-Japanese Catholics in the annual statistical reports, but the Catholic Commission of Japan for Migrants, Refugees, and People on the Move began to gather data on this new type of parishioner and reported that the number had dramatically increased between 1996 and 2005, with foreign parishioners (529,452) exceeding the number of Japanese members (449,925).[18] By 2005, in fact, the percentage of non-Japanese members had reached 81 percent for both the Diocese of Nagoya and Saitama, 69 percent for both Kyoto and Yokohama, 47 percent for Sendai, 46 percent for Niigata, and 45 percent for Tokyo. While the non-Japanese parishioners come from many different countries—China, Vietnam, Korea, and Peru, for example—the two major sources of migrant workers are from Brazil and the Philippines, two countries where the Catholic Church has dominated religious life for centuries.

During the recent decades that the Church has been undergoing internal pluralization due to the arrival of migrant workers, the LDP led governments have been promoting policies of homogenization and an essentialist version of Japanese identity in public education. This is the context for understanding the additional Catholic criticisms of the revised Fundamental Education Law. Tani Daiji, former Bishop of the Saitama Diocese and Chair of the Committee for Refugees and Migrants, for example, appealed to the government for more consideration to be given to the educational needs of the increasing number of non-Japanese children and children of mixed marriages, but to no avail.[19] The Chairperson of the Catholic Schools Educational Committee also expressed grave concerns that the law would eventually allow for state intervention and interference in private schools and, ultimately, lead to the restriction of individual rights and freedom of religious expression.[20] It could eventually have an impact even on some 800 private Catholic schools and their 240,000 students, which would further weaken the clear separation of the state and religion. The Chair of the Social Committee of the Japan Catholic Bishops' Conference, likewise, criticized the new law and argued that the view of education it advances will prove to be an obstacle for educating students appropriately for the future of Japan and international society.[21]

THE ENFORCERS: ISHIHARA AND HASHIMOTO

It appears that disciplinary action against teachers in public schools is likely to continue and, perhaps, increase in the years ahead. On 5 June 2011—in an action resembling that of the Tokyo Education Committee in 2003—the Osaka Prefectural Assembly passed the *Kimigayo jōrei*, an ordinance that requires all teachers and staff employed by public schools in its jurisdiction to stand and sing the Kimigayo at all official school ceremonies. This ordinance, which was pushed through the Assembly by Governor Hashimoto Tōru, had the strong support of both the Osaka branch of the Japan Restoration Party (Nippon Ishin no Kai) and Japan Conference members; in fact, six of the fourteen local representatives who were initially responsible for submitting this proposed ordinance belong to the Japan Conference.

Like Ishihara, the former governor of Tokyo, Hashimoto is another authoritarian figure and "enforcer," a person who has little patience for those who disagree with his position. He also uses social media effectively to promote his views and belittle his opponents. During the time the *Kimigayo jōrei* was being debated in Osaka, media savvy Hashimoto "tweeted" the following message to his 1.18 million followers on Twitter, which clearly indicated that the individual rights guaranteed by the Constitution do not apply to public servants (*kōmuin*):

> What is beneficial for the students is more important than freedom of conscience for the stupid teachers (*baka kyōin*). The teachers at public schools are public servants of Japan. They make their living off of our taxes. If they don't like the national flag and anthem, they should resign from their position. There is freedom not to stand and refrain from singing the national anthem, but only for citizens who are not public servants (*kōmuin*).[22]

The local ordinance passed under Hashimoto's leadership in Osaka, of course, simply reinforced the directives from the Ministry of Education, but it was soon followed with additional action that laid out more clearly the punishments for those who failed to comply.[23] As a result of the hard line stance taken in Tokyo and Osaka, many teachers have since been disciplined, fined, suspended, or reassigned to schools that require a longer commute.

What are we to make of these leaders who ignore the rights of individuals and promote their version of patriotism by force in public schools? Since the strict enforcement of the new educational policy was initiated in 2003 by then Governor Ishihara in the Tokyo Metropolitan Schools, it has become clear that patriotism and devotion to the emperor—a central conviction of the restorationist movement—is not the primary motivation for at least some leaders promoting flag and anthem. While I am unfamiliar with Hashimoto's view of the emperor and Imperial Household, which the Kimigayo celebrates, Ishihara made his personal views very clear some two years after he resigned from the Tokyo governorship and returned to national politics in late 2012.[24] In a 2014 interview in *Bungei shunjū*, Ishihara rather flippantly stated that: "I don't have much interest in the Imperial Household. I don't even sing the national anthem. If I do happen to sing along, I just make up my own lyrics."[25] In short, the national anthem has simply been manipulated and used as a tool of social control by an authoritarian leader who clearly lacks any authentic feelings of respect for the emperor and Imperial Household, which is what the restorationist coalition aims to nurture by restoring patriotic education in the schools.

It is ironic that in pushing this agenda through the school system, the LDP politicians and their network of supporting groups are in fact going against the expressed will of the emperor, the very person who constitutes the *raison d'être* of the entire "restoration" enterprise. In 2004, when questioned by a member of the Tokyo Education Committee about the use of the flag and anthem in the schools, Emperor Akihito responded that it was preferable for it not to be a forced activity.[26] As we have seen, however, neo-nationalists have continued to pursue a policy of coercion in public schools in spite of their expressed devotion to the emperor. It is not just the issue of patriotic education that reveals the growing gap between the far right of the LDP and the Imperial Household. The emperor's own actions—avoidance of Yasukuni Shrine visits since the enshrinement of class-A war criminals in 1978—and recent public statements by both Emperor Akihito and Prince Naruhito, indicates a concern to remember the wartime suffering of Japan's neighbors and express a deep appreciation for the Peace Constitution.[27] This clearly puts them at odds with the larger neonationalistic agenda of Prime Minister Abe and his revisionist supporters. Sooner or later, this growing divide will have to be addressed.[28]

LOCAL CHURCH SUPPORT FOR ACTIVIST TEACHERS

Although various denominations and churches issued letters of concern to the Prime Minister and government officials over the legislation passed by the Diet and the guidelines issued by the Ministry of Education, churches or congregations have been rather slow to become active supporters of individual Christians struggling with legal action in the courts. In July 2008 the Human Rights Committee of the Tokyo Diocese of the Anglican Church finally organized a support group for two Christian teachers appealing disciplinary action: Kishida Shizue, an elementary school music teacher and pianist, and Iguro Yutaka, a teacher in the Tokyo Toritsu High School. In February 2010 this was expanded into an ecumenical trans-denominational support group, which included the Roman Catholic Church and the full range of Protestant churches, including independent evangelical congregations, Baptist churches, the United Church of Christ in Japan, the Reformed Church, and even Non-Church groups (Mukyōkai).[29] These groups and other churches have been organizing special meetings in Tokyo and Osaka to raise the consciousness of Christians over the issues and to provide some moral support for teachers still involved in prolonged lawsuits and hearings over disciplinary action.

For the teachers on the frontlines, however, this was undoubtedly perceived as "too little and too late." In spite of some official statements and letters of support from denominational officials, teachers involved in the lawsuits express exasperation at the lack of support from their own congregation. It appears that many church members tend to embrace a more private and pietistic faith, one that tends to avoid social and political issues, and are more inclined to admonish the "radical" teachers to be good citizens. Japanese Christians are divided over what constitute legitimate grounds for resistance to government or public school directives. Some regard the civic rites simply as "religiously neutral" patriotic expressions and find no problem with going along and have little sympathy for the small number of Christian teachers stirring up trouble and siding with the radical elements of the teachers' union.

At the moment, I only have information on eight Christian teachers who have been involved in ongoing court cases. There are undoubtedly a few more, but it is unlikely that there are many. One reason, as mentioned earlier, is that many of the Japanese Christian teachers are employed by one of the many Catholic and Protestant schools across the country, so the actual number of those facing the challenges in the public schools is relatively small. Another reason is that at most public schools there are usually about five positions assigned for each official ceremony—such as standing at the main gate of the school, serving as receptionist, and so on—which allow the teacher to avoid being in the hall at the time all are expected to stand and sing the anthem (Okada Akira 2006, 5). This has allowed at least a few teachers to avoid disciplinary action in some cases. If a school has a number of teachers known to be opposed to the anthem and likely to refuse to stand and participate, these "escape routes" must be rotated among the teachers so that disciplinary action and punishment can be avoided as long as possible. In this way, some Christian teachers might make it to retirement age before disciplinary action leads to termination of employment.

While the Christian teachers share in common the belief that the new school policies violate the principles of freedom of thought, conscience, and belief guaranteed by the Constitution, they also regard the national anthem as a resurrected element of the civil religion of wartime, which required not only singing the anthem but also shrine visits. Most belong to churches that since the end of the war have made public "confessions" of war responsibility and their compromise with the emperor-centric Shinto religion, and they are concerned not to repeat their mistakes. The Bishops of the Catholic Church in Japan and numerous Protestant churches have published a number of statements and apologies about their collaboration with the government in wartime Japan and have recently warned the faithful that they are now entering a similar period of testing.

Kishida Shizue, a music teacher in Kōritsu Elementary School in Tokyo, is one Christian teacher who regards the requirement as a *fumie* ritual and refuses to participate. A member of the Anglican-Episcopal Church in

Japan (Nippon Sei Kō Kai), Kishida finds it impossible to sing the lyrics of the Kimigayo or even provide piano accompaniment, since that would be supporting an anthem that praises the emperor system and essentially treats the emperor as God. Regarding this as a religious act, Kishida has refused to participate for over a decade. In 2009, at age 59 and one year from retirement, she had already been warned and disciplined 4 times—which included salary cuts—and faced a one-month suspension and transfer to a different school for the final year of her career. On 30 March 2001, she did receive a one-month suspension and 10 percent reduction in her salary for that period. She has been appealing this disciplinary action in the Tokyo courts into late 2013. Since 2005, she had avoided disciplinary action by taking holiday time on the days of the entrance and graduation ceremonies or by entering the hall after the singing of the anthem. Other accounts by Christian teachers recount similar trials and tribulations.[30]

NORMALIZATION AND POLICY EXTENSION TO PUBLIC UNIVERSITIES

As we have seen, the government's policies and efforts to normalize the use of flag and anthem in public schools has been rather effective. It has required some rather heavy-handed enforcement tactics, but most public schools are now in compliance. In fact, within several years of passing the legislation and issuing the stricter policy guidelines the compliance rate for use of flag and anthem at public schools nationwide increased dramatically. While most schools complied, there remained pockets of resistance among teachers, but this diminished quickly as schools resorted to strict disciplinary action. While over 200 teachers in the Tokyo schools were reprimanded and faced disciplinary action in 2004, the number was down to four in 2010.[31] The financial difficulties that can accompany resistance has been sufficient pressure to persuade some teachers to comply, while some have chosen early retirement to avoid a work place that has become a moral and psychological challenge. In my view, this "success" has been achieved at considerable cost and introduced a serious conflict between government policies and the rights of individuals as defined by the Constitution. This is, of course, a Constitution that Prime Minister Abe and his supporters are keen to revise in the not too distant future.

The government is now keen on extending the flag and anthem policy even to national universities. In June 2015, Shimomura Hakubun, the Minister of Education, contacted the presidents of all 86 national universities with a request that the flag and anthem be a part of all official university entrance and graduation ceremonies. The extension of the flag and anthem policy to universities is said to have originated in a statement by Prime Minister Abe at a Budget Committee Meeting of the Diet in April, who expressed his view that it was clearly appropriate for these institutions financed by taxes to similarly follow the new Fundamental Education Law and conduct school ceremonies that include flag and anthem. According to a survey by the Ministry later that year, seventy-four of eighty-six universities responded that the flag would be displayed at the entrance ceremony, but only fifteen indicated that the national anthem would be sung as a part of the program.[32]

The proposed mandatory use of flag and anthem at universities quickly generated a critical response from some academic staff. The faculty union of Tohoku University in Sendai, for example, issued a strong statement in opposition to this policy and organized a meeting to critically engage the policy on 30 June 2015. According to their statement, "the lyrics of the Kimigayo are clearly an expression of one particular political philosophy." Forced use of the anthem, therefore, would violate the Constitution, Articles 19, 21, and 23, which guarantee freedom of thought and conscience, freedom of expression, and academic freedom.[33]

In response to the Ministry's extension of this policy to national universities, the President of Gifu University, Moriwaki Hisataka, attracted considerable media attention when he stated at a 17 February 2016 news conference that the national anthem would not be sung at their ceremonies, although the national flag would be displayed at these events. He rejected the Ministry's explanation that the use of flag and anthem have now become customary (*kanrei*), and while acknowledging that the university had to fulfill its responsibilities as a public institution funded by taxpayers, he firmly stated that it was not the duty of the university "to obey the orders of the state" (*kokka no meirei ni shitagaubeki de wa nai*). It was more appropriate, he explained, for their institution to continue using the old school song, which was a distinctive tradition of the school.[34] It will be interesting to see what additional pressures the government will put on national universities to gain compliance going forward. Perhaps there will be threats of reductions in educational subsidies and research funds on the horizon, which both public and private universities depend upon for their survival.

While Gifu University, a public institution, has expressed strong opposition to this requirement, there is already an unexpected example of a private university with Christian roots that voluntarily incorporated the national flag and anthem into its entrance ceremony in April 2018. Momoyama Gakuin Kyōiku University, known in English as St. Andrew's University of Education, is an institution established by Anglican missionaries over a century ago (1894), which evolved into a university in the postwar period. Given that the Church had issued a strong statement in 2000 in opposition to the government's policy to require use of flag and anthem in public schools, the private institution's use of flag and anthem in 2018 caught the attention of leaders within the Anglican-Episcopal Church in Japan. Church leaders were upset that an institution with Christian roots would adopt the national anthem for their official events. On 3 March 2019, the Justice and Peace Committee of the Anglican Church issued a statement and appealed to the president and school board to stop the planned use of the national anthem in the April 2019 ceremony.[35] It could be that leadership of this institution is simply riding the wave of neonationalism or, perhaps, it could be anticipating that the government will likely extend its flag and anthem policy to all educational institutions receiving government subsidies, and is therefore strategically preparing for its future survival.

CONCLUSION

The patriotic rituals in public schools are now only related to the flag and anthem, but there are fears among religious minorities that shrine visits could very well become a part of the activities promoted by public schools. While this may seem far-fetched to some observers, it is certainly what many neonationalists would like to see happen and there are worrying indicators that the path has been partially prepared for such a development.

Although many Japanese may regard the use of flag and anthem in school ceremonies simply as patriotic rituals and religiously neutral, those promoting them are equally concerned to increase public support for

Yasukuni Shrine by encouraging "official visits" by government officials and through the development of educational materials for public schools. Shortly after the new Fundamental Education Law was passed by the Diet, an animated DVD entitled *Hokori* (Pride) was distributed to public schools under the auspices of the Ministry of Education in 2007. Produced by the Nihon Seinen Kaigisho as a part of the Ministry's "Program for the Development of a New Educational System," it was shown or scheduled for viewing in 93 different locations throughout Japan between February and June. This DVD contains a scene in which the spirit of a deceased soldier appears to a high school girl and invites her back to Yasukuni to remember those who died in defense of the homeland and for their love of country. The DVD as a whole essentially promotes the revisionist history as presented by Yūshūkan, the museum attached to Yasukuni Shrine. On 17 May 2007, Prime Minister Abe was questioned and criticized in the Diet by Ishii Ikuko, a member of the Communist Party, about this controversial DVD and his policies that allowed for it to be produced and distributed under the auspices of the Ministry of Education.[36] This critical response appears to have been effective—at least temporarily—as public showings were apparently stopped and copies do not seem to be available.

There are other signs that Yasukuni Shrine could find a place again in public education. On 27 March 2008, it was announced that school visits to Yasukuni Shrine and other state-protecting shrines (*gokoku jinja*), which had been stopped by GHQ in 1945 and forbidden by a Ministry of Education regulation in 1949, were no longer prohibited. The Ministry of Education has instructed schools that they may arrange such visits as a part of the educational program as long as the visit does not promote a particular religion (one wonders how this will play out). Over the summer months in 2008, the Ministry distributed a document at orientation meetings for prefectural boards of education, which stated this new policy. This new policy was reported on the Japan Conference homepage as an important step in the restoration of a proper relationship between Shinto, the state, and public education.

Given the pluralistic nature of postwar Japanese society, it is not surprising that the range of neonationalistic initiatives promoted by the restorationist coalition have been widely contested by many intellectuals, the teachers' union, and a variety of religious leaders and groups. In the wake of the 1995 Aum incident, we observed a serious concern for "protection from" religions, which largely focused on problematic New Religions known for violence or high-pressure recruitment and fundraising activities. Over the course of two decades, we have seen this evolve into a concern among some of Japan's religious minorities for protection from coercion related to Shinto-related civil-religious obligations in public or national institutions, which were historically the primary carriers of State Shinto. The "politics of inclusion" as practiced by Yasukuni Shrine (enshrinement whether a family requests it or not) and now by public schools (forced teacher participation in leading students in singing the Kimigayo against their will) reveals how government policies are eroding the rights of individuals. There is clearly a clash between those who recognize individual rights and freedoms as fundamental to civil society and those who regard the rights of the individual to be secondary and subservient to the needs of the nation or group. In light of the impact of post-disaster legislation on the school system nationwide, one can appreciate the concerns of religious minorities and others who fear an expansion of coercion as political leaders and groups seek to reshape public institutions.

Given the 2011 Supreme Court decision, there seems little the Christian opposition groups can do to change the situation as far as public schools are concerned. While Christian and non-Christian teachers are likely to be in the courts for some time—processing old appeals or dealing with new lawsuits—the legal battles will be limited to whether punishments were excessive; the right of school principals to expect teachers to obey instructions and lead students in singing the anthem has been legally settled. The larger concern for religious minorities is whether these coercive practices will be expanded in the future, which is closely related to the prime minister's plans for revision of the Constitution. In light of the impact of the flag and anthem legislation in 1999 and the revision of the Fundamental Education Law in 2006, religious minorities are particularly concerned about the possible revision of Articles 20 and 89, which clearly define and protect religious freedom and the separation of religion and state. The constitutional revisions proposed by the LDP represent a serious crisis for religious groups and one to which we now turn our attention.

6

Promoting Constitutional Revision

The Normalization of Nonreligious Shinto

Since the end of the Allied Occupation, a number of conserva-tive political and religious leaders have dreamed of replacing the postwar Constitution (1947)—regarded by many as a foreign impo-sition—with an "autonomous" one (*jishu kenpō*) based on core Japanese values. It was one of the key goals outlined in the charter of the Liberal Democratic Party (LDP) when it was founded in 1955 and was also central to the platform of the League Promoting Ties between Politics and Shinto (Shintō Seiji Renmei), which has represented the political agenda of the National Association of Shrines (Jinja Honchō; NAS) since 1969. Early proponents of constitutional revision were convinced that the Occupation policies and reforms had been too extreme and sought to at least partially restore the emperor-centric values and accompanying duties that had been embedded in the Meiji Constitution. One early leader of the pro-revision-ist camp was Kishi Nobusuke (1896–1987), the maternal grandfather of Prime Minister Abe, which at least partially explains his enthusiasm for this issue today; it has deep roots in his family history.

While the issue of constitutional revision has been taken up from time to time over the decades and numerous drafts have been proposed and cir-culated, it has received renewed focus and attention in post-disaster Japan.[1] The unprecedented triple disaster of 2011—earthquake, tsunami, and nuclear accident—shocked the nation and overwhelmed the leadership of the Democratic Party of Japan (DPJ), which was then governing Japan. The DPJ was already in trouble, but the scale of this disaster and inadequate responses by the national government paved the way for the return of the LDP. After the three-year hiatus under the leadership of three successive DPJ prime ministers, the LDP made a comeback in December 2012, and Abe Shinzō began his second tenure as prime minister. Although he initially focused on revitalizing the Japanese economy, it was clear from the beginning that there was more to his agenda than "Abenomics." Abe's overarching goal has been to restore national pride and create a beautiful Japan—a concern succinctly captured in the title of his best-selling book *Utsukushii kuni e* (2006, 28–29)—and this, he maintains, will only be possible if the laws and Constitution that were put in place during the Occupation period are fundamentally reformed.[2]

Abe was keen on pursuing the revision of the Constitution during his first term as prime minister (2006–2007), but resigned due to "ill health" within a year of pushing through the revision of the Fundamental Education Law. Since being re-elected as prime minister in 2012, he has made constitutional revision one of his key priorities. To facilitate this process, on 1 May 2013 Abe proposed a revision of Article 96, which would allow amendments to be passed by simple majority in the Diet rather than the stipulated two-thirds majority. Due to widespread opposition from both within and outside of his coalition government, Abe was forced to withdraw this proposal and, hence, still faces the high threshold of a two-thirds majority to move forward with his agenda. Nevertheless, the prime minister reiterated his plan to push forward with the proposed revision in 2020, which he announced in a special video message prepared for a public forum hosted by the Japan Conference (Nippon Kaigi) in Tokyo on 3 May 2019, the national holiday that memorializes the postwar Constitution.[3]

In addition to backing by the Japan Conference, Abe's political agenda has continued to receive support from the shrine world. For example, the Tokyo Association of Shinto Shrines, which is a part of the NAS, reaffirmed its backing of his plan for constitutional revision in a public declaration on 14 October 2015. In January the following year, a number of affiliated shrines even used their precincts during the busy *hatsumōde* period—when many Japanese make their first New Year visit to a shrine—to collect signatures from parishioners and visitors in support the LDP proposal.[4] A number of shrines displayed posters promoting constitutional revision—

with Sakurai Yoshiko, the well-known nationalist, as poster girl—and had conveniently arranged tables nearby to solicit signatures in support of the revision.[5] Given that shrines are usually sites for communal festivals and rites of passage, not all parishioners were pleased to see the shrine precincts politicized in this way.[6]

THE PROPOSED REVISIONS TO ARTICLES 20 AND 89

In 2005 the LDP made public its proposed revisions to the postwar Constitution and issued a slightly revised version in 2012.[7] Revision of Article 9—the central pillar of the Peace Constitution—is one key goal of Abe and his supporters, but there are a number of other proposed revisions recommended in the LDP draft that are also a cause of serious concern for the leaders of a wide-range of religious groups. Particularly troubling for religious minorities are the proposed revisions of Articles 20 and 89, which in their current form clearly protect religious freedom and define religion-state separation. According to some critical observers discussed in this chapter, the proposed changes in these articles will lead to the erosion of individual religious rights and freedom of conscience, and will also have serious implications for the status and treatment of the controversial Yasukuni Shrine.

In its current form, Article 20 of the Constitution of Japan (1947) prohibits any state support, promotion, or coercion with respect to religious education or activities. The draft proposal by the LDP suggests an additional phrase of qualification to clause 3 in Article 20, which is also applied to Article 89 as follows:

> Article 20. Freedom of religion is guaranteed to all. The State shall not grant privileges to any religious organization (*Omitted*: *"No religious organization shall exercise any political authority"*).
>
> No person shall be compelled to take part in any religious act, celebration, rite or practice.
>
> The State, local governments and other public entities shall refrain from particular religious education and other religious activities. **However, this provision shall not apply to activities that do not exceed the scope of social rituals or customary practices.** [*tadashi, shakaiteki girei mata wa shūzokuteki kōi no han'i o koenai mono ni tsuite wa, kono kagiri de nai*].

> Article 89. No public money or other property shall be expended or appropriated for the use, benefit or maintenance of **religious activities conducted by** any institution or association, **except for cases set forth in the proviso of the third paragraph of Article 20.**[8]

The highlighted changes and terminology of particular significance here are "social rituals" (*shakaiteki girei*), "customary practices" (*shūzokuteki kōi*), and "this provision shall not apply to" (*kono kagiri de nai*). The new language added and applied to both articles would clearly allow for ritual activity to be redefined as "nonreligious" and reintroduced to public institutions. While Article 89 currently prohibits public funds being expended on or for religious institutions, in its revised form it would allow for public money to be used in support of activities redefined as social ritual or customary practices. The proposed revisions are based on the assumption that one can identify certain actions as "nonreligious," and that these should be outside the scope of the strict application of religion-state separation that was implemented during the Occupation period. It is important to recognize that these proposed revisions constitute an effort to "restore" the distinction between "religion" and "nonreligious" practices, which is clearly reminiscent of the framework and categories that were created to regulate religion and Shinto following the Meiji Restoration until 1945.

Ōishi Yoshio, Professor Emeritus of Constitutional Law at Kyoto University, outlined the validity of this restorationist approach to constitutional interpretation in his Nagoya Higher Court testimony on 7 October 1970, which provides the context for understanding the language eventually adopted in the LDP draft proposal some four decades later:

> I believe that the American Occupation, in causing the Japanese government of that day to develop the current Constitution, undoubtedly held the view that State Shinto belonged to the category of religion. I contend, however, that the Occupation view is only one among many. During the Occupation that view was legally binding. But now the Occupation is over. The authority to interpret the Constitution inheres in Japan's national sovereignty. No longer are we bound by the Occupation interpretation. *We have now returned to the interpretation that prevailed prior to the Occupation.*[9]

A brief review of how this earlier "interpretation" developed is in order before we look more closely at the critical response of some religious groups to the proposed revisions.

BACKGROUND TO PROPOSED REVISIONS

It is worth recalling that it was in response to pressure from the West that Meiji leaders included Article 28 on religious freedom in the 1889 Constitution: "Japanese subjects shall, within limits not prejudicial to the peace and order, and not antagonistic to their duties as subjects, enjoy freedom of religious belief." Shinto was then defined as "nonreligious" and a system of national rites came to be regarded as part of what constituted the "duties" of all imperial subjects. Shinto institutions were overseen and managed by the Bureau of Shrines (Jinja Kyoku), which was established in the Ministry of Home Affairs in 1900. Buddhist temples, Christian churches, and New Religions, on the other hand, were all under the administration of the Bureau of Religion (Shūkyō Kyoku). The emperor-centric values and "nonreligious" Shinto rites were expected to shape life and institutions in the "public sphere."

This understanding was diffused through public education, military training, and the adoption of various ritual practices in government offices.[10] The public school system became the primary vehicle for nurturing a range of ritual practices that were a part of nonreligious Shinto, including shrine visits, the special ritual care of the Imperial portrait (*goshi'nei*), and the reading of the Imperial Rescript on Education (*Kyōiku chokugo*), which became normative and customary practice in all public schools by the Taishō period (1912–1926). Some schools made shrine visits in connection with entrance ceremonies and many introduced field trips to famous national shrines, such as Ise Shrine and Yasukuni Shrine. The spread of these shrine-related rituals extended beyond public schools and also become central to military training exercises. By the mid-1930s, shrine-visiting groups were even formed in prefectural, city, town, and village offices to make pilgrimages to important shrines (Yamamoto and Imano 1973, 378). These rituals not only nurtured loyalty to emperor and nation, but also diffused the idea that these Shinto shrine-related social rituals were separate from those associated with religions (i.e., Buddhism, Christianity, and New Religions). According to Yanagawa and Abe (1983, 294), the restored "interpretation" referred to by Ōishi, which he claims is valid for Japanese in the post-Occupation period, is one that "makes a theoretical separation between traditional community religiosity and the religious beliefs of individual citizens, identifies the former with custom or national morality, and provides a rationale for its support by the state."

This particular understanding of Shinto as a "nonreligious" system of public morality and ritual behavior was seriously challenged in the early months of the Occupation. By early December 1945, Supreme Commander of the Allied Powers's (SCAP) Religions Division head, William Bunce, had hurriedly prepared a detailed memorandum on Shinto in consultation with Japanese scholars, which outlined why State Shinto was regarded as problematic. This document provided the foundation for what is known as the "Shinto Directive," issued on 15 December 1945, which disestablished State Shinto by ending government control of the shrines and the financial support that had been provided to some shrines. No shrines were destroyed, but the Occupation policies ended the public role of Shinto and reduced shrines to the status of voluntary organizations. As already elaborated in a previous chapter, the Directive also required that Shinto elements be removed from all public institutions.

As far as the Occupation authorities were concerned, the various ritual practices that had been categorized as "nonreligious" Shinto by the government were redefined as "religious," and policies were initiated to restrict public officials from supporting or engaging in these practices. Shinto institutions—those shrines that became a part of the NAS in 1946, as well as those independent religious corporations, including Yasukuni Shrine and Meiji Shrine—all survived the Occupation period by embracing a "religious" identity and suppressing their views that Shinto shrines should still have a "public" role and special status as carriers of authentic Japanese tradition. While the registration of shrines as religious corporations (shūkyō hōjin) was necessary for organizational survival, it did not actually transform the older conceptual framework that placed Shinto-related ritual practices in a category separate from that of religion.

The Occupation archives provide extensive evidence of disagreement between SCAP's Religions Division and the Japanese Government's Religious Affairs Office (Shūmuka) over how some ritual activities should be categorized, which reveals serious Japanese resistance to the redefinition of Shinto by the foreign authorities. The Religious Affairs Office staff were the bureaucratic carriers of the "doctrine of the nonreligious nature of shrines" (*jinja hishūkyōron*), which represented the government's position that had been forged over several decades. Since shrine rites were understood to be expressions of patriotism and nonreligious, participation by all Japanese could be required as a civic duty (Scheid 2012, 96). In the early days of the Occupation, a number of public officials in various prefectures continued to participate in Shinto-related rituals and made offerings to shrines as though nothing had changed. The government's Religious Affairs staff were called in to SCAP's Religions Division office to account for these "violations of the Shinto Directive" and reprimanded for failing to adequately educate public officials that "nonreligious" Shinto rituals were no longer officially recognized, and that a clear separation between the government and religion was to be strictly implemented.

Notwithstanding the efforts of the Occupation authorities to eliminate the notion of "nonreligious" Shinto and remove it from public institutions, there is considerable evidence that it survived into the postwar period and shaped the understanding of religion for the vast majority of Japanese. The foreign occupation may have "succeeded in divorcing Shinto from the state and in getting Shinto to identify itself as a religion," as Yanagawa and Abe (1983, 299) explain, but "the Occupation's highly Protestant conception of religion as a faith chosen and believed in by individuals failed to materialize in the new religiously incorporated Shinto."

"RELIGION" AND "CUSTOMARY PRACTICES" IN POSTWAR JAPAN

Survey research indicates that the tendency to distinguish "religion" from "nonreligious" customs or rituals has lingered in the consciousness of postwar generations in spite of the policies SCAP implemented during the Occupation. The NHK Survey of Japanese Religious Consciousness (1984) represents an important benchmark study for consideration of religion in the postwar environment. Some basic patterns discovered in this national survey still characterize religious belief and behavior today. The NHK (1984, 3, 20) survey found that only 33 percent of the sample claimed to have a personal faith of any kind. Of that number, 27 percent identified Buddhism as their faith, 3 percent indicated Shinto, and 2 percent Christianity. The editors explained that when Japanese think of the term "religion" or "faith" they tend to have an image drawn from Christianity, a religion that has a founder, specific teachings or doctrines, and requirements for church membership. When Japanese are asked, "What is your personal faith or religion?," the usual response is that they do not have one (*mushūkyō*) since their beliefs are not so clearly defined and they do not "belong" exclusively to one particular organization. Although most Japanese do not have an articulate faith, the NHK study concluded that they do have a religious consciousness (beliefs and values) and regularly participate in religious actions (household rituals, festivals, annual events, and rites of passage), which the editors designated as a "folk religion."[11]

The *Shūkyō nenkan*, a religion yearbook produced each year by the government's Agency of Cultural Affairs, reported over 100 million Shinto adherents at the time the NHK study published its results. Only 3 percent of the Japanese who claimed to have a personal faith identified "Shinto" as their religion, but over 50 percent of the population regularly participated in annual events and rites of passage at shrines and in household rituals related to the *kamidana*. This suggests that many Japanese still regard their participation in Shinto-related rituals and ceremonies as separate from those that belong in the "religion" category.

More recent survey research indicates that most Japanese claim to be "without religion" (*mushūkyō*) and less than 10 percent of the population claims that they "belong" to a religious organization of any kind (Ishii 2007, 142, 176). Organized religion, especially since the 1995 Aum Shinrikyō subway gas attack, is widely perceived in negative terms as something "gloomy" (*kurai*), "dangerous" (*abunai*), and "closed" (*heisateki*); in short, something to be avoided.[12] Nevertheless, it still remains common for Japanese to participate in annual events (*nenjū gyōji*) and rites of passage (*tsūka girei*) at shrines and temples over the course of the life cycle, but most do not regard their involvement in these events and rituals as "religious" even though they take place in institutions registered with the government as religious corporations. These are simply "customs" (*shūkan*) and individual participation is either voluntary or related to familial obligations. Given this widely held understanding, it would seem reasonable to conclude that the distinction between "religion" and "customary practices" embedded in the proposed revisions to Articles 20 and 89 is one probably shared by the majority of Japanese and unlikely to be perceived as problematic.

The language being used in some postwar Supreme Court decisions indicates that this conceptual framework also continues to shape the deliberation surrounding lawsuits related to Shinto rituals and alleged violations of religion-state separation. The Supreme Court decision in the Tsu City case provides one helpful illustration of what appears to be a taken-for-granted distinction between "religious" and "nonreligious" observances, which has found its way into the proposed revisions. This case began in 1965 as a result of a lawsuit launched by a local citizen against the city for violating the constitutional separation of religion and state by using public funds to pay a Shinto priest to conduct a grounds purification ceremony (*jichinsai*) prior to the construction of a municipal gym. Ravitch (2013, 510–511), a legal scholar, refers to this as the "Shinto as culture" case and summarizes the court proceedings as follows:

> The trial court held that the ceremony was a folk custom and thus not religion for constitutional purposes. The appellate court reversed, holding that the government support for the ceremony violated the principle of separation of church and state. The Supreme Court reversed. It held that the State must be religiously neutral, but not all state connection with religion is prohibited.

The Supreme Court's final decision in 1977 indicated that if the purpose of the activity (*kōi no mokuteki*) was not religious, and the action did not aim to support or promote one particular religion (*shūkyō ni taisuru enjo, jochō, sokushin*) or involve coercion or interference (*appaku, kanshō nado*) in the free practice of another religion, then the activity would not constitute a violation of Article 20.[13] The language and distinction used in the proposed revisions of the articles under consideration is consistent with the distinctions and reasoning of the Supreme Court in this case.[14]

While surveys of religious consciousness of contemporary Japanese indicates that the vast majority of Japanese tend to be comfortable with the notion of "customary rites" or "social rituals" for much of the activity that occurs at sacred sites in the home, shrines, and temples, it is likely that there would still be serious opposition if such a distinction were employed to legitimize "official visits" and government support for the controversial Yasukuni Shrine. Nevertheless, there are many Japanese who would likely support a more relaxed application of religion-state separation that might allow Shinto rites for important national celebrations, including the *Daijōsai*, a ritual related to enthronement of a new emperor, which is now the target of lawsuits for alleged violation of religion-state separation.

Public support for a more relaxed application of religion-state separation has also been generated by what many regarded as an unnatural and unnecessarily strict enforcement of separation in the wake of the 11 March 2011 "triple disaster" in northeastern Japan, which left some 15,894 confirmed dead. The loss of life was so great that it overwhelmed the capacity of crematoriums and religious sites normally used for the care of the dead, and it became necessary to use mass graves. Many bodies were gathered and placed temporarily in a number of public facilities until disposal became possible. These were public facilities where "religious" services could not be conducted since it would be considered a violation of the constitutional separation of religion and state. Shortly after the disaster, conflicts emerged in some communities when some religious practitioners sought to conduct services for the dead in public facilities. While some local governments in Miyagi, Fukushima, and Iwate Prefectures cooperated with religious leaders and allowed these services, this was not the case in some municipalities due to the concern over violating religion-state separation. The Sendai City officials, for example, initially adopted a very strict "separationist" policy and chose not to allow religious services to be conducted by any religious group in public facilities.[15] Even volunteers who offered to chant sutras on behalf of the dead were not allowed to do so in public facilities, even though there was no financial payment by the government involved for the religious services (Momochi 2013, 133–134).

This application of a strict interpretation of religion-state separation in some public facilities generated considerable public debate about the level of cooperation that should be allowed between the government (national, prefectural, and local) and religious actors and organizations in times of disaster. The issue was not just whether religious rituals could be conducted in public facilities, but also whether it was appropriate for local governments to use public funds to support religious facilities that were being used as temporary shelters. For many Japanese, an interpretation of the law that prevents Buddhist priests and other religious actors from entering public facilities to perform memorial services and offer prayers for the victims is an excessive application of the separation principle and one that has prevented the free practice of religion guaranteed by Article 20. These debates and conflicts surrounding the 2011 disaster provide additional evidence for why a variety of religious bodies and the general public might support a more relaxed interpretation of religion-state separation provided by the LDP proposal due to issues unrelated to the usual ones surrounding Shinto rites and Yasukuni Shrine.[16]

RELIGIOUS OPPOSITION TO CONSTITUTIONAL REVISION IN JAPAN

While the language used in the proposed revisions reflects the long-held views and religious sensibilities of many Japanese in contemporary Japan, why is it that some religious bodies, particularly religious minorities, are so concerned about the potential changes to Articles 20 and 89? A number of religious organizations have expressed opposition to the LDP proposal to revise the Constitution, including the Federation of New Religious Organizations of Japan (Shin Nihon Shūkyō Dantai Rengōkai), the Roman Catholic Church, various Protestant denominations, and some priests of the Jōdo Shinshū.

The Federation of New Religious Organizations in Japan, widely referred to as Shinshūren, was established in 1951 as an association of New Religions founded after 1868, which shared a common concern to gain some legitimacy and public recognition and to protect the free practice of religion in postwar Japan. The organization began publishing its own newspaper in 1952, *Shin shūkyō shinbun*, which has covered issues of particular concern to religious minorities. Over the course of several decades, a number of New Religions withdrew from the Federation—Seichō no Ie

in 1957, Sekai Kyūseikyō in 1969, and Bussho Gonenkai Kyōdan in 1972—
due in part to the Federation's public opposition to the renationalization
of Yasukuni Shrine and constitutional revision. Currently, there are some
thirty-five New Religions that are a part of the Federation and over the
past decade the heads of Risshō Kōsei Kai, Gedatsukai, Daiwa Kyōdan, and
Sūkyō Mahikari have taken turns in providing leadership.[17]

In 2004, the Federation inaugurated a Study Group on the Constitution (Kenpō Kenkyūkai), which has continued to address concerns over
the proposals for revision being promoted by Prime Minister Abe and his
supporters in the Diet. At one meeting focused on a review of the LDP's
2012 draft proposal (*Nihon koku kenpō kaisei sōan*), particular concerns
were raised over the introduction of the phrases "social rituals" and "customary practices" to Article 20, which would allow for the national and
local governments to participate in and support some religious rituals
that were recategorized and understood to be merely traditional practices
without religious significance. The Study Group raised the question of who
might be qualified to make this critical decision on behalf of the Japanese
people.

The level of concern raised by the LDP proposal prompted the Federation to prepare a pamphlet to explain the importance of religious freedom
as a fundamental human right, which it has sought to protect throughout
the postwar period. This short publication, *Shinkyō no jiyū to wa nani ka*
(Shinshūren 2016), was meant to provide an accessible guide to these
critical issues and inform the Federation's member communities about
what is at stake in the LDP's proposal. Using a Q & A format, this four-page
pamphlet briefly addresses key issues related to public debates surrounding
religious freedom and the problematic efforts of the government to "revise
the Constitution by reinterpretation" (*kaishaku kaiken*) rather than by
following the proper legal procedures to amend the articles. Of particular
concern was the fact that on 19 September 2015, Abe's government pushed
through security related bills (*anzen hoshō kanren hōan*), which reinterpreted Article 9 to allow for collective self-defense and the deployment of
Japan's Self-Defense Forces overseas to engage in foreign conflicts even in
situations where Japan was not under attack. These bills were enacted in
spite of widespread opposition and days of public protests in front of the

Diet building. An opinion poll conducted by *Asahi shinbun* on 12–13 September revealed that a majority of respondents (54 percent) were opposed to the new security legislation, while only 29 percent supported the government's proposal. According to the pamphlet's afterword, this change of the Constitution by "reinterpretation" set a precedent that could also be used by the government to restrict religious freedom. The pamphlet was prepared with this sense of "impending crisis" (*kikikan*).

The short document addresses the nature of religious freedom in contemporary Japan and explains that it is now a taken-for-granted reality (*atarimae*) due to the protection provided by Article 20 of the Constitution, but notes that before and during the war in Japan and elsewhere people often did not have the freedom to embrace and express their religious faith (Question 3; Shinshūren 2016, 1). It also stresses the importance of religion-state separation for the preservation of religious freedom since propagation of a particular religion by the government would likely lead to an encroachment on religious freedom since it would become difficult for individuals to oppose or resist a religion promoted and backed by the power of the state (Question 7). Again, the religion-state separation guaranteed by Article 20 is seen as providing protection of individual religious rights against coercion by the state (Shinshūren 2016, 3). Overall, the pamphlet indicates a concern over the shifting of too much power from individual decision-making to control by the state.

The Catholic Bishops' Conference has similarly raised concerns about the LDP proposal and published a more detailed and critical response. Given the impact of legalization of the flag and anthem in 1999 and the revision of the Fundamental Education Law in 2006, the Catholic Bishops' are particularly concerned about the plans of the LDP to revise the postwar Constitution's articles pertaining to religion, which they argue will further erode individual rights and extend coercion into other areas. At the 2006 Catholic Bishops' Meeting, a question came up for discussion that brought all of these concerns into focus: "What will we do if our children are forced to participate in shrine visits (*jinja sanpai*) again?" In light of this question and the potential danger to religious freedom, the bishops felt compelled to call a special meeting to address these issues. In 2007 they published the results of their study and deliberation as *Shinkyō no jiyū to seikyō bunri*.[18]

In addition to the sense of crisis generated by the implementation of patriotic education, this volume indicates that their critical engagement today is also based on the wartime experience of the Church and the Bishops' self-reflections over compromises made with the government during that period. Bishop Okada explains that during the postwar period, the Catholic Church has issued a number of statements regarding war responsibility and failure to fulfill its prophetic role during the war (Kattoriku Chūō Kyōgikai 2002). In a statement issued in 2005, which followed the LDP's public announcement of its proposal to revise the Constitution, the Church acknowledged its failure to be prophetic in the wartime period and expressed a determination to remain vigilant in facing the current challenge:

> Peace Message After 60 Years From the End of War World II
> The Road To Peace Based On Nonviolence
> Now Is The Time To Be Prophetic
>
> Before and during the War, and under pressure from the military government, the leaders of the Catholic Church unwillingly admitted visits to Yasukuni and other shrines as 'rites.' We cannot say that this is ancient history and forget about it. Right now we are facing the same crisis again. In the debate about revision of the constitution there are some advocating a relaxation of the principle of separation of Religion and Politics and State trying to get visits to Yasukuni Shrine as 'rites.' The separation of Religion and Politics in Japan (Article 20, number 3 of the Constitution) is a principle born from reflection on the fact that the State, with the emperor at the center, used religion to promote its war effort. This is why protection of the principle of separation of Religion and Politics is for us Japanese an expression of our resolve not to repeat the same mistake.

This perspective is elaborated in some detail in the 2007 volume. The Church has confessed its war responsibility and has apologized to its Asian neighbors for the suffering it caused and asked for their forgiveness (Kattoriku Chūō Kyōgikai 2007, 70–71). According to Bishop Okada, the church must reflect on its history and oppose the LDP efforts to revise the Constitution. Particularly problematic are "official visits" by political leaders to Yasukuni Shrine—an institution that beautifies and justifies the war through its war museum (Yūshūkan)—which would send a message that is in fundamental conflict with the Church's postwar confessions and apologies.

In this book, the former Bishop of Saitama, Tani Daiji, provides a critical analysis of the Draft Constitution proposed by the LDP and its possible implications for students and employees of public institutions. He prefaces his criticism by acknowledging the benefits received from the 1947 Constitution. He states that it was the first time in Japanese history that religious freedom had been truly secured for people of various faiths. Under the Meiji Constitution, there was a conditional or limited religious freedom (*jōken tsuki no shinkyō no jiyū*). State Shinto was defined as "nonreligious" and shrine visits were defined as a civic duty, one that was required even of the colonized peoples in Korea, Manchuria, and Taiwan (Tani 2007, 20). Article 20 of the 1947 Constitution eliminated this kind of coercion.

In its current form, Article 20 prohibits any state support, promotion, or coercion with respect to religious education or activities. As noted earlier, the draft proposal by the LDP, in both the 2005 and 2012 versions, includes an additional phrase of qualification (Clause 3), which prohibits any state support for religious activities that transcend "social ritual or customary practices" (*shakaiteki girei mata wa shūzokuteki kōi*). Tani argues that this will clearly weaken the separation of the state from religion. The language used here would allow for some ritual activity in educational institutions redefined as a "social custom," which approximates the strategy used by the government in relation to shrine visits by teachers and students in the period of State Shinto until 1945. By reintroducing the notion of "nonreligious Shinto," the LDP proposal is setting up a situation in which "coercion"—rather than freedom of conscience—could once again dominate public institutions (Tani 2007, 34).

Although Article 20 in its current form states that individuals cannot be forced to participate in any religious acts or rituals, by redefining these activities as "social rituals" or "national rituals" (*kokuminteki girei*), it would no longer be unconstitutional to require participation. Bishop Tani is concerned that this redefinition of religious rites would provide a legal basis to again require children and teachers at schools, as well as employees at government institutions (*kōmuin*), to participate in shrine visits as a part of their official duties. In short, he fears that shrine rites could eventually be treated as the official ceremonies at school events that now require standing before the Hinomaru flag and singing the national anthem, and students could be forced to participate regardless of conscience or personal religious commitment.

In addition to the problem of coercion for religious minorities, Bishop Tani also argues that there is an additional problematic aim of this revised article, that is, to legitimize and legalize (*gōhōka*) official visits to Yasukuni Shrine recategorized as a "social ritual" (*shakaiteki girei*) or "national ritual" (*kokuminteki girei*). This he regards as a strategy designed to eliminate lawsuits and legal conflict over visits to the shrine by the prime minister and other government officials (Tani 2007, 20–25). This has been a recurring problem since Prime Minister Nakasone's controversial visit in 1985, Prime Minister Koizumi's multiple visits from 2001 to 2006, and Prime Minister Abe's visit in 2013. Similarly, it would make it legal to use public funds for offerings (*tamagushiryō* and *masakaki*, for example) presented to Yasukuni Shrine. In light of these concerns, Tani concludes that the protection of Articles 20 and 89 in their current form is absolutely necessary to preserve religious freedom and avoid coercion in public life.

It is not just religious minorities concerned about the potential fallout of the proposed revisions to these articles. Even mainstream Buddhist denominations have leaders who have offered similar criticisms of the language used in the LDP proposal. Two priests of the Jōdo Shinshū have been among the most outspoken critics of the revisionist agenda. Sugahara Ryūken (2005, 11), for example, a priest in the Honganjiha and head of the Shin-Buddhist Bereaved Families Association (Shinshū Izokukai), disputes the notion that so-called "customary practices" can be regarded as "nonreligious"; in fact, he argues that they are a manifestation of the most "powerful religion," one that is taken for granted as a part of everyday life. Buddhist scholar and anti-Yasukuni activist Hishiki Masaharu (2007, 62) also points out that the educational goal of nurturing "tolerance" in students will inevitably be subverted if things designated as "customs" are no longer subject to the constitutional principle of separation. It will create conditions that will allow "intolerance" to masquerade as "tolerance," but coercion will become the new reality. If the revised law is ever approved, he explains, it will likely be used to identify such Shinto activities as grounds purification ceremonies, as well as Yasukuni Shrine visits, as "customs" and outside of the application of the separation principle. Hishiki argues that if the ambiguous notion of religion (*bakuzen toshita shūkyō*) embedded in this proposed revision is accepted, it will allow the state to have the power to control the people, and the rights normally accorded to individuals—the right not to participate—will disappear (Hishiki 2007, 64–65).

It is interesting to note that the concerns recently raised by religious minorities regarding the proposed revisions and the possible reintroduction of shrine visits to public schools, were actually anticipated in two memorandums prepared by William Woodard, a staff member of SCAP's Religions Division. These were written out of concern over Prime Minister Yoshida's plans to visit Yasukuni Shrine on 18 October 1951, just months before the end of the Occupation. Woodard had advocated for the creation of a neutral war memorial site to serve as an alternative to Yasukuni Shrine and urged Prime Minister Yoshida not to attend the shrine's Fall Festival. He feared that the resumption of "official visits" would be seen as special treatment for Shinto and encourage rightwing elements "to work for the restoration of the prewar status of Yasukuni" and "set the pattern for making local military shrines the official medium for the commemoration of war dead." He argued that this would inevitably lead to government funding of state-protecting shrines (*gokoku jinja*), encourage forced shrine visits, and "tend to place Buddhism, Christianity and other religions on a plain below Shrine Shinto in the eyes of the people."[19]

In an undated draft Memorandum on "Commemoration of War Dead" written about the same time, Woodard raised concerns about the implications for public schools if Yasukuni Shrine were to be recognized again as an institution of the State:

> *The shrine must be kept as a private (Shinto) religious institution* (emphasis in the original). If Yasukuni Shrine is given a semi-official status, if it is allowed to become the accepted official medium for the nation as a whole to commemorate the war dead, the re-establishment of Shrine Shinto as State Shinto in some form may be assumed. This does not mean necessarily that State Shinto with all its ceremonies related to emperor worship will be revived, but the possibility of revival becomes much greater. All that is required as a first step is for the government to treat Yasukuni Shrine as if it were in a class

apart from other religious institutions. *When the pattern has been established official interpretation will declare the shrine to be nonreligious and from then on compulsory attendance by school children is required. Every effort should be put forth to prevent this. Therefore attention must be given now to the establishment of acceptable postwar pattern for commemoration of the war dead.*[20]

As we already noted in a previous chapter, a number of religious and political leaders (Umehara Takeshi and Sono Ayako, and Prime Minister Hatoyama) have advocated for the creation of a religiously "neutral" war memorial site as an alternative to Yasukuni Shrine along the lines of what Woodard and the Religions Division had recommended. The proposal for building an alternative memorial site has also been critically engaged by Japanese scholars in a symposium and subsequent publication,[21] but over half a century later the status quo remains unchanged and conflicts related to this site are unresolved.

In my view, there is sufficient evidence to support the interpretation that the LDP proposal is reintroducing the notion of "nonreligious Shinto," which shaped public policy prior to the Occupation. About this earlier version, historian Sarah Thal (2002, 112) explains that:

> By removing Shinto from the realm of religion, the accumulated rhetoric of decades succeeded in establishing Shinto, in its nineteenth-century form, not as a religious belief but as the fundamental expression of Japanese identity. As advocates insisted, in language that pervaded public discourse until at least 1945, the Way both of the kami and of the Japanese people as a whole, was natural and timeless, public and civic minded, civilized and therefore compatible with the modern, indeed the postmodern, age.... *Using the concept of religion as a political tool, advocates of Shinto confounded the boundaries of church and state, religion and secularism, to shape the very idea of Japaneseness itself.*

History appears to be repeating itself; this view has clearly been revived and embedded in the LDP's proposed revisions to Articles 20 and 89. Religious minorities and some on the political left regard these possible revisions as a threat to individual rights and religious freedom that will likely return Japan to a pre-Occupation state characterized by a "politics of inclusion," which forced all citizens to participate in ritual activity regardless of personal beliefs and commitments.

Legal scholars have identified a significant shift in orientation between the 1947 Constitution and the LDP draft for a new Constitution, which would give priority to the state and public order over the protection of individual rights. "Rather than limiting the power of government," Repeta and Jones (2015, 322) argue, "the LDP would use the constitution to limit the rights of the people." This emphasis clearly echoes the orientation of the Meiji Constitution, in which the language of "duties as subjects" qualified and limited the freedoms of individuals. While the 1947 Constitution imposed "limitations on government power," Repeta (2013, 5) explains, the LDP version would "impose duties on the people."[22] In Article 3 of Chapter 1 of the LDP proposal, which defines the place of the emperor, for example, a clause has been inserted, specifying: "the people must respect the national flag and anthem." This addition represents a reinforcement of the revised Fundamental Education Law (2006) and an expansion of the "duties" applied to public school teachers in Tokyo and Osaka to all Japanese citizens. This is a curious addition for the architects of this proposal to make given their alleged devotion to the emperor and the fact that in 2004 Emperor Akihito himself indicated that human actions taken with reference to the flag and anthem should be "voluntary." It is impossible to predict whether or not new civil-religious duties, such as shrine visits, would actually be added to the list of other duties already spelled out in the LDP proposal, but the fears of religious minorities seem justified given other recent developments.

CHALLENGES FACING ABE'S REVISIONIST AGENDA

The restoration movement has gathered considerable momentum in post-disaster Japan, but Prime Minister Abe's goal of revising the constitution still faces some serious hurdles. The concerns religious leaders raised with regard to Article 20 and 89, however, are unlikely to attract the attention or support of the general public in Japan. Given the climate of public opinion towards organized religion, it is hard to imagine much enthusiasm—even awareness—or public support for efforts aimed at preventing the revision of these articles pertaining to religion. Since the 1995 Aum Shinrikyō subway gas attack, the general public has been more concerned to "protect society from religion" than to "protect religious groups" from state regulation. It is fortunate for religious minorities that these articles are a part of a package deal, which includes proposed revisions to Article 9, which does rouse the interest of vast numbers of Japanese and has mobilized considerable activism against constitutional revision.

In 2004, the Article 9 Association was established by a number of well-known public figures—scholars, authors, public intellectuals, and social activists—to organize citizens to work for the preservation of the Peace Constitution. It quickly expanded across the country as consciousness-raising citizens' movements opposed to the revision of Article 9. By 2008 there were some 6,000 groups registered across the country. Their membership is concerned to recover and preserve the original meaning of the Peace Constitution, that is, prior to the creative "reinterpretation" of Article 9 pushed through by Prime Minister Abe's cabinet in 2015, which expanded the mandate of Japan's military beyond "self-defense" and made it permissible for the government to deploy forces in "collective defense" activities in cooperation with allies in foreign conflicts overseas. According to a survey conducted by the *Nihon keizai shinbun* in April 2015, only 29 percent of those polled actually supported the cabinet's reinterpretation of Article 9, while 52 percent were opposed.[23] The Article 9 Association has continued to expand in response to the new policy advanced by the Abe government and today has some 7,500 groups nationwide.[24]

Public opinion in support of revision is clearly in decline. It is unclear whether this is due to the performance of LDP politicians, the consciousness-raising efforts of the citizens' movements opposed to the revision of Article 9, or growing fears that Japan could very likely be pulled into military conflicts due to the actions of its major ally, the United States. NHK, Japan's national broadcasting organization, has been conducting surveys on constitutional revision for decades and tracking Japanese attitudes on this issue, which has meant following a moving target.[25] In 1974, 31 percent of respondents were in favor of revision and that increased to a peak of 58 percent in 2002. The number of pro-revisionists has been declining under Abe's administration the past several years. It decreased to 43 percent in 2017, and in the most recent survey conducted following the upper house elections (August 2019), it had declined to 28 percent in favor of revision.[26] Respondents were also asked what the current government should focus its attention on going forward, and the replies indicate that Prime Minister Abe's pet project is hardly a pressing concern for the general public; it was ranked last in the list of priorities as follows: social security (26 percent), diplomacy, national security, and economic policy (18 percent), fiscal reform (12 percent), rectification of the disparity gap (9 percent), and finally constitutional revision (7 percent).

Abe and his ruling coalition were able to retain control of the Upper House in the July 2019 election, but were four seats short of the required two-thirds majority needed to push ahead with constitutional revision. This means that Abe will need to recruit additional support from parties outside the coalition, a task that is bound to be difficult. Even within the coalition, however, his work is cut out for him. Yamaguchi Natsuo, leader the LDP coalition partner Kōmeitō, has recently indicated that he is unconvinced constitutional revision is actually necessary. Furthermore, a survey conducted between May and the July election found that only 17 percent of the Kōmeitō Party's candidates indicated their support for the proposed changes to the Constitution.[27] It should also be noted that voter turnout for the July elections was only 48.8 percent, so over half of the eligible voters lacked the motivation to even cast a vote. With such a disillusioned electorate, it is hard to take seriously the prime minister's claim that he has the country's support to move ahead with his agenda. "Despite his electoral victory," as Stephen Nagy recently observed, "the result is not an overwhelming mandate for transformative change. Voters remain very skeptical of revising the Constitution."[28] Even if Abe is able to push his proposal through the Diet—which requires that it pass both houses by a two-thirds majority—it will face the major hurdle of gaining majority support among the Japanese electorate in a national referendum. Popular opinion matters and the survey results cited above indicate that the pro-revisionist camp will need to substantially expand its base of support in order to achieve its goal.

THE GAP BETWEEN NEONATIONALISTS AND THE IMPERIAL HOUSEHOLD

Another important issue related to the debate is where the emperor and Imperial Household stand with regard to the revisionist agenda. As we have documented earlier in this study, the neonationalist coalition is united in its embrace of the emperor as the center of Japanese identity and has pledged to nurture support for the Imperial Household and enhance its place in contemporary Japanese life. Although the emperor constitutes the *raison d'être* of the entire "restoration" enterprise, it has become increasingly clear that the coalition has been advancing a political agenda that is at odds with the values actually embraced by the emperor and the Imperial Household. As we have seen, both Emperors Hirohito and Akihito avoided personal visits to Yasukuni Shrine after it became known that class-A war criminals had been enshrined there. This stance clearly undermines the coalition's aim of restoring "official visits" and government support for the shrine. Emperor Akihito, likewise, put a damper on the promotion of patriotic education after the national flag and anthem legislation was passed by the Diet in 1999. In response to the Tokyo Metropolitan School Board of Education's order in 2003 that required teachers to lead students in singing the anthem or face disciplinary action—a policy the authoritarian Governor Ishihara was determined to strictly enforce—Emperor Akihito expressed his desire that it be a "voluntary" activity.

What about proposals to revise the Peace Constitution? Here, again, the ironic and inconvenient truth is that the views and sympathies expressed by the emperor and other members of the Imperial Household reveal strong support for the current Constitution. At a press conference on his eightieth birthday (23 December 2013), Emperor Akihito spoke with great appreciation for the role of democratic reforms and the new Constitution that accompanied the foreign occupation:

> After the war, Japan was occupied by the allied forces, and based on peace and democracy as values to be upheld, established the Constitution of Japan, undertook various reforms and *built the foundation of Japan that we know today*. I have profound gratitude for the efforts made by the Japanese people at the time who helped reconstruct and improve the country devastated by the war. I also feel that we must not forget the help extended to us in those days by Americans with an understanding of Japan and Japanese culture.[29]

The views expressed by the emperor here are in sharp contrast with those held by Prime Minister Abe and his coalition of supporters.[30] For those in the revisionist camp, the postwar Constitution is an embarrassment and humiliation, a hastily prepared document that a defeated nation was forced to accept. In their view, furthermore, it was the sacrifice of those enshrined in Yasukuni—and not the Constitution imposed during the Occupation—that laid the foundation for Japan's postwar peace and prosperity. This "foundation" is referred to in Yasukuni publications as the cornerstone (*ishizue*), which is a claim that has been repeated by prime ministers and other politicians to explain their official visits to the shrine.[31] This "cornerstone theory" is based largely on emotion rather than historical reality, as John Breen (2008, 158) explains:

> However bravely and selflessly these men sacrificed their lives, it was Japan's defeat by the Allies, the postwar dismantling of Japanese militarism, the implementation of democratic reforms and the restructuring of government under the Occupation, not to mention the hard work of the Japanese people that laid the foundations for postwar prosperity. The consummation of these several processes was none other than the imposition by the Occupation of the postwar Constitution, with its provision for popular sovereignty and pacifism.

Other statements and actions by the emperor provide additional evidence of a deepening gap between the current political leadership not only over the Constitution, but also on how to assess Japan's military past and the country's relationships with those neighbors who were once a part of the Japanese empire. It is worth recalling how incensed rightwing politicians were after Chief Cabinet Secretary Kōno Yōhei (1993) made an apology regarding the suffering of the "comfort women," and Prime Ministers Murayama and Hosokawa (1995) apologized for the pain and suffering caused by Japan's military aggression and colonial rule. It is notable that Emperor Akihito's public recognition and expression of remorse for the suffering inflicted by Japan actually preceded these statements by several years, first in his remarks to South Korean President Roh Tae Woo during his visit to Japan in 1990, and then again two years later on his visit to China. In short, the emperor's "peace diplomacy" set the tone for the brief conciliatory period in Japanese politics of the early-to-mid-1990s.

As the rightward shift in Japanese politics has accelerated in the post-disaster decades, members of the Imperial Household have continued to stress the need for remembering this past, which provides the context for understanding their high regard for the Peace Constitution. The emperor's New Year's message in January 2015 offered the following reflections:

> This year marks the 70th anniversary of the end of World War II, which cost many people their lives. Those who died on the battlefields, those who died in the atomic bombings in Hiroshima and Nagasaki, those who died in the air raids on Tokyo and other cities—so many people lost their lives in this war. I think it is most important for us to take this opportunity to study and learn from the history of this war, starting with the Manchurian Incident of 1931, as we consider the future direction of our country.[32]

Remembering the wartime past and promoting peace have been central to the Imperial Household throughout the Heisei era. In her message to the nation on the occasion of her eighty-third birthday in 2017, for example, Empress Michiko spoke warmly about the Nobel Peace Prize being awarded to the International Campaign to Abolish Nuclear Weapons, an initiative completely avoided and ignored by the Abe government.[33] Her words were widely interpreted as an expression of support for the Peace Constitution and in fundamental tension with the political agenda of Prime Minister Abe.[34]

What should we expect from the new emperor in the Reiwa era? At a press conference on the occasion of his fifty-fourth birthday in February 2014, Crown Prince Naruhito already showed his true colors and indicated that he shared his father Emperor Akihito's deep appreciation and respect for the Peace Constitution, stating that "today's Japan was built with the Japanese Constitution as the cornerstone, and our country is now enjoying peace and prosperity" (*Mainichi shinbun* 23 February 2014). Since his enthronement, Emperor Naruhito's statements have only reinforced this position. At a memorial service on 15 August 2019, he again expressed deep remorse for Japan's wartime past and expressed his hope and prayer for world peace.

It is not surprising that conservative rightwing observers have expressed serious dissatisfaction with members of the Imperial Household and postwar emperors for many of their statements and avoidance of Yasukuni Shrine since the late 1970s. As Shillony (2008, 150–151) has observed, Emperor Hirohito stopped visiting Yasukuni Shrine after learning that class-A war criminals had been enshrined in 1978.[35] Emperor Akihito also steered clear of Yasukuni Shrine throughout the Heisei period. The avoidance of Yasukuni by the recent emperors appears to be particularly troubling for some nationalists. The former outspoken governor of Tokyo, Ishihara Shintarō, for example, after his return to the Diet as a leader of the Japan Restoration Party, questioned Prime Minister Abe on 12 February 2013 about his position on Yasukuni and whether he planned to make an official visit to the shrine that year. In the Q & A session he also urged the prime minister to ask the emperor to resume visits to Yasukuni Shrine. Although he did not respond directly to this proposal, the Prime Minister did express his view that visits to Yasukuni were legitimate and cited the work of a foreign Catholic scholar to support his position.

The statements and peace diplomacy of the Heisei Emperor and Empress ever since have clearly exasperated conservative commentators who have despaired and stated that "a nationalism centered on the Imperial Household is no longer possible" and expressed a need to formulate a "nationalism without the emperor" (*Tennō nuki no nashonarizumu*) (Ōtsuka and Fukuda 1999, 140).[36] Yagi Hidetsugu, a conservative law professor at Reitaku University and a person who is sometimes referred to as the "brain" behind Prime Minister Abe, has raised critical concerns about statements made by the Heisei Emperor and Empress, which he claims "can only be interpreted by the people as expressions of concern or anxiety over the Abe Cabinet's push to revise the Constitution."[37]

The expressions of support for the Peace Constitution by members of the Imperial Household are well documented, but until recently there have been no direct statements or references to Articles 20 and 89, which have been the focus of our concern in this chapter. On 25 August 2018, however, Prince Akishino, the younger brother of Emperor Naruhito, made a rather unexpected comment to the Imperial Household Agency that raised concerns about religion-state separation and expressed his view that public funds should not be used to cover the costs of the *Daijōsai* ritual, a Shinto ceremony scheduled for November 2019 as a part of the enthronement ceremonies for Emperor Naruhito.[38] Needless to say, this was an "unwelcome" comment as far as the current government is concerned, since it has already indicated it will follow the 1990 precedent and use public funds again for the upcoming ritual. In early December 2018, less than four months after

Prince Akishino made his remarks, a lawsuit was filed with Tokyo District Court against the government by 241 plaintiffs, including many Christians and Buddhists, in an effort to prevent public funds from being used again for this Shinto ceremony. While the Tokyo High Court has already dismissed the case, it remains a problem that a member of the Imperial Household holds an interpretation of the Constitution that is more in line with these religious groups. It is ironic that the views and values expressed by the Imperial Household line up with moderate-to-liberal forces in contemporary Japan, while the neonationalist coalition—united in their claim of loyalty and devotion to the emperor—find themselves at odds with the very source of their identity. Sooner or later, this divide will have to be addressed.

CONCLUSION

Takahashi Tetsuya (2008, 107), a professor at the University of Tokyo and one of the most ardent critics of the government, has argued that the neonationalist initiatives we have reviewed here represent an attempt to restore the "triadic system"—military, Yasukuni Shrine, and patriotic education—that characterized the Meiji State. "Sixty years after the end of the Second World War," Takahashi writes, "a twenty-first-century Japanese government is seeking to reconstitute this system, albeit in a new form."[39] Even if the Abe government is unsuccessful in its plan for constitutional revision, it must be acknowledged that the neonationalist coalition has already made great headway toward achieving its restorationist goals by passing legislation and implementing new government policies regulating public life and institutions. "Revision of administrative law," as Helen Hardacre (2011, 201) has astutely observed, can be "a shortcut to constitutional revision."

There is clearly a clash between the values of global civil society, which give priority to individual rights and freedoms, and those values embraced by the religio-political coalition supporting the LDP proposal, which regard the rights of the individual to be secondary and subservient to the needs of the nation or group. Many secularists and religious minorities remain unconvinced that the restorationist vision initially promoted by the NAS and Shinseiren is either "nonreligious" or "essential" for their own identity as Japanese. If the proposed revisions are passed, the extent to which individual citizens enjoy positive religious freedom (to practice their own faith) may not change dramatically, but negative religious freedom—i.e., the freedom to avoid participation in some ritual practices—will clearly be diminished.

Notes

Introduction

1. This broader pattern across various spheres of Japanese society has been analyzed in some detail by Nakano (2015a; 2016) and Tsukada (2017).

2. The genealogy and historical development of the term "religion" (*shūkyō*) is a complicated one. For detailed treatment of how the term has been used and adapted in the Japanese context, see Isomae (2003; 2014), Thal (2002), Josephson (2012), and Krämer (2013). For critical debate on the problems associated with the use of this term in the Japanese context, see Fitzgerald (2003) and Reader (2005; 2016). The fact remains that the term has been used extensively in various ways and is unlikely to disappear. We must find a way to make sense of the multiple meanings and uses of the term.

3. Educational institutions, medical facilities, social welfare institutions, and some nonprofit organizations are also included in this category of *kōeki hōjin*. One of the benefits accorded religious groups registered with the government is permission to engage in various business enterprises, which are subject to a lower tax rate than secular businesses. The assumption here is that their activities benefit the larger society in some way. Serious questions have been raised about this assumption in the wake of the Aum-related violence in the 1990s, given the fact that Aum had been recognized as a *shūkyō hōjin* by the government and its lucrative computer business helped to finance research and the building of facilities for sarin gas production.

4. Shimazono (2001, 88–137) provides a rather detailed treatment of religion and nationalism in the postwar period. I have only highlighted a few key points and changed the order of his discussion here.

5. Although Japan is not the focus of Juergensmeyer's study, he does mention Kōfuku no Kagaku, a New Religion founded by Ōkawa Ryūhō in 1986, as a recent expression of religious nationalism due to its claim that "the Japanese are the new chosen people" (Juergensmeyer 1993, 146).

6. For detailed studies of *Nihonjinron* as an expression of "cultural nationalism," see the studies by Yoshino (1992) and Befu (1992; 2001). While Davis (1992) elaborates the significance of *Nihonjinron* as a new form of "civil religion," Prohl (2004) examines how it is manifested in some of Japan's New Religions.

7. As may be seen in the following table, Demerath's (2007, 16) typology is based on a coaxial framework: one axis has to do with whether the process is an internal (domestic) or external (foreign) one, and the second axis is based on whether the process is non-directed

or directed. A combination of these two axes leads to four types of secularization:

	Internal	External
Non-directed	Emergent	Diffuse
Directed	Coercive	Imperialist

8. The role of human actors in the process of secularization has been emphasized by Fenn (1978) and also appears in the more recent work of Charles Taylor (2007) in his analysis of secularity in Europe as a "project of elites." Helen Hardacre (2011) has extended this perspective to the Japanese context in her analysis of the Meiji Restoration and the formation of modern Japan, which also regards secularization as a top-down process orchestrated and legislated by elites.

9. On this point see Murakami Shigeyoshi (1982, 46–49). For a more focused treatment of the place of Shinto and Yasukuni Shrine in textbooks for elementary school children during this period, see Irie Yōko (2001, 73–78).

10. For a helpful review of Japanese scholarship on "State Shinto" in relation to this distinction between the "narrow" and "broad" definitions, see Okuyama (2011).

11. According to Habermas (1989, 11–12), the process of "privatization" was already rather advanced by the end of the eighteenth century.

12. This "contingency" model is very different from the earlier perspectives on secularization represented by such scholars as Peter Berger and Brian Wilson for whom it was an inevitable and irreversible process. At least in Berger's earlier work, desecularization appeared to be theoretically possible only by a return to a pre-modern and pre-industrial form of society.

13. On these recent developments, see Shimazono (2012; 2013), Inaba and Kurosaki (2013), and McLaughlin (2013a; 2013b).

14. For recent treatments in English, see Okuyama Michiaki (2010), Erica Baffelli (2010), and George Ehrhardt, et al, eds. (2014), and McLaughlin (2018).

15. Shimazono's concerns extend beyond the academic world, which is apparent in his co-authored work based on conversations with political scientist Nakajima Takeshi (2016), which is a focused and critical discussion of religious nationalism in contemporary Japan and whether it will lead to the return of an authoritarian government that resembles the totalitarian system of the prewar period.

16. It is worth noting here that the debate about the usefulness of the term "fundamentalism" for the study of religion has attracted the attention of a number of Japanese scholars. In fact, a symposium was held on the topic at the first annual meeting of the Association for the Study of Religion and Society (Shūkyō to Shakai Gakkai) held in 1993. A number of papers were presented that dealt with fundamentalism in America, Hindu fundamentalism, and Islamic fundamentalism. On the whole, Japanese scholars appeared rather comfortable with the term when applied to religion in America, where fundamentalists proudly adopted the term to identify themselves, but regarded it as a Western and pejorative label with limited value for the study of religion in other cultural contexts. See the published collection of essays edited by Inoue and Ōtsuka (1994).

17. In a 12 October 2015 article, for example, the third Abe cabinet of twenty was referred to as the "Yasukuni sect," since, with the exception of one Kōmeitō member, all belonged to one or more groups within the coalition of the Japan Conference, Shintō Seiji Renmei, and the Diet group promoting visits to Yasukuni Shrine. See http://www.jcp .or.jp/akahata/aik15/2015-10-12/2015101201_01_1.html.

1. Imperialist Secularization

1. Contained in the William Woodard Collection 153, Box 29, Folder 3, PH150 0746: Religion in Japan poster, Prepared and Produced in Tokyo by I & E Section, GHQ, AF-PAC 2 December 1946, Special Collections and University of Oregon Libraries, Eugene, Oregon.

2. Contained in the William P. Woodard Collection 153, Box 15, Folder 5, Division of Special Collections and University Archives, University of Oregon.

3. Memorandum 1944. This document is also available online: http://digital.library .wisc.edu/1711.dl/FRUS.FRUS1944v05. An excerpt of the recommendations section is in Appendix A: 2 of Woodard (1972, 289).

4. The surmise that the memorandum arrived at GHQ in October 1945 finds support in a statement by William Bunce, who played a leading role in SCAP's CIE Religions Division from the fall of 1945. In a 1984 interview with Takemae Eiji, Bunce explained that when preparing the Memorandum and Directive on Shinto he was initially unaware of the so-called "State-War-Navy Coordinating Committee (SWNCC) papers," which included the memorandum under consideration as well as various postwar policy papers for Germany, Austria, and Korea. "It is rather interesting," Bunce goes on to observe, "that some of the material that was in the SWNCC directive *didn't appear in MacArthur's headquarters until well into the month of October*" (Takemae 1987, 198).

5. The acronym "CAA" refers to the Center for Army Analysis.

6. Italicization in quotations has been added for emphasis by the author unless otherwise noted.

7. Iwabuchi Tatsuo (1892–1975), for example, a journalist and a member of the House of Peers who participated in the Constitution Investigation Association (Minkan no Kenpō Kenkyūkai) in the early months of the Occupation, published an opinion piece entitled "Abolish the Yasukuni Shrine" in October 1945 (Iwabuchi 1945).

8. State-War-Navy Coordinating Committee Paper (SWNCC), 150/4.

9. SCAPIN-93 (Supreme Commander for Allied Powers Index); all of the US State Department documents referred to here are now available online at the National Diet Library: http://www.ndl.go.jp/modern/e/img_l/M003/M003-001.html.

10. Part 1 9a, JCS1380/15.

11. Personal information and background on Bunce has been drawn from Woodard 1972 and Takemae's 1984 interview with Bunce (Takemae 1987, 187–210).

12. These documents may be found in Woodard 1972; the "Shinto Directive Staff Study" (3 December 1945) is in Appendix F:1, 322–341. The official document that is

widely referred to as the "Shinto Directive" is actually a memorandum for the Imperial Japanese government on the subject "Abolition of Governmental Sponsorship, Support, Perpetuation, Control, and Dissemination of State Shinto (Kokka Shinto, Jinja Shinto)," issued by GHQ, SCAP Civil Information and Education Section on 15 December 1945; see Appendix B:5, 295–99. In addition to these official documents, Bunce and his staff prepared a major report on religions in Japan in 1948, which was later published as a book (Bunce 1955).

13. The important role played by Kishimoto during the early months of the Occupation has been widely acknowledged (Takagi 1993; Fukuda 1993; Woodard 1972, 62). On Kishimoto's academic career and contribution to religious studies in Japan, see Kitagawa (1964).

14. Professor Anesaki was actually CIE's first choice for the position of advisor, but it became clear that "because of his advanced age and a general state of fatigue due to the war," it would be necessary to employ the younger and more energetic Kishimoto (Woodard 1972, 26).

15. A copy of this diary is held in the Woodard Collection, University of Oregon. See Okuyama (2009) for a more detailed examination of Kishimoto's diary and his activities during the last three months of 1945.

16. According to Shimazono Susumu (2007; 2010), Imperial Household rites, another important element of prewar State Shinto, largely escaped close examination and regulation by the Religions Division, and continued into the postwar period.

17. Woodard (1972, 117) reports on the results of a 1948 survey in Nara prefecture, which "estimated that not more than 10 percent of the teachers in the prefecture were concurrently chief priests, ordinary priests, or part-time priests." While it is highly likely that the number was reduced as a result of the purge, there were still at least some Shinto priests serving as teachers in the public schools.

18. Memorandum on "Religion in Schools," by W. K. Bunce, Chief, Religions Division, Civil Information and Education Section 1 November 1947, 2 (University of Oregon Special Collection 153, Box 23, Folder: SCAP-CIE-Religion-in-Schools 1947).

19. The English translation of Kishimoto's radio broadcast is contained in Woodard 1972, Appendix F:6.

20. Also see the entry for 17 December in the Kishimoto diary.

21. This Ordinance was set to expire at the end of the Occupation along with all other Potsdam ordinances. To avoid confusion and the prospect of processing the dissolution and reincorporation of some 200,000 religious bodies, CIE staff worked closely with religious leaders and officials within the Religious Affairs Section of the Ministry of Education to prepare permanent legislation, the Religious Juridical Persons Law (shūkyō hōjin hō), which was passed by the Diet and replaced the Ordinance on 3 April 1951 (Woodard 1972, 93–102).

22. Woodard (1972, 130) explains, "there is a mistaken impression abroad that the neighborhood associations officially ceased to exist on the day of surrender, but such was not the case. They were active as part of the local government for nearly two years longer, after which they were reorganized as private bodies; but even so in spite of the law

they continued to function very much as semi-official or quasi-official bodies. In fact the leaders of these associations were so active in raising funds for shrine festivals that they were among the chief violators of the principle of religious freedom and the separation of church and state."

23. "MEMO to Chief, R & CR Division; Subject: Religious Affairs Section, 21 January 1948, 2. The Memo (1–2) also explains that: "a strong governmental agency with administrative supervision over religions supplemented by religions officers on the prefectural level has existed in Japan since the Meiji Restoration. Japanese, accordingly, do not find it easy to conceive of religions without governmental control and supervision. Japanese religionists are conditioned to such control; Japanese officialdom takes it for granted."

24. See page 4 of the "Instructions to agencies of the Occupation Forces in the field of Japanese Religions," General Headquarters, Supreme Commander for the Allied Powers, Civil Information and Education Section, Religions Division, 25 March 1946. Contained in the William P. Woodard Papers, Collection 153, Box 15, Folder 5, Division of Special Collections and University Archives, University of Oregon.

25. "Memorandum for the Record, Subject: Talk to Chaplains' Association," 14 May 1946, 1–2. Contained in the William P. Woodard Papers, Collection 153, Box 13, Folder 4, Division of Special Collections and University Archives, University of Oregon.

26. This was issued by Lt. Col. D. R. Nugent, Chief of the Civil Information & Education Section, General Headquarters, Supreme Commander for the Allied Powers, 29 August 1946; contained in the William P. Woodard Papers, Collection 153, Box 13, Folder 4, Division of Special Collections and University Archives, University of Oregon.

27. The foremost historian of the Occupation period, Takemae Eiji, describes in some detail the misbehavior of soldiers and sailors in the first few days of the Occupation, which were reported by the Japanese press before SCAP issued and enforced censorship codes. "According to newspaper accounts," he writes, "GIs committed 931 serious offenses in the Yokohama area during the first week of occupation, including 487 armed robberies, 411 thefts of currency or goods, 9 rapes, 5 break-ins, 3 cases of assault and battery and 16 other acts of lawlessness. In the first 10 days of occupation, there were 1,336 reported rapes by US soldiers in Kanagawa Prefecture alone" (Takemae 2003, 67; Dower 1999, 579).

28. For more on the CCD's operations, see the detailed study by Yamamoto Takeyoshi (2013) in Japanese and the helpful treatments by John Dower (1999, 407–408) and Monica Braw (1991, 44).

29. The original Gordon W. Prange Collection of print publications from the Occupation period is in the Special Collections and University Archives at the University of Maryland; I have accessed the microform copy available at the UCLA Richard C. Rudolph East Asian Library.

30. Chōkoku, May 1946, 7; this document is a part of the Gordon W. Prange Collection, University of Maryland; I have used the microform copy provided by UCLA.

31. Shūkyō kōron. 16/1, 15 (March 1947), 11; Gordon W. Prange Collection, University of Maryland; I have used the microform copy provided by UCLA. Shūkyō kōron was a journal published from 1935 to 1966 by the Shūkyō Mondai Kenkyūsho.

32. See, for example, Kishimoto (1963, 240–241); Jinja Shinpōsha (1971, 54); Wittner (1971). More in-depth studies have appeared recently that draw more extensively on various archives and provide details on the various actors—General MacArthur, Occupation staff, ecumenical church committees and missionaries, as well as some Japanese Christians (Kagawa Toyohiko, for example). Ray A. Moore's *Soldier of God: MacArthur's Attempt to Christianize Japan* (2011) and Okazaki Masafumi's *Nihon senryō to shūkyō kaikaku* (2012) are particularly important additions to this field of research. In addition to drawing on these studies, I have also been gathering considerable documentation of this quasi-official support of Christianity by many individuals in the Occupation from both the National Archives (SCAP/CIE Records) and various Protestant and Catholic archives.

33. Letter to Father General, 31 December 1945, from Fr. Byrne, Kyoto, p. 2. Byrne Correspondence, Box 3.

34. William P. Woodard Papers, Collection 153, Box 29, Folder 1, Division of Special Collections and University Archives, University of Oregon.

35. The articles were in the *Akahata* on 22 and 28 February, and preserved in the William P. Woodard Papers, Collection 153, Box 29, Folder 4, Division of Special Collections and University Archives, University of Oregon.

36. See chapter 6 of Moore (2011) for more detailed treatment.

37. In this chapter I have only been able to address the situation of Shinto institutions in occupied Japan. See Matsutani Motokazu (2003) for a helpful study of the fate of Shinto in Korea at the end of the war. Unlike the situation in Japan, Matsutani (2003) notes that some 136 Shinto shrines or sacred precincts were burned or destroyed in the first ten days after the end of the war (8.4 percent of the 1,141 Shinto sites in Korea). Although some Japanese residing in Korea sought to preserve the shrines, the Colonial Government maintained its position that Shinto was not a religion and proceeded to dismantle shrines and remove sacred objects to return them to Japan.

2. Shinto Responses to the Occupation

1. See Hardacre (2017, 425–436) for details on the funding of shrines from the early Meiji period until 1945, including overseas shrines in Japan's expanding empire.

2. Jinja Honchō is rendered in various ways in English. Here I am following Breen and Teeuwen (2010, 5) and their shorthand NAS.

3. See Creemers (1968, 48–53, 67–77) for a more detailed treatment of these three Shinto organizations and their role in forming this new association.

4. The Japanese report entitled "Jinja Shintō no genjo" (12 pages) is on file with an abbreviated English summary entitled "The Present State of Shrine Shinto" from a statement received from Jinja Honchō, June 1950, in the Daniel Clarence Holtom Papers, Special Collections, Honnold/Mudd Library, Claremont University Consortium.

5. "Jinja Shintō no genjo," 11.

6. This same report states that the association was also working on the development of a unified doctrine and suggested that *Jinja Shintō kōwa* (Lectures on Shrine Shinto)

by Ono Sokyō, a Jinja Honchō priest and former chief of the association's educational department, provided a useful text that represented current thinking about doctrinal matters.

7. On this point, see the document entitled "Disposition of State-Owned Land Used By Religious Institutions," SCAPIN (CIE) 13 Nov. 46 (AG 603), in Woodard 1972, 300–301), Appendix B:8.

8. Woodard 1972, Appendix B:5, 298.

9. This document is contained in Woodard 1972, Appendix B: 300–301, section 3f. Paragraph 3f was not rescinded until 14 August 1951.

10. See Fukuda's own reflections about these meetings (Fukuda 1988, 9–10; 1993, 535) as well as the accounts by Jinja Shinpōsha (1971, 77); Shibukawa (1967, 201–202; 1993, 519).

11. This meeting is recorded in the 21 November entry of Kishimoto's diary. In the analysis to follow, I have gleaned information from several sources published as part of Yasukuni Jinja 1983–1984; particularly helpful is the memorandum "Yokoi Tokitsune kōjutsu, Yasukuni shūsen oboegaki," contained in vol. 2, 81–85. This is based on an oral statement made by Yokoi on 29 October 1966. Also useful is the head priest's report to Woodard on 17 May 1949, contained in vol. 2, 74–78.

12. Yasukuni Jinja 1983–1984, vol. 1, 412. Sakamoto regularly appears in both the Religions Division records and Yasukuni Shrine accounts. He served as secretary at the meetings between Yokoi and Bunce and, as noted above, was assigned to work with Woodard in a two-year study of Yasukuni and *gokoku* shrines, which began in the summer of 1946.

13. Yasukuni Jinja 1983–1984, vol. 1, 481–482.

14. Yasukuni Jinja 1983–1984, vol. 2, 18–19.

15. "Outline of Discussion Between Lt. Bunce and Second Priest Yokoi/GHQ-21 January 1946/Interpreter Mr. Kishimoto/Note Taker—Mr. Sakamoto," in the William Woodard Collection, University of Oregon. This discussion is also recorded in Yasukuni Jinja (1983–1984, vol. 2, 31).

16. Yasukuni Shrine historical records provide extensive documentation of the range of activities that had become a regular and expected part of shrine life.

17. Irie (2001, 73–78) provides a helpful discussion of this shift in policy that involved new restrictions (*gorakusei o kinjite*) to eliminate some of the entertainment aspects of the shrine and promote its solemnization (*sōgonka*). This account shows as well how these new developments were reflected in the representation and treatment of Yasukuni Shrine in textbooks for elementary school children.

18. Zushi (2007, 56–57) notes that the insurance company in question, Fukoku Chōhei Hoken Sōgo Kaisha, began renting the Yūshūkan after its office building in Hibiya was taken over by the Occupation administration in 1946.

19. Yasukuni Jinja 1(983–1984, vol. 2, 18–19).

20. Tsukuba was related to the Imperial family and had served as a member of the House of Peers (Kizokuin) since 1925. During Tsukuba's tenure, the Chinreisha was built within the shrine precincts as a site for the commemoration of non-Japanese war dead. The question about the possible enshrinement of class-A war criminals was debated while

he was head priest, but he was cautious and did not proceed with this in spite of considerable pressure. It was his successor, Matsudaira Nagayoshi (1915–2005), who came from a military background (he had served in the Navy during the war and in the Self-Defense Force after 1954), who quickly processed the enshrinement of the class-A war criminals on 17 November 1978, just three months after his appointment as head priest. Details regarding these priests are recorded in Yasukuni Jinja (1983–1984, vol. 2; 1984, 299–300); see also Breen (2008, 8–11).

21. Yasukuni Jinja 1983–1984, vol. 1, 293–294, 297.

22. Yasukuni Jinja 1983–1984, vol. 2, 74–78. Details on the start of new rituals are also in Moriya 1973, 183–185.

23. Breen and Teeuwen (2010, 6) have highlighted the competing roles of several individuals with very different orientations in shaping the development of postwar Shinto. While Ashizu Uzuhiko sought to promote the unification of "the Japanese people under the spiritual guidance of the emperor," Yanagita emphasized the local traditions of kami worship, and Orikuchi Shinobu thought the future survival of Shinto would require it to be transformed "from an ethnic religion into a universal one." Yanagita's recommendation that these folk traditions and festivals become more central was clearly more compatible with the adaptations required to survive the Occupation, while those of Ashizu became more influential once the Occupation ended.

24. See also Miyata (1999) for a more detailed analysis of Yanagita's views in relation to State Shinto and his Yasukuni Shrine lectures in 1946.

25. Yasukuni Shrine accounts mention a variety of distinctive groups that emerged and contributed to ceremonial events (Eitai Kagura Kō, Kenka Kō) and fundraising activities (Kensen Kō).

26. See Woodard's 12 October 1951 memorandum "Attendance of Prime Minister Yoshida at Yasukuni Shrine" and an undated memorandum by Woodard on "Commemoration of War Dead."

27. In addition to these two volumes introduced here, similarly critical views of the Occupation and appeals for restoration can be gleaned from numerous other books and magazines, such as *Gekkan wakaki* and *Yasukuni*, published by the Association of Shinto Shrines and Yasukuni Shrine during the postwar decades.

28. Debates regarding an alternative memorial site have resumed in recent years. It is clearly a complicated issue that is unlikely to be resolved in the foreseeable future. The issue was the focus of a 2002 symposium, the results of which were published in Inoue and Shimazono (2004). This volume provides a wide range of pro and con views on proposals for an alternative to Yasukuni Shrine.

29. Here I am drawing on the historical account of the first fifteen years of their activities (Shintō Seiji Renmei 1984) and the regular updates on the Shinseiren homepage: http://www.sinseiren.org/. Other helpful resources on their history, membership and activities include Ōhara Yasuo (2010b, 35–105) and John Breen and Mark Teewen (2010, especially chapter 6).

30. See http://www.jinjahoncho.or.jp/honcho/index4.html (accessed 28 April 2014).

31. These victories were recognized at a workshop held in connection with the Fifty

Year Anniversary of Jinja Honchō and interpreted by Abe Yoshiya as evidence the the Shinto world had made some strides in recovering some of the "public" aspects of Shinto that had been lost due to the privatization policy of the Occupation (see "Sengo no jinja 50 nen o kenshō suru," *Gekkan wakaki*, No. 558, April 1, 1996, 50–51.

32. On this point, see Jinja Shinpōsha (1971, 158) and Haruyama (2006, 65).

33. An examination of Yasukuni's own website (http://www.yasukuni.or.jp/) as well as a number of scholarly studies reveal the distinctively Shinto and "religious" nature of the rituals that occur in the shrine's precincts (John Breen 2004).

3. Disasters and Social Crisis

1. These figures are drawn from the report available on the Kobe City website; see http://www.city.kobe.lg.jp/safety/hanshinawaji/revival/promote/img/English.pdf.

2. For a detailed treatment of the political and legal response to Aum, see Mullins (2001).

3. It is worth remembering that the problems posed by Aum were somewhat exaggerated. At its peak the movement had managed to attract no more that ten thousand members, so the vast majority of young people found the level of commitment and demands of religious practice required by membership in such a group to be wholly unattractive.

4. While Umehara shared with many other Japanese this sense of moral crisis, he did not embrace the solution advanced by the neonationalists we will consider below. He rejects the attempts to revive what he refers to as Tennōkyō and *shūshin kyōiku*, which characterized wartime Japan, as well as their view that the Imperial Rescript on Education represents authentic Japanese tradition. He argues that all of this was part of a manufactured system that does not truly represent the best of Japanese tradition. Rather, he draws on Buddhist ethical teachings and Shinto traditions that predated Tennōkyō (i.e., State Shinto) in the development of his vision of moral education (Umehara 2010).

5. In the year preceding the subway gas attack, Aum's lawyer initiated a lawsuit against Kobayashi for slandering the group through his writings and public statements, a legal action that was dropped in September 1995, just months after Aum's deviant behavior became fully revealed (reported in the *Asahi shinbun*, 15 September 1995, morning edition).

6. For additional information on Kobayashi's conflict with Aum, see Nathan (2004, 127–128).

7. See Oguma and Ueno (2003) and Saaler (2005) for more detailed treatments of this group.

8. The controversial statements and apologies are available on the official sites below: Chief Cabinet Secretary Kōno Yōhei's statement on the result of the study on the issue of "comfort women" (4 August 1993, http://www.mofa.go.jp/policy/women/fund /state9308.html); Prime Minister Hosokawa Morihiro's Policy Speech to the 127th Session of the National Diet (23 August 1993, http://japan.kantei.go.jp/127.html); and Prime Minister Murayama Tomiichi's Statement "On the occasion of the 50th anniversary of the war's end" (15 August 1995, http://www.mofa.go.jp/announce/press/pm/murayama/9508.html).

9. Opposition from a number of groups—conservative LDP politicians, the Association of Shinto Shrines, the Japan Association of War-ereaved Families, and veterans—meant that Murayama was unable to gain adequate support in the Diet for his statement and was only able to issue it from the office of the Prime Minister. Nihon o Mamoru Kai and Nihon o Mamoru Kokumin Kaigi, two forerunners of the Japan Conference (Nippon Kaigi), which will be discussed below, were also strongly opposed to the Murayama apology and launched a signature campaign to document support for their critical assessment of the Prime Minister's statement (Nelson 2003, 456–457; Nakano 2015, 38; Sugano 2016, 51–53; Aogi 2016, 183–188).

10. Ishihara made this statement following a visit to Yasukuni Shrine in August 2001. Opinion polls at the time indicated that roughly 50 percent of the Japanese agreed with Hosokawa, so Ishihara's critical reaction and perspective on the war should not be regarded as the mainstream view.

11. Nakano (2016, 24) likens this shift to a pendulum, which "is not simply swinging right and left hanging from a fixed point, but instead, the supporting point too is shifting rightward each time the pendulum swings to the right." He argues that this means the larger political environment is shifting right, which is apparent in the DPJ, whose policy positions are considerably to the right of the earlier Socialist positions. For a more detailed treatment of this process, see Nakano (2015).

12. http://www.sinseiren.org/ouenshiteimasu/ouensimasu.htm (accessed 14 December 2018).

13. The Diet group in support of Yasukuni Shrine is known as "Heiwa o Negai Shin no Kokueki o Kangaeru Yasukuni Sanpai o Shiji Suru Wakate Kokkai Giin no Kai."

14. See the following videos for Yamatani's explanation of her May 2010 promotion of Ise Shrine pilgrimages: http://www.nicovideo.jp/watch/1271036516 and http://www.nicovideo.jp/watch/1275963427.

15. Reported in *Shūkan kinyōbi*, No. 797, 30 April 2010, 36–37.

16. It is worth noting that Mori was a founding member of Shinseiren's debating club for Diet members (Kokkai Giin Kondankai) and was involved in the formation of a similar group in the Japan Conference (Yamazaki 2016, 81).

17. The Japanese phrase used here for "natural religiousness" is *shūkyōteki na jōsō*, which might also be rendered as "religious sensibilities." Both the original Japanese and English translation of Mori's 26 May 2000 press conference remarks may be found online at http://www.kantei.go.jp/foreign/souri/mori/2000/0526press.html (access 15 August 2011).

18. In *Kokoro* 184 (1 February 2013, 1–2). This issue of the magazine also provides a report on the lower house elections in December and a list of the 218 candidates recommended by Shinseiren and elected for office, which represents a substantial block out of the total number of 722 Diet members.

19. Here I am summarizing some of the key points highlighted in the article entitled "Genyaku no jinja gūji ga 'Nippon Kaigi ya Jinja Honchō no iu dentō wa dentō janai' 'kaiken de zentaishugi ni gyaku modori suru' to makkō hihan," contained in the online

magazine, *Litera* (https://lite-ra.com/2016/06/post-2296.html), which draws on the *Shūkan kinyōbi* (27 May 2016) piece. A similar piece entitled "Genyaku gūji ga Nippon Kaigi o hihan, zentaishugi no kowasa ni keikai o" featuring Miwa appeared in the online publication, *AERAdot* (1 January 2017, https://dot.asahi.com/aera/2017011100219.html?page=1). For a more detailed analysis and treatment, see Miwa's blog post from 11 October 2016 (http://hiyoshikami.jp/hiyoshiblog/?p=369).

20. These figures have been gleaned from Ishii's handy collection of the postwar surveys on religion (2007, 17, 26–29, 52).

21. Fuwa (2007, 51), for example, highlighted the close connection between the leadership of the Japan Conference and Yasukuni Shrine; at the time of his study, the chairperson of the Conference and three of the four vice-chairs at the time were also serving as representatives of Yasukuni Shrine's parishioners association (*sōdaikai*), and the chief priest of Yasukuni Shrine was also serving on the Board.

22. For very helpful analysis of this "wave of books," see Saito, Nogawa, and Hayakawa (2018), with an "Introduction" by Sven Saaler. For a concise overview of the Japan Conference in English, see the article by Tawara (2017), one of the leading researchers on this organization as well as the debate over revisionist textbooks, along with Tomomi Yamaguchi's "Introduction."

23. For some earlier scholarly treatment in English of the organizational structure, finances, and strategy of the Japan Conference, see Masshardt (2009, especially chapter 3).

24. Here I am paraphrasing the information widely available in Nippon Kaigi publications and on the official homepage.

25. See also the appendix (*shiryō*) section of Tawara (2016, 1–26), which provides detailed tables of information he collected on Japan Conference members at various levels of government and the religious bodies represented on the board and involved in supporting the Japan Conference initiatives to some degree.

26. There is a great deal of anecdotal evidence to support this interpretation. Guthmann's (2017, 209) recent study of "Nationalist Circles in Japan Today," for example, reports on an interview with a local leader of the Japan Conference who is fully convinced that Shinto is a nonreligious "national custom."

27. The information included in the Table on the Board composition is for 2017 and available on the website; http://www.nipponkaigi.org/about/yakuin.

28. See Tawara (2016, appendix section 11–12).

29. See Tsukada (2015) for detailed treatment of the relationship of representative New Religions to this conservative political agenda.

30. On Genshi Fukuin's nationalistic version of Christianity, see my earlier treatment of indigenous Christian movements (Mullins 1998, 125–127).

31. This information has been gleaned from the Nippon Kaigi homepage (accessed 7 August 2011 and 14 December 2018): http://www.nipponkaigi.org/. There are also Youtube resources on the homepage about the history and purpose of the organization.

32. This information is based on interviews with Ishii and data reported in Ukai Hidenori's *Jiin shōmetsu* (2015, 160–163, 240–241). The projections for the future of Buddhist

temples in these declining municipalities are similarly pessimistic with estimates of between 20–45 percent of temples disappearing for most denominations.

33. See https://s3.amazonaws.com/media.cloversites.com/35/35524cd0-9b31-4449-a3dd-eec3f8a61dbe/documents/Rev._Masanobu_New_Years_Message.pdf. The "new" stance of Seichō no Ie—its seclusion in the forests and its shift from being a rightwing organization to one on the left—was the focus of an article in *Shūkan daiamondo*, a weekly magazine. While this New Religion is shifting left, the article notes that Sōka Gakkai appears to be shifting right as its political party Kōmeitō continues to cooperate with the Abe administration as a part of the coalition government (13 October 2018, 46–47).

34. For updates on Seichō no Ie activities, see http://www.jp.seicho-no-ie.org/.

35. Official data for each prime minister is available at the government homepage: http://japan.kantei.go.jp/archives_e.html; www.kantei.go.jp/jp/rekidai/ichiran.html; additional information has been gleaned from multiple sources.

36. See Tawara (2013, 45–58) for one of the early critical examinations of the composition of Abe's Cabinet members and the increase in the number belonging to Shinseiren and the Japan Conference from 2006 (the first Cabinet) to 2012 (second Cabinet). See also the material prepared by Tawara, "The Abe Cabinet: An Ideological Breakdown," 28 January 2013, prepared by the Children and Textbooks Japan Network 21 (Kodomo to Kyōkasho Zenkoku Netto 21), an NGO organized in 1998 to critically engage the revisionist textbook movement (translated by Matthew Penny). For recent figures on Shinseiren and an overview of how representative religious groups line up in relation to Abe's political agenda, see "Abe Teikoku Shūkyō," *Shūkan asahi* (11 April 2014, 21). Information on Shinseiren membership and Abe's 2015 Cabinet were gleaned from the Shinseiren homepage and the official Japanese government (Kantei) homepage.

37. This table is an adaptation of information provided by Tawara Yoshifumi and his NGO, the Children and Textbooks Japan Network 21 (Kodomo to Kyōkasho Zenkoku Netto 21), organized in 1998 to critically engage the revisionist textbook movement. The data for 2012 appears in the article, "The Abe Cabinet: An Ideological Breakdown," (28 January 2013). The latest update for October 2018, also provided by Tawara Yoshifumi online in "Dai yonji Abe Shinzō naikaku no chō takaha (kyokuu) no daijintachi" (http://peacephilosophy.blogspot.com/2018/10/4the-continuing-or-worsening-far-right.html) and reported in *Akahata* (10 October 2018, https://www.jcp.or.jp/akahata/aik18/2018-10-03/2018100301_01_1.html).

38. See the articles, "Abe Shushō ga naikaku kaizō tō yakuin jinji," *Akahata* (3 October 2018) and "Fukudaijin mo 'Yasukuni' ha bakari," *Akahata* (8 October 2018).

39. These official statements are contained in Katorikku Chūō Kyōgikai 2002.

40. For more detailed analysis of the divisions within the Catholic Church today and the complicated history of the relationship with Shinto and shrine rites, see Breen (2003; 2009; 2010) and Mullins (2010b).

41. It is worth noting that, in the case of Sono Ayako, support for Yasukuni represents a fundamental change. In a 1985 article, she advocated that a new religiously neutral war memorial site be built as an alternative to Yasukuni (Sono 1985). She developed her early

position while serving as a member of the committee formed by Nakasone's government to review the issue of Yasukuni *sanpai* by prime ministers and other government officials. By 2005, however, she had joined other neonationalists and declared, "I will visit Yasukuni" (Sono 2005a; 2005b). Her husband, Miura, is the editor of *Yasukuni jinja o tadashiku rikai suru tame ni* (Miura 2005), a volume in which he expresses his own appreciation for Yasukuni Shrine as a Japanese Catholic.

4. The Politics of Yasukuni Shrine

1. The homepages and publications of these organizations provide ample evidence of the centrality of Yasukuni Shrine in their agenda. They are especially keen to promote and normalize official state visits to the shrine by the Prime Minister and other government officials. For example, the Eirei ni Kotaeru Kai, an association within the Japan Conference, has for many years been organizing annual gatherings at Yasukuni Shrine on 15 August to honor the war dead and continue their appeal for government representatives, the prime minister in particular, to fulfill their duty by making official visits to the shrine.

2. Documents discovered by *Asahi shinbun*, revealed that shrine representatives had asked the Health and Welfare Ministry not to reveal to the public (hence the term "secretly") that the personnel records had been transferred to the shrine to facilitate the enshrinement of the war criminals. See Takenaka (2007) for detailed treatment of the controversy over the enshrinement of war criminals.

3. Even the conservative *Sankei shinbun* investigated and confirmed that the Shōwa Emperor stopped visiting Yasukuni Shrine after the enshrinement of class-A war criminals in 1978, and recognized it as a "turning point" (*bunkiten*) in the relationship between the Imperial Household and the controversial shrine. This article further reported that the Heisei Emperor, Akihito, had similar concerns over such enshrinements in Yasukuni and prefectural *gokoku* shrines. In 1996, in advance of a planned visit to the Tochigi prefecture *gokoku* shrine in Utsunomiya, for example, the Imperial Household Agency inquired whether or not class-A war criminals were enshrined there ("Shōwa Tennō Gokoku Jinja Gosanpai A-kyū Gōshigo Todaeru," *Sankei shinbun*, 7 August 2006).

4. The record of these Advisory Committee (known in Japanese as the *Kakuryō no Yasukuni Jinja sanpai mondai ni kannsuru kondankai*) meetings and the materials reviewed by the advisory committee in 1984 and 1985 are available online, and a part of the larger collection of Yasukuni Shrine-related documents in the National Diet Library (http://www.ndl.go.jp/jp/diet/publication/document/2007/200704/1027-1126.pdf).

5. On the divided opinions of the committee, see Hardacre (1989, 151), and Reid (1991, 50 n. 31).

6. In this statement, Fujinami recognized the concerns of some critics who claimed that shrine visits by officials will lead to a "revival of prewar State Shinto and militarism" (*senzen no Kokka Shintō oyobi gunkoku shugi no fukkatsu*). He indicated that care would be taken so that does not happen, but made no reference to the recommendation that a religiously "neutral" memorial site be created as an alternative to Yasukuni Shrine. His statement

is available online: http://www.kantei.go.jp/jp/singi/tuitou/dai2/siryo1_7.html (last accessed 2 October 2015).

7. This explanation is found on page 98 of the final report: http://www.ndl.go.jp/jp/diet/publication/document/2007/200704/1027-1126.pdf.

8. More details about this incident and Matsudaira's response may be found in *Mainichi shinbun* "Yasukuni Shuzaihan" (2007, 76–78). NHK News coverage of the 15 August 1985 visit is available at the following site, which includes Nakasone's clear explanation to reporters that he was engaging in an "official" (*kōshiki sanpai*) visit as prime minister and it was an appropriate action for Cabinet members: http://cgi2.nhk.or.jp/archives/tv60bin/detail/index.cgi?das_id=D0009030198_00000.

9. As David Reid (1991, 51) has noted, these rulings indicate "that 'separation issues' have been reduced to 'religious freedom'" issues. Unless coercion can be proved, there is no religious freedom issue, and if there is no religious freedom issue, there is no separation issue."

10. This special issue also contained essays by some of the others who served on the advisory committee as well as Murakami Shigeyoshi, a well-known historian and critic of Yasukuni Shrine and the system of State Shinto.

11. Carol Gluck (1993, 72), for example, observes the close relationship between Umehara and former Prime Minister Nakasone, whose vision for "internationalization" was linked to "the revival of a cultural nationalism unencumbered by remembrance of the wartime past." Similarly, Margaret Sleeboon's (2004, 114) treatment of the founding of Nichibunken, includes a quotation from the co-authored work by Nakasone and Umehara (1996, 80), in which Umehara acknowledges that his critics on the left viewed him to be an "ultranationalist" like Nakasone and regarded Nichibunken as "an organ of nationalist propaganda."

12. Sono's close association with the government and ruling Liberal Democratic Party is apparent from the personal information provided on the government site: http://www.kantei.go.jp/jp/m-magazine/backnumber/2002/sono.html.

13. Although Umehara does not refer to this committee member by name, I suspect that it was Etō Jun (1932–1999), a "pro-Yasukuni" literary critic who until his death provided intellectual support for those in the government promoting Yasukuni Shrine and the particular "memory" of the war as represented by Yūshūkan. Ann Sherif (2007, 141) has noted Etō's disappointment with what he felt was an over-emphasis on the legal and constitutional dimension of the Yasukuni issue and lack of attention to "cultural issues" in the Committee's deliberations.

14. Some might regard Chidorigafuchi—not far from Yasukuni Shrine—as an appropriate memorial site since it is regarded as a sacred space but with no official religious affiliation, but Sono suggests it is probably too small to serve as an adequate alternative.

15. The statements of Hyde and Lantos are available on the US government House of Representatives homepage in the Hearing Record entitled "Japan's Relationship With Its Neighbors: Back to the Future," (14 September 2006, http://commdocs.house.gov/committees/intlrel/hfa29883.000/hfa29883_0f.htm).

16. It should also be noted here that Asō is still promoting the renationalization of Yasukuni Shrine and proposes that it could be done by registering it under a new "special" category of organization and removing it from its current status as a religious corporation, which would then allow the shrine to be financially supported by the government again (see his personal homepage: http://www.aso-taro.jp/lecture/talk/060811.html).

17. Reported in the *Asahi shinbun* (11 August 2009).

18. Reported in the *Asahi shinbun* (12 and 22 April 2014).

19. See https://www.facebook.com/akieabe/posts/10153324319836779. It was "liked" by 8,632 people and shared by 567. She is followed by 72,099 people on Facebook, so her visits to Yasukuni Shrine are likely to have a ripple effect and wider impact.

20. Abe has indicated he would avoid visiting the shrine for the 2019 Spring Festival (21–23 April) over concern that it might create a negative response from China just before hosting the G20 June summit in Osaka (reported in the *Jiji*, 17 April 2019).

21. For a critical treatment of claims regarding Fr. Bruno Bitter, see Mullins (2010b). Professor Doak's pro-Yasukuni perspective, which Prime Minister Abe and other nationalists clearly appreciate, appears in his 2006 interview in *Shokun*, his chapter in Breen (2008, 47–67), and in his more recent book in Japanese (2016; see especially chapter 3).

22. Miyaji's remarks are from an interview conducted by Woodard on 15 October 1946, and recorded by Dr. Hiyane Antei (1892–1970), a Protestant scholar who later taught the history of religion at Aoyama Gakuin University and Tokyo Union Theological Seminary. The interview was published two decades later in *Contemporary Religions in Japan* (1966), a journal edited by Woodard, as "An Interview with Dr. Naokazu Miyaji."

23. See Haruyama (2006) for a helpful introduction to the Yasukuni related materials preserved in the National Diet Library.

24. The legal action against Yasukuni Shrine over postwar enshrinements actually began in the late 1960s, when Tsunoda Saburō and a number of other members of the Association for War-bereaved Christian Families requested that the names of their family members be removed from the shrine register. See Takenaka (2015, 142–162) for treatment of this early case as well as others launched by Taiwanese, Koreans, and civilians from Okinawa.

25. Here I am only summarizing some key points elaborated by the Osaka District Court judges in their final decision (81 pages) on 26 February 2009 (copy distributed after the court hearing; personal archive).

26. For helpful overviews of the Nakaya case, see Hardacre (1989, 153–157), and Reid (1991, 52–54). The full statement of the Supreme Court decision (1 June 1988) may be found in *Minshu* 42 (5), 1988.

27. This brief synopsis draws on the Osaka High Court decision (26 February 2009), the debriefing by the plaintiffs and activists in a meeting following the decision, and a more detailed treatment of Yasukuni Shrine and religion-state issues by Hishiki (2003; 2007).

28. This movement refers to itself today as the *Yasukuni Gōshi Iya desu Ajia Nettowāku*.

29. Copies of these documents were provided by Sugahara.

30. Another significant difference between Arlington and Yasukuni not mentioned by Sugahara in this latest appeal is that Yasukuni enshrines, deifies, and pacifies the spirits of the deceased according to Shinto rituals and beliefs, while Arlington only conducts military ceremonies. It does allow, however, for families to organize additional religious rituals or memorial services according to their own religious faith (https://www.arlington-cemetery.mil/Funerals/About-Funerals, accessed 16 May 2020).

31. This appeared in *Nippon no ibuki*, the monthly magazine of Nippon Kaigi (April 2014) no. 317, 24.

32. I am grateful to Date Kiyonobu, Sophia University, Tokyo, for bringing this story and source to my attention. In addition to the article, his 15 August 2013 speech on which the article is based, is available on the Nippon Kaigi Youtube channel: https://www.youtube.com/watch?v=TEAez31LoQQ. It should be noted that the primary purpose of the speech was to oppose proposals to create an alternative memorial site to Yasukuni Shrine, since that would violate the promise made to the soldiers who offered their lives for the nation (*senbotsusha ni taisuru yakusoku ihan da*).

33. It is not entirely clear how Matsuhashi's proposal would actually solve the issue as he states that the *bunshi* procedure—dividing the spirits—so that they could be enshrined in Tōgō Jinja as well, would not actually remove them from Yasukuni Shrine. Nevertheless, he suggests that the focus of ritual care of these problematic spirits could be shifted to Tōgō Jinja and defuse the situation surrounding Yasukuni Shrine.

34. See Breen (2004, 77–81) for a detailed analysis of the rites of apotheosis and propitiation.

35. In an earlier period—the late 1930s and early 1940s, for example—such disrespectful words regarding the emperor would have been labeled lèse majesté (*fukeizai*), or a criminal offense, and grounds for arrest.

36. His critical comments were originally made to ten staff members at a 20 June 2018 study meeting, which were later leaked to the press (Kobori 2018, 95).

37. Reported in the *Sankei shinbun* (10 November 2017, https://www.sankei.com/life/news/171110/lif1711100005-n1.html?fbclid=IwAR30PMVEPn5NrPr93edSd-DLMuaNiHH18rhx-LjTQbZ7872Ne1DfgxoXym6A).

38. I accompanied this lay Catholic group to Yasukuni Shrine back in 2008, and have in my files the lay leader's written comments about our conversations that day, which he had posted on his personal homepage.

39. Ikegami first reported on his field research on Yasukuni in the special issue of *Gendai shūkyō* (2006) devoted to issues surrounding care of the dead, which I have drawn on here. A more detailed treatment has been published in a supplementary chapter in the new edition of his *Shisha no kyūsaishi* (2019, 294–335).

5. Patriotic Education

1. Other important dimensions of this restoration movement in public education, which we are unable to take up here, include the Ministry of Education's approval of

revisionist history textbooks for junior high schools in 2001 prepared by the Society for the Creation of New History Textbooks (Atarashii Rekishi Kyōkasho o Tsukuru Kai), a group organized in 1996, and the Ministry's reintroduction of patriotic moral education textbooks to elementary and junior high schools from 2002. See Saaler (2005; 2016) for helpful treatment of these developments.

2. These figures for the number of Christian schools are reported in International Institute for the Study of Religions (1998), but the total number of teachers employed by these schools is not included.

3. For additional historical background on the place of the Hinomaru and Kimigayo in postwar Japan, see Cripps (1996) and Tanaka (2000, 242–245). Tanaka's treatment includes an examination of the use of these symbols during the Occupation period and a survey of their reappearance and expanding use in schools and society. His study also includes the statistics reported by the Ministry of Education, which indicate the increase in the percentage of schools (elementary, junior high, high school) following the guidelines for use of the flag and anthem in 1985, 1992, and 1999.

4. Even though the bill was passed by the Diet, it did not actually represent the view of the majority of Japanese on this issue. When the national flag and anthem legislation was being debated, for example, an opinion poll conducted by the *Mainichi shinbun* (14 July 1999) found that 43 percent were in favor of official recognition of the Hinomaru as the national flag, while some 52 percent were opposed or in favor of a more careful debate and discussion; similarly, 36 percent were in favor of official recognition of Kimigayo, while some 58 percent were opposed or in favor of more serious debate.

5. For the original Japanese record of Prime Minister Obuchi's explanation on 29 June 1969, see http://sdaigo.cocolog-nifty.com/kokkikokkasingirokushoroku.pdf.

6. The 12 March 1999 "Appeal Regarding Hinomaru and Kimigayo" and other official statements introduced in this paper are contained in the volumes edited by the Catholic Bishops' Conference (2002; 2007; 2008).

7. The Protestant groups involved in the 9 August 1999 declaration *"Hinomaru, Kimigayo no hōseika ni kōgi suru seimei"* were the ecumenical National Christian Council of Japan (Nihon Kirisuto Kyōgikai), the Japan Evangelical Association (Nihon Fukuin Dōmei), the Reformed-Presbyterian Church (Nihon Kirisuto Kyōkai), and the Reformed Church in Japan (Nihon Kirisuto Kaikakuha Kyōkai).

8. In 1990, for example, 118 teachers were disciplined for refusing to comply and in 1991 some 220 (Niioka 2004, 241).

9. See Tanaka (2000) for a more detailed treatment on what has occurred in schools in various locations across Japan since the 1999 legislation was passed by the Diet.

10. There are a number of accounts and collections of documents regarding the lawsuit; see, for example, *Ryōshinteki "Hinomaru-Kimigayo" Kyohi*, eds. (2004), the accounts and explanations by Okada Akira (2007; 2013), one of the few Christian school teachers involved in this legal action, and the homepage of the support group for the teachers involved in the legal action (http://yobousoshouhome.blogspot.co.nz/2006/03/introduction.html).

11. For a critical documentary account of these developments, see *Fukiritsu Kimigayo* [Against Coercion], which appeared in 2006.

12. This comparison with the *fumie* ritual is also reported by Isomura Kentarō (*Asahi shinbun*, 8 August 2009) with reference to the words of Kishida Shizue, a music teacher supported by the Anglican Church in her legal struggle against the Tokyo School Board. She explained her experience with reference to Endō Shūsaku's novel, *Silence* (*Chinmoku*), which deals with the *fumie* policy adopted by the Tokugawa authorities to control deviant behavior.

13. The 2004 Letter "In Order to Make Peace Set Your Heart To That Of a Child," addressed to "All Our Brothers and Sisters," (74) is included in *The Catholic Bishops' Conference of Japan Yearbook 2008* (Katorikku Chūō Kyōgikai 2008, 72–77).

14. The English version appeared in the *Japan Christian Activity News: The Newsletter of the National Christian Council in Japan*, No. 736, Spring/Summer 2004, 15–16.

15. See Ōsaki Motoshi (2007) for a helpful historical overview of the movement to revise the education law, with particular reference to the problem of religious education.

16. As reported in *Jiji tsūshin* (7 February 2007), this book went through nine printings and sold over half a million copies within a year of its release, making it the best-selling book out of some six hundred titles published by *Bungei shunjū* since 1998.

17. The original Japanese here is *jinkaku no kansei o mezasu kyōiku kara kokusaku ni shitagau ningen*. This viewpoint appears in a letter from the Chair of the Social Committee of the Japan Catholic Bishops' Conference to Prime Minister Abe Shinzō and Ibuki Bunmei, the Minister of Education, Science, Sports and Culture, dated 2 November 2006. This letter is contained in the 2008 Yearbook edited by the Catholic Bishops' Conference of Japan (Katorikku Chūō Kyōgikai 2008, 298–301). A comparison of the old and new laws—with the changes highlighted—is available on the homepage of the Ministry of Education: http://www.mext.go.jp/b_menu/kihon/about/06121913/002.pdf.

18. The Catholic Commission's report and these statistics were made available online some years ago, but are no longer preserved on the site (http://www.jcarm.com/). For a more detailed treatment of the impact of the increase of non-Japanese parishioners, see my earlier study (Mullins 2011b).

19. See his 21 April 2006 Letter Addressed to Prime Minister Koizumi, included in *The Catholic Bishops' Conference of Japan Yearbook 2008* (Katorikku Chūō Kyōgikai 2008, 289).

20. See his 26 September 2006 letter to Prime Minister Abe and Ministry of Education, included in *The Catholic Bishops' Conference of Japan Yearbook 2008* (Katorikku Chūō Kyōgikai 2008).

21. See his 2 November 2006 letter to Prime Minister Abe in the *The Catholic Bishops' Conference of Japan Yearbook 2008* (Katorikku Chūō Kyōgikai 2008 298–301).

22. Tweet posted on 19 May 2011; https://twitter.com/t_ishin.

23. These developments in Osaka were reported widely by the Japanese media. See, for example, the article in the 4 June 2011 *Asahi shinbun*, entitled "Osakafu, Kimigayo jōrei

seiritsu kyōshokuin ni kiritsu saishō gimuzuke," and the 5 June 2011 *Japan Times* piece, "Anthem ordinance obliges Osaka teachers to stand, sing 'Kimigayo.'"

24. Ishihara resigned two months early from his fourth term as governor of Tokyo after he secured a seat in the Diet as a member of the new Japan Restoration Party in December 2012, a party he initially led in cooperation with Hashimoto Tōru.

25. The interview by Nakamori Akio appeared in *Bungei shunjū* (March 2014, 406–419), and was reported on subsequently in the online biz-journal on 3 March 2014 (http://biz-journal.jp/2014/03/post_4279.html).

26. The original Japanese here is *yahari, kyōsei ni naru to iu koto de wa nai koto ga nozomashii*, reported in the *Asahi shinbun*, 28 October 2004. A spokesperson of the Imperial Household Agency commented later that he thought the emperor was trying to say that "it would be best if the flag was raised and the anthem sung spontaneously or voluntarily" (http://www.asahi.com/edu/news/TKY200410280332.html).

27. For example, see the emperor's 2015 New Year address: http://www.kunaicho. go.jp/okotoba/01/gokanso/shinnen-h27.html.

28. Ben-Ami Shillony (2008, 158) has noted that this growing gap and tension has led some intellectuals to talk about the need to develop a new form of Japanese nationalism without the emperor (*tennō nuki nashonarizumu*). This is, of course, unthinkable for the groups who are a part of the restorationist coalition.

29. The initial Anglican support group was called the Hinomaru Kimigayo Kyōsei Mondai ni Torikumukai, which became the Hinomaru Kyōsei ni Hantaishi, Shinkyō no Jiyū o Motomeru Chō Kyōha no Kai once other denominations joined in this initiative. I am grateful to Uchida Mari for providing me with documents and records of this group's activities and the expansion in the range of participating denominations and individual churches or congregations. Here I am drawing on data contained in a 31 March 2010 report of the support group, which lists the supporting denominations and individual churches, as well as the number of individuals (2,458) who signed their appeal submitted to the Tokyo Metropolitan School Board.

30. Kishida's experience is briefly recounted in the article "Fumie toshite no Saishō, Kokki Kokka Hō seiritsu 10 nen," *Asahi shinbun* (8 August 2009). For additional accounts by Christian teachers about their struggles with the public school system and the courts, see Okada Akira (2006; 2007; 2013) and Satō Miwako (2009). For a helpful treatment of Sato's experience in English, see Tanaka Nobumasa (2005).

31. Reported in the *Asahi shinbun* (19 April 2010).

32. Reported in the *Nihon keizai shinbun* (16 June 2015, https://www.nikkei.com/ article/DGXLASDG16H73_W5A610C1CR8000/) and the *Akahata* (17 June 2015, http://www.jcp.or.jp/akahata/aik15/2015-06-17/2015061701_02_1.html).

33. This initial response is available online: http://www.tohokudai-kumiai.org/ docs15/gs150630.pdf.

34. Here I am drawing on the coverage provided by *Mainichi shinbun* and *Akahata* on 18 February 2016.

35. Reported in the *Kirisuto shinbun* (24 April 2019, http://www.kirishin.com /2019/04/24/24657/).

36. The initial debate between Ishii and Abe can be viewed on Youtube: http://www .youtube.com/watch?v=z4ewxDkZcsU (uploaded on 24 May 2007). The Communist Party also produced some critical written statements about this DVD; see *Akahata* (18 May 2007, http://www.jcp.or.jp/akahata/aik07/2007-05-18/2007051803_01_0.html).

6. Promoting Constitutional Revision

1. Winkler (2011, 61) has identified some twenty-seven drafts. We are concerned here with the 2005 LDP draft proposal, which was slightly revised in 2012.

2. In addition to this popular book, see the policy paper posted on his homepage, which also explains that Constitutional revision is indispensable in order to be liberated from the "postwar regime" established by the Occupation of Japan (http://www.s-abe .or.jp/policy/consutitution_policy).

3. Reported in the *Asahi shinbun digital* (3 May 2019, https://www.asahi.com/arti-cles/ASM534RQ3M53UTFK005.html).

4. The Tokyo Branch of the Association of Shinto Shrines (Tokyoto Jinja Chō) maintains the link with this "declaration" and a PDF form for the faithful to use in collecting signatures for this campaign (http://www.tokyo-jinjacho.or.jp/kenpou/).

5. Sakurai, with over 50,000 followers on Facebook and regular appearances on TV, has a significant public presence and influence.

6. For one critical treatment of this development, see Kajita Yōsuke (2016, http:/ /lite-ra.com/2016/01/post-1863.html).

7. The LDP draft proposal is available online: https://jimin.jp-east-2.storage.api.nif-cloud.com/pdf/news/policy/130250_1.pdf. For an explanation of the changes proposed in this document, see also the LDP's Q & A on proposed revisions: https://jimin.jp-east-2 .storage.api.nifcloud.com/pdf/pamphlet/kenpou_qa.pdf.

8. I am relying on the draft translation provided by the LDP for the 2012 proposed revision (https://www.voyce-jpn.com/ldp-draft-constitution); for the original Japanese, see http://constitution.jimin.jp/draft/.

9. Quoted in Yanagawa and Abe (1983, 294).

10. See Yamamoto and Imano (1973; 1976) for detailed treatments of the spread of these nonreligious social and national rituals (*kokkateki gyōji ni kansuru gishiki*) in the public schools and other public offices.

11. What the NHK editors referred to as "folk religion," and Ama Toshimaru (1996) designates as "natural religion," has also been referred to by Swyngedouw (1993b, 61–63) as Nipponkyō or the "religion of Japaneseness." As yet there is not a scholarly consensus on how to refer to this dominant form of Japanese religiosity, but it approximates what Max Weber (1946, 287–289) referred to as "mass religiosity," which was distinct from "virtuoso religiosity" that he documented in various cultural contexts and religious traditions. One alternative term suggested by Reader and Tanabe (1998, 29) is "common

religion," which is defined as "a set of sentiments, behavior, practices, beliefs, customs, and the like that is shared by the vast number of people and is common to all classes and groups in society, including the elites (aristocratic, economic, religious) and ordinary." Whichever term is finally adopted, most scholars would agree that *mushūkyō* is not something that can be equated with a secular or atheistic worldview.

12. These negative images and attitudes toward organized religions were reported by sociologist Nishiyama Shigeru, which were gleaned from his 1985 survey of the religious consciousness of first- and second-year university students (Mullins 1992, 237). For several decades survey research has revealed that the majority of Japanese view organized religions as untrustworthy and regard the proselytizing activities of some groups as intrusive. Surveys conducted after the 1995 Aum Shinrikyō subway gas attacks revealed that many respondents were concerned about the dangers associated with organized religions and supported the idea of revising the laws regulating religion so that the authorities would be allowed to monitor problematic religious groups more closely; see the survey results reported by Ishii (2007, 25, 102–105).

13. See Forfar (1996) for an English summary of the case.

14. The Supreme Court is sending out mixed messages, as Ravitch (2014, 720) has noted, given that it ruled in 1997 that the use of public funds for offerings (*tamagushiryō*) to Yasukuni Shrine and the prefectural *gokoku* shrine by Ehime Prefecture's government officials was a clear violation of Article 20, since it could be viewed by the public as support for a particular religion.

15. In Sendai City, for example, a prefab building in Aoba Ward was used to temporarily hold some twenty-four unidentified bodies under the care of twelve city employees. No arrangements were made for religious services on behalf of the deceased. A Buddhist association asked to be able to provide for sutra chanting and prayers, but city officials declined their offer since their religious activities in a public facility would violate religion-state separation. Similar incidents occurred at a number of crematoria and facilities managed by local governments (Tajika 2014, 22–23). The issue was complicated by the fact that local governments were ill prepared to deal with the pluralistic religious situation, that is, how to fairly manage the variety of religious groups—Buddhist, Christian, Shinto—offering their religious services for the deceased.

16. An opinion piece in the conservative *Sankei shinbun* provides one example of an appeal for a more "relaxed" or "lenient" application of religion-state separation in such disaster situations (see the 2 May 2013 edition: http://www.sankei.com/politics/news/130502/plt1305020015-n1.html).

17. Information on the Federation is available on the homepage: http://www.shin-shuren.or.jp/index.php.

18. See Katorikku Chūō Kyōgikai (2007). Some of the Bishops' earlier official statements engaging these issues are contained in Katorikku Chūō Kyūgikai (2002).

19. GHQ, SCAP, Civil Information and Education Section, Intra-Section Memorandum on "Attendance of Prime Minister Yoshida at Yasukuni Shrine," from William P. Woodard to the Acting Chief, RCR, 12 October 1951, 109–110, National Diet Library Collection.

20. Draft Memorandum on "Commemoration of War Dead" from William Woodard to the Acting Chief, RCR, p. 112, National Diet Library Collection; the Memorandum refers to a *Tokyo shinbun* article (11 September 1951) and the typed text includes handwritten additions and corrections; it is unclear whether a final draft of this document was actually submitted.

21. See Kokusai Shūkyō Kenkyūsho (2004).

22. Sasaki (2018, 10) similarly argued that the government may be observing democratic procedures in the process of constitutional revision, but "what the LDP is seeking to accomplish in the revised Constitution is unequivocally undemocratic in that it expects people to give up their rights and freedoms in exchange for greater government control."

23. The results of this survey by the *Nihon keizai shinbun* (20 April 2015) were reported in the editorial "Yoron no ayaui chōkō: Seisaku no sanpi to naikaku shijiritsu," *Chūgai nippō*, 29 April 2015. The survey also asked respondents about the impact of "Abenomics"; only 17 percent reported that the "economic recovery" had positively benefited them, while 78 percent claimed no improvement in their situation.

24. See the official site of the Article 9 Association (Kyūjō no Kai) for additional information: http://www.9-jo.jp/index.html.

25. The results of the NHK Surveys are available online: https://www.nhk.or.jp/bunken/research/yoron/index.html.

26. A two-day telephone poll conducted by Kyodo News following the upper house election in July 2018 reported similar findings: only 32.2 percent were in favor of constitutional revision while 56.0 percent opposed the LDP proposal being pushed by Abe (https://english.kyodonews.net/news/2019/07/db65fe83e96f-update1-56-oppose-amending-constitution-under-abe-govt-kyodo-poll.html).

27. The results of the survey conducted between May and July 2019 were reported in the article by Yoshitaka Isobe, "Survey: Ruling Parties Wide Apart on Revising the Constitution" (3 July 2019, http://www.asahi.com/ajw/articles/AJ201907030048.html). See Hardacre (2005) for earlier treatment of the restraining role of Kōmeitō Party members with regard to the revisionist plans of the LDP.

28. Stephen R. Nagy, "Voter Disillusion Tempered by Realism," *The Japan Times* (23 July 2019).

29. The full record of his remarks and responses to questions are available online: http://www.kunaicho.go.jp/e-okotoba/01/press/kaiken-h25e.html.

30. One can only speculate about the possible influence of the liberal and pacifist education the emperor received from his English tutor, Elizabeth Vining, a Quaker, for four years (1946–1950), who was followed by another Quaker tutor, Esther Rhodes, for an additional seven years until 1957. Freedom of conscience and pacifism are two central values of the Quaker Christian tradition and they seem to have been absorbed by the Prince in a formative decade. Empress Michiko received a Catholic education and graduated from Sacred Heart University, so it would not be surprising if that background shaped her attitudes and statements during the Heisei period. On the range of Christian influences on the Imperial Household, see Shillony's (2008) detailed study.

31. For more details on the "cornerstone theory," see John Breen (2008, 156–158).

32. The full message is available in both the original Japanese and English translations online: http://www.kunaicho.go.jp/e-okotoba/01/gokanso/shinnen-h27.html, last access 14 May 2015.

33. In spite of Japan's firsthand experience of atomic bombs in Hiroshima and Nagasaki, the Japanese government did not adopt the United Nations Treaty for the Abolition of Nuclear Weapons (2017). According to Japan's Foreign Ministry, this was due to concerns over North Korea's development of nuclear capabilities and a missile program: "If Japan participates in a treaty that categorically makes nuclear weapons illegal, nuclear deterrence will lose its justification, which could then expose the lives and properties of Japanese citizens to danger. This will cause a problem for the security of Japan." This statement appears in the section on "The Views of the Japanese Government," in Chapter 3 of the *Diplomatic Bluebook 2018* (https://www.mofa.go.jp/policy/other/bluebook/2018/html/chapter3/c030104.html).

34. For more details on this, see the article "Michiko Kōgō ga tanjōbi danwa de Abe seiken ni kaunta-! Abe ga mushi shita ICAN Nōberu Shō no igi o kyōchō, han heito shisei mo senmei ni," *Litera* (22 October 2017, https://lite-ra.com/i/2017/10/post-3533-entry.html) and "Symbol of the State: Empress Michiko's Honest Words Resonate with the People," *Mainichi shinbun* (31 October 2018, https://mainichi.jp/english/articles/20181031/p2a/00m/0na/010000c).

35. This Q & A session is available on Youtube: https://www.youtube.com/watch?v=8dFrUopgujM (uploaded 15 April 2015).

36. For background on this point, see Shillony (2008, 137–162), who notes that conservatives have been disgruntled about the stance of the emperors on these issues for some time.

37. The original Japanese here is *ryō heika no go hatsugen ga, Abe naikaku ga susumeyō toshiteiru kenpō kaisei e no kenen no hyōmei no yō ni kokumin ni uketomerare kanenai*. See "Heisei saigo no kenpō kinenbi ni Tennō Kōgō no goken hatsugen o furikaeru! Heiwa no tsuyoi omoi, Abe kaiken e no kikikan"(3 May 2018), which discusses Yagi Hidetsugu's controversial criticism published several years earlier in the May 2014 issue of *Seiron* (https://lite-ra.com/2018/05/post-3990_2.html).

38. Reported in the *Mainichi shinbun* (25 August 2018, https://mainichi.jp/english/articles/20180825/p2a/00m/0na/019000c).

39. See Takahashi's earlier studies (2004; 2005) for a more detailed analysis and critique of the neonationalistic agenda with regard to Yasukuni Shrine and education reform.

Bibliography

Abe Shinzō 安倍晋三. 2006. *Utsukushii kuni e* 美しい国へ. Tokyo: Bungei Shunjū.

Abe, Yoshiya 阿部美哉. 1968. "Religious Freedom Under the Meiji Constitution (Part 1)." *Contemporary Religions in Japan* 9: 268–338. doi. org/bjc4

———. 1993. "Senryōgun ni yoru kokka Shintō no kaitai to tennō no ningenka: GHQ ni yoru waga kokutai henkaku" 占領軍による国家神道の解体と天皇の人間化—GHQによるわが国体の変革. In *Senryō to Nihon shūkyō* 占領と日本宗教, ed. Ikado Fujio 井門富二夫, 73–118. Tokyo: Miraisha.

Akashi Hirotaka 明石博隆 and Matsuura Sōzō 松浦総三, eds. 1975. *Shōwa tokkō dan'atsushi: Shūkyōjin ni taisuru dan'atsu* 昭和特高弾圧史—宗教人に対する弾圧. Tokyo: Taihei Shuppansha.

Almond, Gabriel A., Emmanuel Sivan, and R. Scott Appleby. 1995. "Explaining Fundamentalism." In *Fundamentalisms Comprehended*, vol. 5, Martin E. Marty and R. Scott Appleby, eds., 425–444. Chicago: University of Chicago Press.

———. 2003. *Strong Religion: The Rise of Fundamentalisms around the World*. Chicago: University of Chicago Press.

Ama Toshimaru 阿満利麿. 1996. *Nihonjin wa naze mushūkyō na no ka* 日本人はなぜ無宗教なのか. Tokyo: Chikuma Shobō.

Anderson, Benedict. 1983 (1991). *Imagined Communities*. Revised edition. New York: Verso.

Aogi Osamu 青木理. 2016. *Nippon Kaigi no seitai* 日本会議の正体. Tokyo: Heibonsha.

Asahi Sonorama Henshūbu, ed. 1973. *Makkāsā no namida: Burunō Bitteru shinpu ni kiku* マッカーサーの涙—ブルノー・ビッテル神父に聞く. Asahi Sonorama.

Ashizu Uzuhiko 葦津珍彦. 1987 (2006). *Kokka Shintō to wa nan datta no ka* 国家神道とは何だったのか. Tokyo: Jinja Shinpōsha. [new edition includes notes and commentary by Sakamoto Koremaru].

Asō Tarō 麻生太郎 and Miyazaki Tetsuya 宮崎哲弥. 2008. "Hoshu saisei wa ore ni makasero" 保守再生はオレにまかせろ. *Shokun* 諸君 40/2: 24–43.

Asō Tarō and Watanabe Shōichi 渡部昇一. 2006a. "Jishu dokuritsu o mamorinuku Nihon: Yasukuni jinja no sonzai o Katorikku wa ikkanshite mitomete iru" 自主独立を守り抜く日本—靖国神社の存在をカトリックは一貫して認めている. *Voice* 344 (August): 106–115.

———. 2006b. "A Talk with the Foreign Minister." *Japan Echo* (October): 9–12.

Azegami Naoki 畔上直樹. 2009. "*Mura no chinju*" to senzen nihon: "*Kokka Shintō*" no chiiki shakaishi 「村の鎮守」と戦前日本—「国家神道」の地域社会史. Tokyo: Yūshisha.

Bae Boo-Gil. 裴 富吉. 2007. "Yasukuniteki genrishugi to sen seki mondai (1): A kyū senpan gōshi o meguru shisōshiteki bunseki" 靖国的原理主義と戦責問題(1)—A級戦犯合祀をめぐる思想史的分析. *Chūō Gakuin Daigaku Ningen: Shizen Ronsō* 25 (August): 3–46.

———. 2008. "Yasukuniteki genrishugi to sen seki mondai (2): A kyū senpan gōshi o meguru shisōshiteki bunseki." *Chūō Gakuin Daigaku Ningen: Shizen Ronsō* 26 (January): 35–81.

Baffelli, Erica. 2010. "Sōka Gakkai and Politics in Japan." *Religion Compass* 4: 746–756. doi.org/10.1111/j.1749-8171.2010.00252.x

Befu, Harumi. 1992. "Symbols of Nationalism and *Nihonjinron*." In *Ideology and Practice in Modern Japan*, Roger Goodman and Kirsten Refsing, eds., 26–46. London: Routledge.

———. 2001. *Hegemony of Homogeneity: An Anthropological Analysis of Nihonjinron*. Rosanna, Victoria: Trans Pacific Press.

Bellah, Robert N. 1967. "Civil Religion in America." *Daedalus* 96: 1–21. doi.org/10.1162/001152605774431464

Berger, Peter L. 1967. *The Sacred Canopy: Elements of a Sociological Theory of Religion*. New York: Anchor Books.

Bitter, Bruno S. J. 1972. Review of *The Allied Occupation of Japan 1945–1952 and Japanese Religions*, by William Woodard. *Monumenta Nipponica* 27: 483–484. doi.org/10.2307/2383835

Bitter-MacArthur Correspondence. File R6–5 (OMS) Correspondence. MacArthur Memorial Foundation Archives, Norfolk, Virginia.

Bocking, Brian. 1995. "Fundamental Rites? Religion, State, Education and the Invention of Sacred Heritage in post-Christian Britain and pre-War Japan." *Religion* 25: 227–247. doi.org/10.1006/reli.1995.0021

Borton, Hugh. 1967. *American Pre-surrender Planning for Postwar Japan.* Occasional Papers of the East Asian Institute. New York: Columbia University.

Braw, Monica. 1991. *The Atomic Bomb Suppressed: American Censorship in Occupied Japan.* New York: M. E. Sharp.

Breen, John. 1998. "Japan's Postwar Paradox: Between God and Man." *History Today*, 48/5: 2–5.

———. 2003. "Shinto and Christianity: A History of Conflict and Compromise." In *Handbook of Christianity in Japan*, ed. Mark R. Mullins, 249–276. Leiden: Brill.

———. 2004. "The Dead and the Living in the Land of Peace: A Sociology of Yasukuni Shrine." *Mortality* 9: 76–93. doi.org/10.1080/1357627041000165255o

———, ed. 2008. *Yasukuni, the War Dead and the Struggle for Japan's Past.* New York: Columbia University Press.

———. 2009. "The Danger is Ever Present: Catholic Critiques of the Yasukuni Shrine in Postwar Japan." *Japan Mission Journal* 63/2: 111–122.

———. 2010. "Popes, Bishops and War Criminals: Reflections on Catholics and Yasukuni in Postwar Japan." *Asia-Pacific Journal* 8/9/3: 1–16. www.japanfocus.org/-John-Breen/3312

———. 2010. "Resurrecting the Sacred Land of Japan: The State of Shinto in the Twenty-First Century." *Japanese Journal of Religious Studies* 37/2: 295–315. doi.org/bfvb

Breen, John and Mark Teeuwen, eds. 2000. *Shinto in History: Ways of the Kami.* Richmond, Surrey: Curzon Press.

———. 2010. *A New History of Shinto.* Chichester: Wiley-Blackwell.

Bruce, Steve. 2008. *Fundamentalism*. Cambridge: Polity Press.

Bunce, William K. 1955. *Religions in Japan: Buddhism, Shinto, Christianity*. Tokyo: Charles E. Tuttle.

Byrne Correspondence. Patrick J. Byrne Papers. Boxes 3 and 5. Maryknoll Fathers and Brothers Archives, Maryknoll Mission Archives, Maryknoll, New York.

Byrne-MacArthur Correspondence. File R6-5 (OMS) Correspondence. MacArthur Memorial Foundation Archives, Norfolk, Virginia.

Casanova, José. 1994. *Public Religions in the Modern World*. Chicago: University of Chicago Press.

Catholic Church vis-à-vis Yasukuni. 1945. Box 85, Folder 4. William Woodard Special Collection (153). Special Collections and University Archives, University of Oregon Libraries.

Creemers, Wihelmus H. M. 1968. *Shrine Shintō After World War II*. Leiden: E. J. Brill.

Cripps, Denise. 1996. "Flags and Fanfares: The Hinomaru Flag and Kimigayo Anthem." In *Case Studies on Human Rights in Japan*, Roger Goodman and Ian Neary, eds., 76–108. Richmond, Surrey: Curzon Press, Japan Library.

Davie, Grace. 2013. *The Sociology of Religion: A Critical Agenda*. Los Angeles: Sage.

Davis, Winston. 1977. *Toward Modernity: A Developmental Typology of Popular Religious Affiliations in Japan*. East Asia Papers Series. Ithaca, NY: Cornell University Press.

———. 1991. "Fundamentalism in Japan: Religious and Political." In *Fundamentalisms Observed*, vol. 1, Martin E. Marty and R. Scott Appleby, eds., 782–813. Chicago: University of Chicago Press.

———. 1992. *Japanese Religion and Society: Paradigms of Structure and Change*. Albany: State University of New York Press.

Demerath, N. J. III. 2007. "Secularization and Sacralization Deconstructed and Reconstructed." In *The Sage Handbook of the Sociology of Religion*, James Beckford and N. J. Demerath III, eds., 57–80 (online version, 1–25). London and Los Angeles: Sage. sk.sagepub.com/reference/hdbk_socreligion/n4.xml

Dillon, Michele. 2012. "Jürgen Habermas and the Post-Secular Appropri-
ation of Religion: A Sociological Critique." In *The Post-Secular in
Question: Religion in Contemporary Society*, Philip Gorski, David
Kyuman Kim, and John Torpey, eds., 249–278. New York: NYU
Press.

Doak, Kevin ケヴィン・ドーク and Ikehara Mariko 池原麻理子. 2006. "Sanpai
wa 'seinaru mono' e no apurōchi da" 参拝は「聖なる者」へのアプ
ローチだ. *Shokun* (August): 24–35.

———. 2008. "A Religious Perspective on the Yasukuni Shrine Controversy." In *Yasukuni, the War Dead and the Struggle for Japan's Past*,
ed. John Breen, 47–69. New York: Columbia University Press.

———. 2016. *Nihonjin ga kizukanai sekaiichi subarashii kuni, Nihon* 日本
人が気づかない世界一素晴らしい国・日本. WAC Bunko 232. Tokyo:
Wakku.

Doi Takako. 2007. "Key Note Speech." In the *Report Inter-religious Conference on Article 9 of the Japanese Peace Constitution*, Nov. 29–Dec. 1:
23–34.

Dower, John W. 1999. *Embracing Defeat: Japan in the Wake of World War II*.
New York: W. W. Norton & Company.

Duke, Benjamin C. 1973. *Japan's Militant Teachers: A History of the Left-
Wing Teachers' Movement*. Honolulu: University of Hawai'i Press.

Eger, Max. 1980. "Modernization and Secularization in Japan: A Polemical
Essay." *Japanese Journal of Religious Studies* 7: 7–24. doi.org/bg6h

Ehrhardt, George, Axel Klein, Levi McLaughlin, and Steven R. Reed, eds.
2014. *Komeito: Politics and Religion in Japan*. Research Monograph
18. Berkeley: Institute of East Asian Studies.

Eisenstadt, Shmuel Noah. 1999. *Fundamentalism, Sectarianism, and Revolution: The Jacobin Dimension of Modernity*. Cambridge: Cambridge University Press.

Fenn, Richard K. 1978. *Toward a Theory of Secularization*. Monograph
Series Number 1. Norwich, Conn.: Society for the Scientific Study
of Religion.

Fitzgerald, Timothy. 1993. "Japanese Religion as Ritual Order." *Religion* 23:
315–341. doi.org/10.1006/reli.1993.1027

———. 2003. "'Religion' and the 'Secular' in Japan: Problems in history, social anthropology, and the study of Religion." *Electronic Journal of Contemporary Japanese Studies*, Discussion Paper 3. http://www.japanesestudies.org.uk/discussionpapers/Fitzgerald.html

Forfar, David. 1996. "Individuals Against the State? The Politics of Opposition to the Re-emergence of State Shintō." In *Case Studies on Human Rights in Japan*, Roger Goodman and Ian Neary, eds., 245–276. Richmond, Surrey: Curzon Press, Japan Library.

Frykenberg, Robert Eric. 1993. "Hindu Fundamentalism and the Structural Stability of India." In *Fundamentalisms and the State: Remaking Polities, Economies, and Militance*, Martin E. Marty and R. Scott Appleby, eds., 233–255. Chicago: University of Chicago Press.

Fukuda Shigeru 福田繁. 1988. "Kenshō: GHQ no shūkyō seisaku" 検証—GHQの宗教政策. *Shūmu jihō* 宗務時報 78: 1–24.

———. 1993. "Kenshō: GHQ no shūkyō seisaku" 検証—GHQの宗教政策. In *Senryō to Nihon shūkyō* 占領と日本宗教, ed. Ikado Fujio 井門富二夫, 521–560. Tokyo: Miraisha.

Fukuda Shigeru, Shibukawa Ken'ichi 渋川謙一, Kawawada Yuiken 河和田唯賢, Abe Yoshiya 阿部美哉, and Ōie Shigeo 大家重夫. 1984. "Zadankai: Shūsen chokugo no shūmu gyōsei" 座談会—終戦直後の宗務行政. *Shūmu jihō* 宗務時報 65: 1–36.

Fuwa Tetsuzō 不破哲三. 2007. "Kenpō taiketsu no zentaizō o tsukamō: Kenpō kaiseiha wa donna Nihon o tsukurō toshiteiru ka" 憲法対決の全体像をつかもう—憲法改正派はどんな日本をつくろうとしているのか. *Zen'ei* 前衛 (July): 13–66.

Gellner, Ernest. 1995. "Fundamentalism as a Comprehensive System: Soviet Marxism and Islamic Fundamentalism Compared." In *Fundamentalisms Comprehended*, vol. 5, Martin E. Marty and R. Scott Appleby, eds., 277–287. Chicago: University of Chicago Press.

Gluck, Carol. 1993. "The Past in the Present." In *Postwar Japan as History*, ed. Andrew Gordon, 64–95. Berkeley: University of California Press.

Guthmann, Thierry. 2017. "Nationalist Circles in Japan Today: The Impossibility of Secularization." *Japan Review* 30: 207–225.

Habermas, Jürgen. 1989 (1991). *The Structural Transformation of the Public Sphere: An Inquiry into a Category of Bourgeois Society*. Thomas Burger and Frederick Lawrence, trans. Cambridge, Mass.: MIT Press.

———. 2006. "Religion in the Public Sphere." *European Journal of Philosophy*, 14: 1–25. doi.org/10.1111/j.1468-0378.2006.00241.x

Hardacre, Helen. 1989. *Shintō and the State, 1968–1988*. Princeton: Princeton University Press.

———. 1993. "The New Religions, Family, and Society in Japan." In *Fundamentalisms and Society: Reclaiming the Sciences, the Family, and Education*, Martin E. Marty and R. Scott Appleby, eds., 294–310. Chicago: University of Chicago Press.

———. 2003. "After Aum: Religion and Civil Society in Japan." In *The State of Civil Society in Japan*, Frank J. Schwartz and Susan J. Pharr, eds., 135–153. Cambridge: Cambridge University Press.

———. 2005. "Constitutional Revision and Japanese Religions." *Japanese Studies* 25/3: 235–247. doi.org/10.1080/10371390500342725

———. 2011. "Revision of Administrative Law as Shortcut to Constitutional Revision." In *Japanese Politics Today: From Karaoke to Kabuki Democracy*, Takashi Inoguchi and Purnendra Jain, eds., 201–217. New York: Palgrave Macmillan.

———. 2017. *Shinto: A History*. New York: Oxford University Press.

Harootunian, Harry. 2006. "Japan's Long Postwar: The Trick of Memory and the Ruse of History." In *Japan After Japan: Social and Cultural Life From the Recessionary 1990s to the Present*, Tomiko Yoda and Harry Harootunian, eds., 98–121. Durham: Duke University Press.

Haruyama Meitetsu 春山明哲. 2006. "Yasukuni Jinja to wa nanika: Shiryō kenkyū no shiza kara no joron" 靖国神社とはなにか—資料研究の視座からの序論. *The Reference* 56/7: 49–75.

Hishiki Masaharu 菱木政晴. 2003. "Some Thoughts on the Yasukuni Court Case." *Japan Mission Journal* 57/2: 98–104.

———. 2007. *Shiminteki jiyū no kiki to shūkyō: Kenpō, Yasukuni Jinja, seikyō bunri* 市民的自由の危機と宗教—憲法、靖国神社、政教分離. Tokyo: Hakutakusha.

Hiyane, Antei. 1966. "An Interview with Dr. Naokazu Miyaji." Interview by William P. Woodard, 15 October 1946. *Contemporary Religions in Japan* 7: 143–153. doi.org/bh92

Hobsbawm, Eric. 1983. "Introduction: Inventing Traditions." In *The Invention of Tradition*, Eric Hobsbawm and Terence Ranger, eds., 1–14. Cambridge: Cambridge University Press.

Holtom, Daniel C. 1943 (1947). *Modern Japan and Shinto Nationalism: A Study of Present-Day Trends in Japanese Religions*. Chicago: University of Chicago Press.

———. 1946. "New Status of Shintō." *Far Eastern Survey* 15/2: 17–20.

Holtom Correspondence. Daniel Clarence Holtom Papers. Box 1, Folder 3. Personal Correspondence. Special Collections, Honnold/Mudd Library, Claremont University Consortium.

———. 1945. "The Shintō Dilemma." Unpublished paper. Daniel Clarence Holtom Papers. Box 2, File 42. Special Collections, Honnold/Mudd Library, Claremont University Consortium.

Ikado Fujio 井門富二夫, ed. 1993. *Senryō to Nihon shūkyō* 占領と日本宗教. Tokyo: Miraisha.

Ikegami, Eiko. 2000. "A Sociological Theory of Publics: Identity and Culture as Emergent Properties in Networks." *Social Research* 67/4: 989–1029.

———. 2005. *Bonds of Civility: Aesthetic Networks and the Political Origins of Japanese Culture*. New York: Cambridge University Press.

Ikegami Yoshimasa 池上良正. 2019. *Shisha no kyūsaishi: Kuyō to hyōi no shūkyōgaku* 死者の救済史——供養と憑依の宗教学. Chikuma Gakugei Bunko 1-61-1. Tokyo: Chikuma Shobō.

Ikegami Yoshimasa, Sueki Fumihiko 末木文美士, and Shimazono Susumu 島薗 進. 2006. "Taidan: Shisha no koe o kiku: irei to tsuitō o megutte" 対談——死者の声を聞く〜慰霊と追悼を巡って. *Gendai shūkyō* (June): 6–13.

Inaba Keishin 稲場圭信 and Kurosaki Hiroyuki 黒崎浩行, eds. 2013. *Shinsai fukkō to shūkyō* 震災復興と宗教. Tokyo: Akashi Shoten.

Inagaki Hisakazu 稲垣久和. 2006. *Yasukuni Jinja kaihōron: Hontō no tsuitō to wa nani ka* 靖国神社「解放」論——本当の追悼とはなにか. Tokyo: Kobunsha.

Inoue Nobutaka 井上信孝. 1991. *Kyōha Shintō no keisei* 教派神道の形成. Tokyo: Kōbundō.

———. 2002. "The Formation of Sect Shinto in Modernizing Japan." *Japanese Journal of Religious Studies* 29: 405–427. doi.org/bgcm

———. 2003. *Japanese College Students' Attitudes Towards Religion: An Analysis of Questionnaire Surveys from 1992 to 2001.* Tokyo: Kokugakuin University.

———. 2009. "Religious Education in Contemporary Japan." *Religion Compass* 3: 580–594. doi.org/10.1111/j.1749-8171.2009.00159.x

Inoue Nobutaka and Ōtsuka Kazuo 大塚和夫, eds. 1994. *Fuandamentalizumu to wa nanika: Sezokushugi e no chōsen* ファンダメンタリズムとは何か—世俗主義への挑戦. Tokyo: Shinyōsha.

Inoue Nobutaka and Shimazono Susumu, eds. 2004. *Atarashii tsuitō shisetsu wa hitsuyō ka* 新しい追悼施設は必要か. Tokyo: Pelican.

Irie Yōko 入江曜子. 2001. *Nihon ga "kami no kuni" datta jidai: Kokumin gakkō no kyōkasho o yomu* 日本が「神の国」だった時代—国民学校の教科書をよむ. Tokyo: Iwanami Shoten.

Ishihara Shintarō 石原慎太郎. 2014. "Akutagawa shō to watakushi no paradokushikaru na kankei" 芥川賞と私のパラドクシカルな関係. Interviewed by Nakamura Akio 中森昭夫. *Bungei shunjū* 文藝春秋 68: 406–419.

Ishii Kenji 石井研士. 2007 (1997). *Dēta bukku: Gendai Nihonjin no shūkyō* データブック現代日本人の宗教. Tokyo: Shinyosha.

———. 2010. "Purorōgu: Jinja Shintō wa suitai shita ka" プロローグ—神社神道は衰退したか. In *Shintō wa doko he iku no ka* 神道はどこへいくのか. Ishii Kenji, ed., 11–30. Tokyo: Perikansha.

Isomae Jun'ichi 磯前順一. 2003. *Kindai Nihon no shūkyō gensetsu to sono keifu: Shūkyō, kokka, Shintō* 近代日本の宗教言説とその系譜—宗教・国家・神道. Tokyo: Iwanami Shoten.

———. 2014. *Religious Discourse in Modern Japan: Religion, State, and Shintō.* Leiden: Brill.

Itoh, Mayumi. 2001. "Japan's Neo-Nationalism: The Role of the Hinomaru and Kimigayo Legislation." Japan Policy Research Institute Working Paper No. 79 (July). www.jpri.org/publications/workingpapers/wp79.html

Iwabuchi Tatsuo 岩淵辰雄. 1945. "Abolish the Yasukuni Shrine." *Contemporary Japan* (April–December): 237–239.

Jeans, Roger B. 2005. "Victims or Victimizers? Museums, Textbooks, and the War Debate in Contemporary Japan." *The Journal of Military History* 69: 149–195. doi.org/10.1353/jmh.2005.0025

Jinja Honchō Sōgō Kenkyūsho 神社本庁綜合研究所, ed. 2010. *Sengo no jinja, Shintō: Rekishi to kadai* 戦後の神社・神道―歴史と課題. Tokyo: Jinja Shinpōsha.

Jinja Honchō Statement. "The Present State of Shrine Shinto" (Jinja Shintō no genjō 神社神道の現状). English and Japanese (11 pp.) versions submitted in June 1950. Daniel Holtom Papers. Box 3, Folder 22. Special Collection, Honnold/Mudd Library, Claremont, California.

Jinja Shinpōsha 神社新報社, ed. 1969. *Shintō shirei to Sengo no Shintō* 神道指令と戦後の神道. Tokyo: Jinja Shinpōsha.

———, ed. 1971. *Shintō shirei to sengo no Shintō* 神道指令と戦後の神道. Tokyo: Jinja Shinpōsha.

———, ed. 2008. *Kenshō Jinja Honchō rokujū nen* 検証神社本庁六十年. Tokyo: Jinja Shinpōsha.

Jinja Shinpō Sōkan Rokujū Shūnen Kinen Shuppan Iinkai 神社新報創刊六十周年記念出版委員会, ed. 2008. *Kenshō Jinja Honchō rokujū nen: Senjin no ashiato* 検証神社本庁六十年―先人の足跡. Tokyo: Jinja Shinpōsha.

Josephson, Jason Ānanda. 2012. *The Invention of Religion in Japan.* Chicago: University of Chicago Press.

Juergensmeyer, Mark. 1993. *The New Cold War? Religious Nationalism Confronts the Secular State.* Berkeley: University of California Press.

———. 1996. "The Worldwide Rise of Religious Nationalism." *Journal of International Affairs* 50: 1–20.

Kajita Yōsuke 梶田陽介. 2016. "Zenkoku kakuchi no jinja ga hatsumōde kyaku o neratte kaiken no shomei o atsume! Nippon Kaigi, Jinja Honchō ga shimei, senzen fukkatsu mokuteki o kakusu hiretsu na teguchi" 全国各地の神社が初詣客を狙って改憲の署名を集めよう！日本会議・神社本庁が指令、戦前復活の目的を隠す卑劣な手口. *Litera* (5 January): 1–5. lite-ra.com/2016/01/post-1863.html

Katō Genchi. 1971 (1926). *A Study of Shintō: The Religion of the Japanese Nation*. New York: Barnes & Noble.

Katorikku Chūō Kyōgikai カトリック中央協議会 ed. 2002. *Katorikku kyōkai no shakai mondai ni kansuru kōteki hatsugen shū* カトリック教会の社会問題に関する公的発言集. Tokyo: Katorikku Chūō Kyōgikai.

———. 2007. *Shinkyō no jiyū to seikyō bunri* 信教の自由と政教分離. Tokyo: Katorikku Chūō Kyōgikai.

———. 2008. *Nihon Katorikku Shikyō Kyōgikai Iyābukku* 2008 日本カトリック司教協議会イヤーブック2008. Tokyo: Katorikku Chūō Kyōgikai.

Kawano, Satsuki. 2005. *Ritual Practice in Modern Japan*. Honolulu: University of Hawai'i Press.

Kisala, Robert and Mark R. Mullins, eds. 2001. *Religion and Social Crisis in Japan: Understanding Japanese Society Through the Aum Affair*. Basingstoke, UK and New York: Palgrave and St. Martin's Press.

Kishimoto Hideo 岸本英夫. 1945. "Diary, 1945" (*Shōwa nijūnen nikki* 昭和二十年日記). Box 56, Folder 1. William Woodard Special Collection (153). Special Collections and University Archives, University of Oregon Libraries.

———. 1963. "Arashi no naka no Jinja Shintō" 嵐の中の神社神道. In *Sengo shūkyō kaisō roku* 戦後宗教回想録, ed. Shinshūren Chōsa Shitsu 新宗連調査室, 195–294. PL Kyōdan.

Kitagawa, Joseph. 1964. "Hideo Kishimoto (1903–1964)." *History of Religions* 4: 172–173. doi.org/10.1086/462502

Kiyama Masayoshi 木山正義. 1981. "Yasukuni Jinja to Burunō Bitteru shinpu" 靖国神社とブルノー・ビッテル神父. *Yasukuni* やすくに 323 (1 July).

Kobayashi Yoshinori 小林よしのり. 1996. *Shin gōmanizumu sengen* 新ゴーマニズム宣言. Tokyo: Gentōsha.

———. 1998. *Sensōron* 戦争論. Tokyo: Gentōsha.

———. 2001. *Shin gōmanizumu sensōron 2* 新ゴーマニズム戦争論(2). Tokyo: Gentōsha.

———. 2005. *Yasukuniron* 靖国論. Tokyo: Gentōsha.

———. 2006. *Iwayuru A kyū senpan* いわゆるA級戦犯. Gentōsha.

———. 2010a. *Shōwa Tennō ron* 昭和天皇論. Gentōsha.

———. 2010b. *Shūshinron* 修身論. Gentōsha.

Kobori Kunio 小堀邦夫. 2018. "Yasukuni Jinja wa kiki ni aru" 靖国神社は危機にある. *Bungei shunjū* 文藝春秋 96: 94–101.

Kokusai Shūkyō Kenkyūsho 国際宗教研究所, ed. 1998. *Kyōiku no naka no shūkyō* 教育の中の宗教. Tokyo: Shinshokan.

———.2004. *Atarashii tsuitō shisetsu wa hitsuyō ka* 新しい追悼施設は必要か. Tokyo: Pelican.

Krämer, Hans Martin. 2013. "How 'Religion' Came to Be Translated as *Shūkyō*: Shimaji Mokurai and the Appropriation of Religion in Early Modern Japan." *Japan Review* 25: 89–111.

Madsen, Richard. 2011. "Secularism, Religious Change, and Social Conflict in Asia." In *Rethinking Secularism*, Craig Calhoun, Mark Juergensmeyer, and Jonathan Van Antwerpen, eds., 248–269. Oxford: Oxford University Press.

Mainichi Shinbun "Yasukuni" Shuzaihan 毎日新聞「靖国」取材班. 2007. *Yasukuni Jinja sengo hishi: A kyū senpan o gōshishita otoko* 靖国戦後秘史—A級戦犯を合祀した男. Tokyo: Mainichi Shinbunsha.

Martin, David. 1978. *A General Theory of Secularization*. New York: Harper and Row.

Marty, Martin E. and R. Scott Appleby, eds. 1991. *Fundamentalisms Observed*, vol. 1. Chicago, University of Chicago Press.

———. 1993. *Fundamentalisms and Society: Reclaiming the Sciences, the Family, and Education*. Chicago: University of Chicago Press.

———. 1995. *Fundamentalisms Comprehended*, vol. 5. Chicago: University of Chicago Press.

Maruyama Masao. 1974. *Studies in the Intellectual History of Tokugawa Japan*. Trans. Mikiso Hane. Princeton: Princeton University Press.

Masshardt, Brian J. 2009. "Demonstrating Democracy: Citizen Politics in Japan and Yasukuni Shrine, 2001–2006." PhD diss., University of Hawai'i.

Matsudo Yukio. 2001. "Back to Invented Tradition: A Nativist Response to National Crisis." In *Religion and Social Crisis in Japan: Understanding Japanese Society through the Aum Affair*, Robert J. Kisala and Mark R. Mullins, eds., 163–177. Basingstoke UK and New York: Palgrave and St. Martin's Press.

Matsuhashi Teruo 松橋暉男. 2008. *Maboroshi no kigō* 幻の揮毫. Tokyo: Mainichi Ones.

Matsutani Motokazu. 松谷基和. 2003. "Minami Chōsen ni okeru Bei Senryōgun no Shintō seisaku: GHQ/SCAP no Shintō seisaku to no hikaku no shiten kara" 南朝鮮における米占領軍の神道政策—GHQ/SCAP の神道政策との比較の視点から. *Gendai Kankoku Chōsen kenkyū* 現代韓国朝鮮研究 3: 64–77.

McLaughlin, Levi. 2013a. "What Have Religious Groups Done After 3.11? Part 1: A Brief Survey of Religious Mobilization after the Great East Japan Earthquake Disasters." *Religion Compass* 7: 294–308. doi.org/10.1111/rec3.12057

———. 2013b. "What Have Religious Groups Done After 3.11? Part 2: From Religious Mobilization to 'Spiritual Care.'" *Religion Compass* 7: 309–325. doi.org/10.1111/rec3.12056

———. 2018. *Soka Gakkai's Human Revolution: The Rise of a Mimetic Nation in Modern Japan.* Honolulu: University of Hawai'i Press.

Memorandum 1944. "Memorandum: Freedom of Worship" (15 March 1944). In *Foreign Relations of the United States Diplomatic Papers, 1944. The Near East, South Asia, and Africa, the Far East*, vol. 5, United States Department of State. Washington, DC: US Government Printing Office.

Minamiki, George, S. J. 1985. *The Chinese Rites Controversy from Its Beginning to Modern Times.* New Orleans: Loyola University Press.

Mishima Mitsuya 三島みつや. 2016. "Genyaku no jinja gūji ga 'Nippon Kaigi ya Jinja Honchō no iu dentō wa dentō janai' 'kaiken de zentaishugi ni gyaku modori suru' to makkō hihan" 現役の神社宮司が「日本会議や神社本庁の言う伝統は伝統じゃない」「改憲で全体主義に逆戻りする」と真っ向批判. *Litera* (June). lite-ra.com/2016/06/post-2296.html

Miura Shumon 三浦朱門.1998. *Nihonjin o dame ni shita kyōiku: Kodomo ni waga shinnen o kyōsei subeshi* 日本人をダメにした教育—子供に我が信念を矯正すべし. Tokyo: Kairyūsha.

———, ed. 2005. *Yasukuni jinja tadashiku rikai suru tame ni* 靖国神社正しく理解するために. Tokyo: Kairyūsha.

Miwa Takahiro 三輪隆裕. 2016a. "Jinja Honcho (Nippon Kaigi) no mihatenu yume" 神社本庁（日本会議）の見果てぬ夢, *Hiyoshikami* (blog). 11 October 2016. hiyoshikami.jp/hiyoshiblog/?m=201610

———. 2016b. "Shinseiren no shisō no mondai ten" 神政連の思想の問題点, *Hiyoshikami* (blog). 12 June 2016. hiyoshikami.jp/hiyoshiblog/?cat=1&paged=10

———. 2017. "Gen'yaku gūji ga Nippon Kaigi o hihan: Zentaishugi no kowasa ni keikai o" 現役宮司が日本会議を批判―全体主義のこわさに警戒を. *Aera* (12 January). dot.asahi.com/aera/2017011100219.html?page=1

Miyata Noboru 宮田 登. 1999. "Kokka Shintō" 国家神道. In *Shūkyō to seikatsu* 宗教と生活. Kindai Nihon bunkaron 近代日本文化論, vol. 9, Aoki Tamotsu 青木保, et al., eds., 39–54, Tokyo: Iwanami Shoten.

Momochi Akira 百地 章. 2013. "Shūkyō hō to giseisha no sōsō, tsuitō, irei: Higaisha no kokoro no kea mo fukumete" 宗教法と犠牲者の葬送・追悼・慰霊―被災者の心のケアも含めて. *Shūkyō hō* 宗教法 32: 129–142.

Moore. Ray A. 1979. "Reflections on the Occupation of Japan." *Journal of Asian Studies* 38: 721–734. doi.org/10.2307/2053910

———. 2011. *Soldier of God: MacArthur's Attempt to Christianize Japan.* Portland, M.E.: MerwinAsia.

Moriya Shūryō 森谷秀亮. 1973. *Yasukuni Jinja ryaku nenpyō* 靖国神社略年表. Tokyo: Yasukuni Jinja.

Morris, Ivan I. 1960. *Nationalism and the Right Wing in Japan: A Study of Post-war Trends.* London: Oxford University Press.

Mullins, Mark R. 1992. "Japan's New Age and Neo-New Religions: Sociological Interpretations." In *Perspectives on the New Age*, James R. Lewis and J. Gordon Melton, eds., 232–246. Albany: State University of New York Press.

———. 1998. *Christianity Made in Japan: A Study of Indigenous Movements.* Nanzan Library of Asian Religion and Culture, vol. 3. Honolulu: University of Hawai'i Press.

———. 2001. "The Legal and Political Fallout of the 'Aum Affair.'" In *Religion and Social Crisis in Japan: Understanding Japanese Society*

Through the Aum Affair, Robert Kisala and Mark R. Mullins, eds., 72–86. Basingstoke, UK and New York: Palgrave and St. Martin's Press.

———. 2010a. "From 'Departures' to 'Yasukuni Shrine': Caring for the Dead and Bereaved in Contemporary Japanese Society." *Japanese Religions* 35: 101–112.

———. 2010b. "How Yasukuni Shrine Survived the Occupation: A Critical Examination of Popular Claims." *Monumenta Nipponica* 65: 89–136. doi.org/10.1353/mni.0.0109

———. 2011a. "Religion in Contemporary Japanese Lives." In *Routledge Handbook on Japanese Culture and Society*, Theodore C. Bestor and Victoria Lyon Bestor, eds., 63–74. London: Routledge.

———. 2011b. "Between Inculturation and Globalization: The Situation of Roman Catholicism in Contemporary Japanese Society." In *Xavier's Legacies: Catholicism in Modern Japanese Culture*, ed. Kevin Doak 169–192. Vancouver: University of British Columbia Press.

———. 2012a. "Secularization, Deprivatization, and the Reappearance of 'Public Religion' in Japanese Society." *Journal of Religion in Japan* 1: 61–82. doi.org/10.1163/221183412x628442

———. 2012b. "The Neo-nationalist Response to the Aum Crisis: A Return of Civil Religion and Coercion in the Public Sphere?" *Japanese Journal of Religious Studies* 39: 99–125. doi.org/bfs6

———. 2013. "Sacred Sites and Social Conflict: Yasukuni Shrine and Religious Pluralism in Japanese Society." In *Religious Pluralism, State and Society in Asia*, ed. Chiara Formichi, 35–50. London: Routledge.

———. 2015. "Japanese Responses to 'Imperialist Secularization': The Postwar Movement to Restore Shintō in the 'Public Sphere.'" In *Multiple Secularities Beyond the West: Religion and Modernity in the Global Age*. Marian Burchardt, et. al. eds., 141–167. Boston: DeGruyter.

———. 2016. "Neonationalism, Politics, and Religion in Post-disaster Japan." In *Disasters and Social Crisis in Contemporary Japan: Political, Religious, and Sociocultural Responses*, Mark R. Mullins and

Koichi Nakano, eds., 107–131. Basingstoke, UK and New York: Palgrave Macmillan Press.

———. 2017a. "Shinsaigo no Nihon ni okeru neo nashonarizumu" 震災後の日本におけるネオナショナリズム. Trans. Saitō Kōta 齋藤公太. In *Tettei kenshō:Nihon no ukeika* 徹底検証—日本の右傾化, ed. Tsukada Hotaka 塚田穂高, 128–147. Tokyo: Chikuma Shobō.

———. 2017b. "Becoming a Multicultural Church in the Context of Neo-Nationalism: The New Challenges Facing Catholics in Japan." In *"Scattered & Gathered": Catholics in Diaspora*, William Cavanaugh and Michael Budde, eds., 112–130. Portland: Wipf & Stock/Cascade Books.

———. 2018. "Public Intellectuals, Neo-nationalism, and the Politics of Yasukuni Shrine." In *Japanese Studies Down Under: History, Politics, Literature and Art*, International Research Center for Japanese Studies Symposium Proceedings 23, Guo Nanyan and Shogimen Takashi, eds., 145–160. Kyoto: Kokusai Nihon Bunka Kenkyū Sentā.

Munakata Iwao. 1976. "The Ambivalent Effects of Modernization on Traditional Folk Religion." *Japanese Journal of Religious Studies* 3: 99–126. doi.org/bhb3

Murakami Shigeyoshi 村上重良. 1970. *Kokka Shintō* 国家神道. Tokyo: Iwanami Shoten.

———. 1982. *Kokka Shintō to minshū shūkyō* 国家神道と民衆宗教. Tokyo: Yoshikawa Kōbunkan.

Nagoshi Futaranosuke 名越二荒之助, ed. 1999. *Dai tōa sensō no hiwa* 大東亜戦争の秘話, vol. 3. Tokyo: Tendensha.

Nakajima Takeshi 中島岳志 and Shimazono Susumu. 2016. *Aikoku to shinkō no kōzō: Zentaishugi ga yomigaeru no ka* 愛国と信仰の構造—全体主義はよみがえるか. Tokyo: Shūeisha.

Nakamura Naofumi 中村直文. 2007. *Yasukuni: Shirarezaru senryōka no kōbō* 靖国—知られざる占領下の攻防. NHK Shuppan.

Nakano Kōichi 中野晃一. 2015. *Ukeika suru Nihon seiji* 右傾化する日本政治. Tokyo: Iwanami Shoten.

———. 2016. "New Right Transformation in Japan." In *Disasters and Social Crisis in Japan: Political, Religious, and Sociocultural Responses*,

Mark R. Mullins and Nakano Kōichi, eds., 23–41. New York: Palgrave Macmillan, 2016.

Nakano Tsuyoshi 中野 毅. 1993. "Amerika no tai-nichi shūkyō seisaku no keisei" アメリカの対日宗教政策の形成. In *Senryō to Nihon shūkyō*, ed. Ikado Fujio, 27–72. Tokyo: Miraisha.

———. 2004. *Sengo Nihon no shūkyō to seiji* 戦後日本の宗教と政治. Tokyo: Hara Shobō.

Nakasone Yasuhiro 中曽根康弘 and Umehara Takeshi 梅原猛. 1996. *Seiji to tetsugaku: Nihonjin no aratanaru shimei o motome* 政治と哲学—日本人の新たなる使命を求め. Tokyo: PHP Kenkyūsho.

Nathan, John. 2004. *Japan Unbound: A Volatile Nation's Quest for Pride and Purpose*. Boston: Houghton Mifflin.

Nelson, John K. 2000. *Enduring Identities: The Guise of Shinto in Contemporary Japan*. Honolulu: University of Hawai'i Press.

———. 2003. "Social Memory as Ritual Practice: Commemorating Spirits of the Military Dead at Yasukuni Shinto Shrine." *Journal of Asian Studies* 62: 443–467. doi.org/10.2307/3096245

NHK Hōsō Yoron Chōsasho. 1984. *Nihonjin no shūkyō ishiki* 日本人の宗教意識. Tokyo: Nihon Hōsō Shuppan Kyōkai.

Niioka Masayuki 新岡昌幸. 2004. "Gakkō ni okeru 'Hinomaru' 'Kimigayo' mondai no kenpō, kyōiku hōgakutaki kentō" 学校における「日の丸」「君が代」問題の憲法・教育法学的検討. *Hokkaido Department of Law Junior Research Journal* 10: 235–264.

Nishiyama Toshihiko 西山俊彦. 2006. *Yasukuni gōshi torikeshi soshō no chūkan hōkoku: Shinkyō no jiyū no kaifuku o motomete* 靖国合祀取消し訴訟の中間報告—信教の自由の回復を求めて. Tokyo: San Paulo Shuppan.

———. 2007. "Naze 'Yasukuni jinja gōshi torikeshi soshō' genkoku to natta no ka" なぜ「靖国神社合祀取消し訴訟」原告となったのか. *Zen'ya* 前夜 10: 67–73.

Nitta Hitoshi. 2000. "Shinto as a 'Non-Religion': The Origin and Development of an Idea." In *Shinto in History: Ways of the Kami*. John Breen and Mark Teeuwen, eds., 252–271. Richmond, Surrey: Curzon Press.

———. 2008. "And Why Shouldn't the Prime Minister Worship at Yasukuni? A Personal View." In *Yasukuni, the War Dead and the Struggle for Japan's Past*, ed. John Breen, 1–22. New York: Columbia University Press.

Noguchi Tsunegi 野口恒木. 1984. "Waga Kokka Shintō to Amerika no Kōmin Shūkyō" 我が国家神道とアメリカの公民宗教. *Yasukuni* (1 January): 5–8.

O'Brien. David M. and Yasuo Ohkoshi. 1996. *To Dream of Dreams: Religious Freedom and Constitutional Politics in Postwar Japan*. Honolulu: University of Hawai'i Press.

Oguma Eiji 小熊英二 and Ueno Yōko 上野陽子. 2003. *'Iyashi' no nashonarizumu: Kusa no ne hoshu undō no jishō kenkyū* 「癒し」のナショナリズム―草の根保守運動の実証研究. Tokyo: Keio University Press.

Ōhara Yasuo 大原康男. 2010a. "Sengo shuppatsu ten" 戦後出発点. In *Sengo no jinja, Shintō: Rekishi to kadai* 戦後の神社・神道―歴史と課題, ed. Jinja Shinpō Sōkan Rokujū Shūnen Kinen Shuppan Iinkai 神社新報創刊六十周年記念出版委員会, 3–31. Tokyo: Jinja Shinpōsha.

———. 2010b. "Jinja to seiji" 神社と政治. In *Sengo no jinja, Shintō: Rekishi to kadai*, ed. Jinja Shinpō Sōkan Rokujū Shūnen Kinen Shuppan Iinkai, 35–105. Tokyo: Jinja Shinpōsha.

Okada Akira 岡田 明. 2006. *Kokki, kokka no "kyōsei" ni tsuite* 国旗・国歌の「強制」について. March, booklet version 2: 1–26.

———. 2007. *Shisō, ryōshin, shinkyō no jiyū ni tsuite kangaetekita koto: Toritsu kōkō ni okeru kokki, kokka kyōsei no naka de* 思想・良心・信教の自由について考えてきたこと―都立高校における国旗・国歌強制の中で. Pamphlet No. 5, [based on a presentation at the Reformed Church in Japan, 15 August, 2007].

———. 2013. "Hinomaru, Kimigayo 'kyōsei' no mondai no kako, genzai, mirai" 日の丸・君が代「強制」の問題の過去・現在・未来. In *Shinkō no ryōshin no tame no tatakai* 信仰の良心のための戦い, ed. Kimigayo Kyōsei Hantai Kirisutosha no Tsudoi 君が代強制反対キリスト者の集い, 9–42. Tokyo: Inochi no Kotobasha.

Okada Takeo 岡田武夫. 2007. "Senzen, senchū to sengo no Katorikku kyōkai no tachiba: 1936 nen no Fukyō Seishō shishin 'Sokoku ni taisuru shinja no tsutome' no saikōsatsu" 戦前・戦中と戦後のカトリック

教会の立場: 1936年の布教聖省指針『祖国に対する信者のつとめ』の再考察. In *Shinkyō no jiyū to seikyō bunri* 信教の自由と政教分離, ed. Katorikku Chūō Kyōgikai カトリック中央協議会, 59–80. Tokyo: Katorikku Chūō Kyōgikai.

Okada Yoneo 岡田米夫他, ed. 1966. *Jinja Honchō nijū nenshi* 神社本庁二十年史. Tokyo: Jinja Hochō.

Okazaki Hisahiko 岡崎久彦. 2002. "Senryō ga nokoshita kizu ato" 占領が残した傷跡. *Yasukuni*, 1 October: 6–7.

Okazaki Masafumi. 2010. "Chrysanthemum and Christianity: Education and Religion in Occupied Japan, 1945–1952." *Pacific Historical Review* 79: 393–417. doi.org/10.1525/phr.2010.79.3.393

———. 2012. *Nihon senryō to shūkyō kaikaku* 日本占領と宗教改革. Tokyo: Gakujutsu Shuppankai.

Okuyama Michiaki 奥山道明. 2009. "Kishimoto Hideo no Shōwa 20 nen" 岸本英夫の昭和20年. *Tōkyō Daigaku shūkyōgaku nenpō* 東京大学宗教学年報 26: 19–34.

———. 2010. "Sōka Gakkai as a Challenge to Japanese Society and Politics." *Politics and Religion* 4: 83–96.

———. 2011. "State Shinto in Recent Japanese Scholarship: Review Article." *Monumenta Nipponica* 66: 123–145. doi.org/10.1353/mni.2011.0019

Ōsaki Motoshi 大崎素史. 2007. "Kyōiku kihon hō kaisei no rekishi to mondai ten: Shūkyō kyōiku no shiten kara" 教育基本法改正の歴史と問題点—宗教教育の視点から. *Gendai shūkyō* 現代宗教: 39–62.

Oskin, Becky. 2017. "Japan Earthquake & Tsunami of 2011: Facts and Information." *Live Science* (13 September). www.livescience.com/39110-japan-2011-earthquake-tsunami-facts.html

Ōtsuka Eiji 大塚英志 and Fukuda Kazuya 深田和也. 1999. "Tennō nuki no nashonarizumu o ronzu" 天皇抜きのナショナリズムを論ず. *Shokun* 49: 140–153.

Pfister, Paul S. J. 1955. "The Church and Shinto Rites: A Historical Note." *Missionary Bulletin* 9/5: 264–265.

Powles, Cyril. 1976. "Yasukuni Jinja Hōan: Religion and Politics in Contemporary Japan." *Pacific Affairs* 49: 491–505. doi.org/10.2307/2755500

Prohl, Inken. 2004. "Religion and National Identity in Contemporary Japan." In *Civil Society, Religion and Nation: Modernization in Intercultural Context: Russia, Japan, Turkey*, Rerrit Steunebrink and Evert van der Zweerde, eds., 135–150. Amsterdam: Rodopi.

Ravitch, Frank S. 2013. "The Shinto Cases: Religion, Culture, or Both—The Japanese Supreme Court and Establishment of Religion Jurisprudence." *Brigham Young University Law Review* 505: 505–520. digitalcommons.law.msu.edu/cgi/viewcontent.cgi?article=1578&-context=facpubs

———. 2014. "The Japanese Prime Minister's Visits to the Yasukuni Shrine Analyzed under Articles 20 and 89 of the Japanese Constitution." *Michigan State International Law Review* 22/3: 713–730.

Reader, Ian. 2005. "Of Religion, Nationalism, and Ideology: Analyzing the Development of Religious Studies in Japan." *Social Science Japan Journal* 8: 119–124. doi.org/10.1093/ssjj/jyho51

———. 2012. "Secularisation R.I.P.? Nonsense!: The 'Rush Hour Away from the Gods' and the Decline of Religion in Contemporary Japan." *Journal of Religion in Japan* 1: 7–36. doi.org/10.1163/221183412x628370

———. 2016. "Problematic Conceptions and Critical Developments: The Construction and Relevance of 'Religion' and Religious Studies in Japan." *Journal of the Irish Society for the Academic Study of Religions* 3: 198–218.

Reader, Ian and George J. Tanabe, Jr. 1998. *Practically Religious: Worldly Benefits and the Common Religion of Japan*. Honolulu: University of Hawai'i Press.

Reid, David. 1991. *New Wine: The Cultural Shaping of Japanese Christianity*. Berkeley: Asian Humanities Press.

Repeta, Lawrence. 2007. "Politicians, Teachers and the Japanese Constitution: Flag, Freedom and the State." *The Asia-Pacific Journal: Japan Focus*: 1–7. www.japanfocus.org/-Lawrence-Repeta/2355

———. 2013. "Japan's Democracy at Risk: The LDP's Ten Most Dangerous Proposals for Constitutional Change." *SRRN* (22 July): 1–12. doi.org/10.2139/ssrn.2325179

———. 2016. "Nationalism and the Law: Japan's Tale of Two Constitutions." In *Asian Nationalisms Reconsidered*, ed. Jeff Kingston, 70–82. London: Routledge.

Repeta, Lawrence and Colin P. A. Jones. 2015. "State Power versus Individual Freedom: Japan's Constitutional Past, Present, and Possible Futures." In *Japan: The Precarious Future*, Frank Baldwin and Anne Allison, eds., 304–328. New York: NYU Press.

Roemer, Michael K. 2012. "Japanese Survey Data on Religious Attitudes, Beliefs, and Practices in the Twenty-First Century." In *Handbook of Contemporary Japanese Religions*, John Nelson and Inken Prohl, eds., 23–58. Leiden: Brill.

Rots, Aike. 2017. *Shinto, Nature and Ideology in Contemporary Japan: Making Sacred Forests*. London: Bloomsbury.

Rubenstein, Richard L. 1989. "Japan and Biblical Religion: The Religious Significance of the Japanese Economic Challenge." In *Social Consequences of Religious Belief*, ed. William Reace Garrett, 116–117. New York: Paragon House.

Ruoff, Kenneth J. 2001. *The People's Emperor: Democracy and the Japanese Monarchy, 1945–1995*. Harvard East Asian monographs 211. Cambridge: Harvard University Asia Center.

Saaler, Sven. 2005. *Politics, Memory and Public Opinion: The History Textbook Controversy and Japanese Society*. Munich: Iudicium Verlag.

———. 2016. "Nationalism and History in Contemporary Japan." *The Asia-Pacific Journal: Japan Focus* 14/20/7: 1–17. apjjf.org/2016/20/Saaler.html

Saito Masami, Nogawa Motokazu, and Hayakawa Tadanori. 2018. "Dissecting the Wave of Books on Nippon Kaigi, the Rightwing Mass Movement that Threatens Japan's Future." Trans. Miho Matsugu. *The Asia-Pacific Journal: Japan Focus* 16/19/1: 1-33.

Saitō Yoshihisa 斉藤吉久. 2007. "Tōkyō Daishikyōsama, naze Nihon no rekishi no anbu bakari o furēmuappu suru no deshō" 東京大司教様、なぜ日本の歴史の暗部ばかりをフレームアップするのでしょう. *Seiron* 正論 423: 256–264.

Sakamoto Koremaru 阪本是丸. 1994a. *Kokka Shintō keisei katei no kenkyū* 国家神道形成過程の研究. Tokyo: Iwanami Shoten.

———. 1994b. "Shintō Fuandamentarizumu mōsō" 神道ファンダメンタリズム妄想. In *Fuandamentarizumu to wa nanika: Sezokushugi e no chōsen* ファンダメンタリズムとは何か―世俗主義への挑戦, Inoue Nobutaka and Ōtsuka Kazuo 大塚和夫, eds., 178–179. Tokyo: Shinyōsha.

———. 2000. "The Structure of State Shinto: Its Creation, Development and Demise." In *Shinto in History: Ways of the Kami*, John Breen and Mark Teeuwen, eds., 272–294. Richmond, Surrey: Curzon Press.

———. 2005. *Kindai no jinja Shintō* 近代の神社神道. Tokyo: Kōbundō.

Sasaki Tomoyuki. 2018. "The Constitution Must Be Defended: Thoughts on the Constitution's Role in Japan's Postwar Democracy." *The Asia Pacific Journal: Japan Focus* 16/20/3: 1–16. apjjf.org/2018/20/Sasaki.html

Satō Miwako 佐藤美和子. 2009. "Hinomaru, Kimigayo, to tamashii no jiyū" 日の丸、君が代、と魂の自由. *Fukuin to sekai* 福音と世界 64/4: 36–42.

Scheid, Bernhard. 2012. "Shinto Shrines: Traditions and Transformations." In *Handbook of Contemporary Japanese Religions*, John Nelson and Inken Prohl, eds., 75–105. Leiden: Brill.

Seaton, Philip. 2005. "Reporting the 2001 Textbook and Yasukuni Shrine Controversies: Japanese War Memory and Commemoration in the British Media." *Japan Forum* 17: 287–309. doi.org/10.1080/09555800500283786

Seikyō Kankei o Tadasu Kai 正教関係を正す会, ed. 1993. *Zoku jitsurei ni manabu "seikyō bunri": Konna koto made kenpō ihan?* 続実例に学ぶ「正教分離」―こんなことまで憲法違反? Tokyo: Tendensha.

———. 2001. *Zoku jitsurei ni manabu "seikyō bunri": Konna koto made kenpō ihan?* 続実例に学ぶ「正教分離」―こんなことまで憲法違反? Tokyo: Tendensha.

———. 2011. *Shin jitsurei ni manabu "seikyō bunri": Konna koto made kenpō ihan?* 新実例に学ぶ「正教分離」―こんなことまで憲法違反? Tokyo: Tendensha.

Seraphim, Franziska. 2006. *War Memory and Social Politics in Japan, 1945–2005*. Harvard East Asian monographs 278. Cambridge: Harvard University Asia Center.

Sherif, Ann. 2007. "Lost Men and War Criminals: Public Intellectuals at Yasukuni Shrine." In *Ruptured Histories: War, Memory, and the Post-Cold War in Asia*, Sheila Miyoshi Jager and Rana Mitter, eds., 122–149. Cambridge: Harvard University Press.

Shibukawa Ken'ichi 渋川謙一. 1967. "Senryōka no Yasukuni jinja" 占領下の 靖国神社. *Shintōshi kenkyū* 神道史研究 15/5–6: 185–206.

———. 1993. "Senryō seisaku to Shintōkai no taiō" 占領政策と神道界の 対応. In *Senryō to Nihon shūkyō*, ed. Ikado Fujio, 497–520. Tokyo: Miraisha.

Shillony, Ben-Ami. 2008. "Conservative Dissatisfaction with the Modern Emperors." In *The Emperors of Modern Japan*, 137–162. Leiden: Brill.

Shimazono Susumu 島薗 進. 2001. *Posutomodan no shinshūkyō: Gendai Nihon no seishin jōkyō no teiryū* ポストモダンの新宗教―現代日本の 精神状況の底流. Tokyo: Tōkyōdō.

———. 2005. "State Shinto and the Religious Structure of Modern Japan." *Journal of the American Academy of Religion*, 73: 1077–1098. doi.org /10.1093/jaarel/lfi115

———. 2007. "State Shinto and Religion in Post-War Japan." In *The Sage Handbook of the Sociology of Religion*, James A. Beckford and N. J. Demerath III, eds., 697–709. London: Sage.

———. 2009. "State Shinto in the Lives of the People: The Establishment of Emperor Worship, Modern Nationalism, and State Shinto in Late Meiji." *Japanese Journal of Religious Studies* 36: 93–124. doi.org /bfwv

———. 2010. *Kokka Shintō to Nihonjin* 国家神道と日本人. Tokyo: Iwanami Shoten.

———. 2012. "Japanese Buddhism and the Public Sphere: From the End of World War II to the Post-Great East Japan Earthquake and Nuclear Power Plant Accident." *Journal of Religion in Japan* 1: 203–225. doi.org/10.1163/22118349-12341237

———. 2014. *Kokka Shintō to senzen, sengo no Nihonjin: "Mushūkyō" ni naru mae to ato* 国家神道と戦前・戦後の日本人―「無宗教」になる 前と後. Kawai Booklet 39. Tokyo: Kawai Bunka Kyōiku Kenkyūjo.

Shinshūren (Shin Nihon Shūkyō Dantai Rengōkai 新日本宗教団体連合会). 2016. *Shinkyō no jiyū wa nanika* 信教の自由は何か. Tokyo: Shinshūren.

Shintō Seiji Renmei 神道政治連盟, ed. 1984. *Shinseiren jūgo nenshi* 神政連十五年史. Tokyo: Shintō Seiji Renmei Chūō Honbu.

Sleeboon, Margaret. 2004. *Academic Nations in China and Japan: Framed in Concepts of Nature, Culture and the Universal*. London: RoutledgeCurzon.

Sono Ayako 曽野綾子. 1985. "Shūkyō o tokutei shinai aratana kinenbyō no setsuritsu o" 宗教を特定しない新たな記念廟の設立を. *Jurist* 848: 32–34.

———. 2005a. "Yasukuni ni mairimasu" 靖国に参ります. *Shokun.* September, 36–41.

———. 2005b. "I Will Visit Yasukuni." *Japan Echo*, December: 51–54.

———. 2011. *Tamashii o yashinau kyōiku aku kara manabu kyōiku* 魂を養う教育悪から学ぶ教育. Tokyo: PHP.

———. 2012. *Kokka no toku* 国家の徳. Tokyo: Sankei Shinbun Shuppan.

———. 2015. "*Rōdōfusoku to imin*" 労働不足と移民. *Sankei shinbun* 産経新聞,11 February.

Sugahara Ryūken 菅原龍憲. 2005. *Yasukuni to iu ori kara no kaihō* 靖国という檻からの解放. Tokyo: Nagata Bunshōdō.

———. 2007. *Gōshi torikeshi: Yasukuni mondai no kakushin o tou* 合祀取り消し—靖国問題の核心を問う [self-published booklet].

Sugano Tamotsu 菅野 完. 2016. *Nippon kaigi no kenkyū* 日本会議の研究. Tokyo: Fusōsha.

Suzuki Tomi. 2012. "Introduction: History and Issues in Censorship in Japan." In *Censorship, Media, and Literary Culture in Japan: From Edo to Postwar*, Suzuki Tomi, Toeda Hirokazu, Hori Hikari, and Kazushige Munakata, eds., 7–21. Tokyo: Shinyōsha.

Swyngedouw, Jan. 1967. "The Catholic Church and Shrine Shinto." *The Japan Missionary Bulletin* 21: 579–584, 659–663.

———. 1993a. "Katorikku kyōkai no tenkai - senjika to sengo: Shūkyō shakai-gakuteki na ichi kōsatsu カトリック教会の展開・戦時下と戦後—宗教社会学的な一考察. In *Senryō to Nihon shūkyō*, ed. Ikado Fujio, 321–42. Tokyo: Miraisha.

———. 1993b. "Religion in Contemporary Japanese Society." In *Religion & Society in Modern Japan*, Mark R. Mullins, Shimazono Susumu, and Paul L. Swanson, eds., 49–72. Berkeley: Asian Humanities Press.

Tajika Hajime 田近 肇. 2014. "Dai kibo shizen saigai no seikyō mondai" 大規模自然災害の政教問題. *Rinshōhō kenkyū* 臨床法務研究 13: 15–39.

Takagi Kiyoko 高木きよ子. 1993. "Kishimoto hakushi to senryō jidai no shūkyō seisaku" 岸本博士と占領時代の宗教政策. In *Senryō to Nihon shūkyō*, ed. Ikado Fujio, 423–436. Tokyo: Miraisha.

Takahashi Seiju 高橋正樹. 1998. "Kyōsei no saki ni mieru mono" 強制の先に見えるもの. In the *Ryōshinteki "Hinomaru, Kimigayo" kyohi* 良心的「日の丸・君が代」拒否, ed. "Hinomaru, Kimigayo" Futō Shobun Tekkai o Motomeru Hishobunsha no Kai 「日の丸・君が代」不当処分撤回を求め被処分者の会, 176–179. Tokyo: Akashi.

———. 2004. "Kyōsei no saki ni mieru mono" 強制の先に見えるもの. In *Ryōshinteki "Hinomaru, Kimigayo" kyohi* 良心的「日の丸・君が代」拒否, ed. "Hinomaru-Kimigayo" Futō Shobun Tekkai o Motomeru Hishobunsha no Kai, 176–179. Tokyo: Akashi.

Takahashi Tetsuya 高橋哲哉. 2004. *Kyōiku to kokka* 教育と国家. Tokyo: Kōdansha.

———. 2005. *Yasukuni mondai* 靖国問題. Tokyo: Chikuma Shobō.

———. 2008. "Legacies of Empire: the Yasukuni Shrine Controversy." In *Yasukuni, the War Dead and the Struggle for Japan's Past*, ed. John Breen, 105–124. New York: Columbia University Press.

Takayama, K. Peter. 1988. "The Revitalization of Japanese Civil Religion." *Sociological Analysis* 48: 328–341. doi.org/10.2307/3710871

Takemae Eiji 竹前栄治. 1987. "Religious Reform under the Occupation of Japan: Interview with Dr. W. K. Bunce." *Tōkyō Keizai Daigaku kaishi* 東京経済大学会誌 150: 187–219.

———. 1988. *Nihon no senryō*: GHQ *kōkan no shōgen* 日本の占領—GHQ 高官の証言. Tokyo: Chūō Kōronsha.

———. 2003. *The Allied Occupation of Japan*. Trans. and adapted by Robert Ricketts and Sebastian Swann. New York: Continuum.

Takenaka, Akiko. 2007. "Enshrinement Politics: War Dead and War Criminals at Yasukuni Shrine." *The Asia-Pacific Journal: Japan Focus* 5/6: 1–9. apjjf.org/-Akiko-TAKENAKA/2443/article.html

———. 2015. *Yasukuni Shrine: History, Memory, and Japan's Unending Postwar.* Honolulu: University of Hawai'i Press.

Tanaka Nobumasa 田中伸尚. 2000. *Hinomaru-Kimigayo no sengoshi* 日の丸・君が代の戦後史. Tokyo: Iwanami Shoten.

———. 2005. "Conscience and a Music Teacher's Refusal to Play the National Anthem." Trans. Joshua A. Fogel. *The Asia Pacific Journal: Japan Focus* 3/1: 1–7. apjjf.org/-Nobumasa-Tanaka/2167/article.html

———. 2012. *Rupo ryōshin to gimu: "Hinomaru, Kimigayo" ni kōu hitobito to* ルポ良心と義務—「日の丸・君が代」に抗う人びと. Tokyo: Iwanami Shoten.

Tani Daiji 谷大二. 2007. "Jimintō shinkenpō sōan o kenshō suru" 自民党新憲法草案を検証する. In *Shinkyō no jiyū to seikyō bunri*, ed. Katorikku Chūō Kyōgikai, 17–44. Tokyo: Katorikku Chūō Kyōgikai.

Taniguchi Masanobu 谷口雅宣. 2014. *Shūkyō wa naze tokai o hanareru ka* 宗教はなぜ都会を離れるか. Tokyo: Nihon Kyōbunsha.

Tawara Yoshifumi 俵義文. 2013. "Abe naikaku no kyokuu takaha jinmyaku no keifu" 安倍内閣の極右タカ派人脈の系譜. *Zen'ei* 前衛 892: 45–58.

———. 2016. *Nippon Kaigi no zenbō: Shirarezaru kyodai soshiki no jittai* 日本会議の全貌—知られざる巨大組織の実態. Tokyo: Kadensha.

———. 2017. "What is the Aim of Nippon Kaigi, The Ultra-Right Organization that Supports Japan's Abe Administration." "Introduction" by Tomomi Yamaguchi, trans. William Brooks and Lu Pengqiao. *The Asia-Pacific Journal: Japan Focus* 15/21/1: 1–23. apjjf.org/2017/21/Tawara.html

Taylor, Charles. 2007. *A Secular Age.* Cambridge: Harvard University Press.

Teeuwen, Mark. 1996. "Jinja Honchō and Shrine Shintō Policy." *Japan Forum* 8: 177–188. doi.org/10.1080/09555809608721568

———. 1999. "State Shinto: An 'Independent Religion'?" *Monumenta Nipponica* 54: 111–121. doi.org/10.2307/2668275

Thal, Sarah. 2002. "A Religion That Was Not a Religion." In *The Invention of Religion: Rethinking Belief in Politics and History*, Derek R.

Peterson and Darren R. Walhof, eds., 100–114. New Brunswick, New Jersey: Rutgers University Press.

Toeda Hirokazu. 2012. "The Home Ministry and GHQ/SCAP as Censors of Literature: Media Regulations and the Battle Over Expression in the 1920s–40s Japan." In *Censorship, Media, and Literary Culture in Japan: From Edo to Postwar*, Suzuki Tomi, Toeda Hirokazu, Hori Hikari, and Kazushige Munakata, eds., 96–107. Tokyo: Shinyōsha.

Tokoro Isao 所功. 2007. *Yōkoso Yasukuni Jinja e* ようこそ靖国神社へ. Kindai Shuppansha.

Tomioka Morihiko 富岡盛彦. 1960. "Jinja Honchō jūgo nen no ayumi" 神社本庁15年の歩み. *Gekkan wakaki* 月刊若木 137: 48.

Toyoda, Maria A. and Aiji Tanaka. 2002. "Religion and Politics in Japan." In *Religion and Politics in Comparative Perspective: The One, the Few, and the Many*, Ted Gerard Jelen and Clyde Wilcox, eds., 269–286. Cambridge: Cambridge University Press.

Tsukada Hotaka 塚田穂高. 2012. "Cultural Nationalism in Japanese Neo-New Religions: A Comparative Study of Mahikari and Kōfuku no Kagaku." *Monumenta Nipponica* 67: 133–157. doi.org/10.1353/mni.2012.0015

———. 2015. *Shūkyō to seiji no tentetsuten: Hoshu gōdō to seikyō itchi no shūkyō shakaigaku* 宗教と政治の転轍点―保守合同と政教一致の宗教社会学. Tokyo: Kadensha.

———. ed. 2017. *Tettei kenshō Nihon no ukeika* 徹底検証日本の右傾化. Tokyo: Chikuma Shobō.

Ueda Kenji. 1979. "Contemporary Social Change and Shinto Traditions." *Japanese Journal of Religious Studies* 6: 303–327. doi.org/bg7h

Uesugi Satoshi 上杉 聰. 2007. "Shūkyō uyoku to gendai Nihon no nashonarizumu" 宗教右翼と現代日本のナショナリズム. *Nenpō Nihon gendaishi* 年報日本現代史 12: 163–186.

———. 2016. *Nippon Kaigi to wa nani ka: "Kenpō kaisei" ni tsuki susumu karuto shūdan* 日本会議とは何か―「憲法改正」に突き進むカルト集団. Tokyo: Gōdō Shuppan.

Ukai Hidenori 鵜飼秀徳. 2015. *Jiin shōmetsu: Ushinawareu "chihō" to "shūkyō."* 寺院消滅―失われる「地方」と「宗教」. Tokyo: Nikkei BP.

Umehara Takeshi 梅原猛. 1985. "*Kōshiki sanpai no meritto to demeritto*" 公式参拝のメリットとデメリット. *Jurist* 848: 10–16.

———. 1995. *Kokoro no kiki o sukue: Nihon no kyōiku ga oshienai mono* 心の危機を救え—日本の教育が教えないもの. Tokyo: Kōbunsha.

———. 2004a. "Yasukuni wa Nihon no dentō kara mendatsu shiteiru" 靖国は日本の伝統から免立つしている. Interview in *Sekai* 世界, no. 730, September: 72–78.

———. 2004b. "Official Visits to Yasukuni Shrine Invite the Revenge of Reason." Trans. by Steven Platzer. *The Asia Pacific Journal: Japan Focus* 2/4: 1–3. apjjf.org/-Umehara-Takeshi/1947/article.html

———. 2005. "What is Japanese Tradition?" Trans. Yusei Ota and Gavan McCormack. *Asia Pacific Journal Japan Focus* 3/7: 1–3. apjjf.org/-Umehara-Takeshi/2128/article.html

———. 2006. *Kami koroshi no Nihon: Hanjidaiteki mitsugo* 神殺しの日本—反時代的密語. Tokyo: Asahi Shinbunsha.

———. 2010. *Nihon no dentō to wa nani ka* 日本の伝統とは何か. Tokyo: Minerva Shobō.

US Government Records. 1947. "Opinions regarding future of Yasukuni Shrine." GHQ, SCAP Civil Information and Education Section, Intra-Section Memorandum from W. P. Woodard to Mr. Bunce, 6 January 1947, RG No. 331, Box 5933. National Archives and Record Administration, Washington, DC.

Veer, Peter van der. 1994. "Hindu Nationalism and the Discourse of Modernity: The Vishva Hindu Parishad." In *Accounting for Fundamentalisms: The Dynamic Character of Movements*, Martin E. Marty and R. Scott Appleby, eds., 653–668. Chicago: University of Chicago Press.

Watanabe, Chie. 2019. *Becoming One: Religion, Development, and Environmentalism in a Japanese NGO in Myanmar*. Honolulu: University of Hawai'i Press.

Weber, Max. 1946. *Essays in Sociology*. Translated, edited, and with an Introduction by H. H. Gerth and C. Wright Mills. New York: Oxford University Press.

Winkler, Christian G. 2011. *The Quest for Japan's New Constitution: An Analysis of Visions and Constitutional Reform Proposals 1980–2009.* London: Routledge.

Wittner, Lawrence S. 1971. "MacArthur and the Missionaries: God and Man in Occupied Japan." *Pacific Historical Review* 40: 77–98. doi.org/10.2307/3637830

Wohlrab-Sahr, Monika and Marian Burchardt. 2012. "Multiple Secularities: Toward a Cultural Sociology of Secular Modernities." *Comparative Sociology* 11: 875–909. doi.org/10.1163/15691330-12341249

Woodard, William P. 1972. *The Allied Occupation of Japan 1945–1952 and Japanese Religions.* Leiden: Brill.

———. n.d. "Annex: Dr. Hideo Kishimoto." Box 55 (7 pages). William Woodard Special Collection 153. Special Collections and University Archives, University of Oregon Libraries.

———. 1947. "Opinions regarding future of Yasukuni Shrine." GHQ, SCAP Civil Information and Education Section, Intra-Section from W. P. Woodard to Mr. Bunce, 6 January 1947. RG No. 331, Box 5933. National Archives and Record Administration, Washington, DC.

Yamamoto Taketoshi 山本武利. 2013. *GHQ no ken'etsu, chōhō, senden kōsaku* GHQの検閲・諜報・宣伝工作. Tokyo: Iwanami Shoten.

Yamamoto Yoshinobu 山本信良 and Imano Toshihiko 今野敏彦. 1973. *Kindai kyōiku no tennōsei ideorogī: Meijiki gakkō gyōji no kōsatsu* 近代教育の天皇制イデオロギー——明治期学校行事の考察. Tokyo: Shinsensha.

———. 1976. *Taishō, Shōwa kyōiku no tennōsei ideorogī 1: Gakkō gyōji shūkyōteki seikaku* 大正・昭和教育の天皇制イデオロギー〈1〉——学校行事の宗教的性格. Tokyo: Shinsensha.

Yamazaki Masahiro 山崎雅弘. 2015. *Senzen kaiki: "Dai nipponbyō" no saihatsu* 戦前回帰——「大日本病」の再発. Tokyo: Gakken Kyōiku Shuppan.

———. 2016. *Nippon Kaigi: Senzen kaiki e no jōnen* 日本会議——戦前回帰への情念. Tokyo: Shūeisha Shinsho.

Yanagawa Keiichi and Abe Yoshiya. 1983. "Cross-Cultural Implications of a Behavioral Response." *Japanese Journal of Religious Studies* 10: 289–307. doi.org/bg3v

Yasukuni Jinja. 1983–1984. *Yasukuni jinja hyakunen shi shiryōhen* 靖国神社百年史資料篇. 3 vols. Tokyo: Yasukuni Jinja.

———. 1987. *Yasukuni jinja hyakunen shi jireki nenpyō* 靖国神社百年史事歴年表. Tokyo: Yasukuni Jinja.

Yoda Tomiko. 2006. "A Roadmap to Millennial Japan." In *Japan After Japan: Social and Cultural Life From the Recessionary 1990s to the Present*, Tomiko Yoda and Harry Harootunian, eds., 16–53. Durham: Duke University Press.

Yokota Kōichi 横田耕一. 1988. "Kanyō naki shakai no kanyōron: Jieikan gōshi iken soshō daihōtei hanketsu o megutte" 寛容なき社会のかん要論―自衛官合祀違憲訴訟大法廷判決をめぐって. *Hōgaku seminā* 法学セミナー 33/8: 14–23.

Yoshino Kosaku. 1992. *Cultural Nationalism in Contemporary Japan: A Sociological Enquiry*. London: Routledge.

Young, Issac. 2009. "Shut Up and Sing: The Rights of Japanese Teachers in an Era of Conservative Educational Reform." *Cornell International Law Journal* 42: 157–192.

Young, James R. 1948. "The Menace of Shintoism." *The United States Naval Institute Proceedings* 74/542: 463–465.

Zushi Minoru 辻子 実. 2003. *Shinryaku jinja: Yasukuni shisō o kangaeru tame ni* 侵略神社―靖国思想を考えるために. Tokyo: Shinkansha.

———. 2007. *Yasukuni no yami ni yōkoso: Yasukuni Jinja, yūshūkan hikō-shiki gaidobukku* 靖国の闇にようこそ―靖国神社・遊就館非公式ガイドブック. Tokyo: Shakai Hyōronsha.

Permissions

The author and publisher wish to thank the following institutions and individuals for permission to reproduce the photographs and illustrations on the following pages of this volume:

1. Imperialist Secularization

p. 34 Courtesy of the Special Collections and University of Oregon Libraries, William Woodard Collection 153, Box 29, Folder 3, PH150 0746: Religion in Japan poster, Prepared and Produced in Tokyo by I & E Section, GHQ, AFPAC 2 December 1946, Special Collections and University of Oregon Libraries, Eugene, Oregon.

p. 40 Courtesy of Peter Bunce and the W. K. Bunce Family Personal Collection; William K. Bunce at Matsuyama Number Twelve Higher School (Kōtō Gakkō), in the late 1930s, and as a staff member of the Religions Division, 17 March 1948.

p. 43 Courtesy of Peter Bunce and the W. K. Bunce Family Personal Collection; Religions Division staff field trip with Japanese scholars to Tsurugaoka Hachimangū, Kamakura, 1946.

p. 43 Courtesy of Peter Bunce and the W. K. Bunce Family Personal Collection; Religions Division staff field trip to Tenrikyō, Tokyo, June 1946.

p. 44 Courtesy of Peter Bunce and the W. K. Bunce Family Personal Collection; Religions Division staff field trip to Mt. Nikkō and Rinnōji, 1946.

2. Shinto Responses to the Occupation

p. 64 Courtesy of Peter Bunce and the W. K. Bunce Family Personal Collection; Yasukuni Shrine in wartime Japan (1). No date.

p. 65 Courtesy of Peter Bunce and the W. K. Bunce Family Personal Collection; Yasukuni Shrine in wartime Japan (2). No date.

4. The Politics of Yasukuni Shrine

Photographs on pp. 117, 133, 139 are from the author's personal collection.

The author would like to express appreciation to the following publishers and journals for permission to use and adapt previously published materials in this volume:

2018 "Public Intellectuals, Neo-nationalism, and the Politics of Yasukuni Shrine." In *Japanese Studies Down Under: History, Politics, Literature and Art*, International Research Center for Japanese Studies Symposium Proceedings 23, Guo Nanyan and Shogimen Takashi, eds., 145–160.

2017 "Religion in Occupied Japan: The Impact of SCAP's Policies on Shinto." In *Belief and Practice in Imperial Japan and Colonial Korea*, ed. Emily Anderson, 229–248. Singapore: Palgrave Macmillan Press.

2016 "Neonationalism, Politics, and Religion in Post-disaster Japan." In *Disasters and Social Crisis in Contemporary Japan: Political, Religious, and Sociocultural Responses*, Mark R. Mullins and Koichi Nakano, eds., 107–131. Basingstoke/NY: Palgrave Macmillan Press.

2015 "Japanese Responses to 'Imperialist Secularization': The Postwar Movement to Restore Shinto in the 'Public Sphere.'" In *Multiple Secularities Beyond the West: Religion and Modernity in the Global Age*. Marian Burchardt, Monika Wohlrab-Sahr, and Matthias Middell, eds., 141–167. Berlin: De Gruyter.

2013 "Sacred Sites and Social Conflict: Yasukuni Shrine and Religious Pluralism in Japanese Society." In *Religious Pluralism, State and Society in Asia*, ed. Chiara Formichi, 35–50. Routledge.

2012 "Secularization, Deprivatization, and the Reappearance of 'Public Religion' in Japanese Society." *Journal of Religion in Japan* 1: 61–82.

2012 "The Neo-nationalist Response to the Aum Crisis: A Return of Civil Religion and Coercion in the Public Sphere?" *Japanese Journal of Religious Studies* 39: 99–125.

2010 "How Yasukuni Shrine Survived the Occupation: A Critical Examination of Popular Claims." *Monumenta Nipponica* 65: 89–136.

Index